DEVOTIONS

January

"Friend, your sins are forgiven."

— *Luke 5:20*

W9-BAA-749

Gary Wilde, Editor | **Margaret Williams,** Project Editor | Photo John Foxx | Stockbyte | Thinkstock®

DEVOTIONS® is published quarterly by Standard Publishing, Cincinnati, Ohio, www.standardpub.com. © 2012 by Standard Publishing. All rights reserved. Topics based on the Home Daily Bible Readings, International Sunday School Lessons. © 2010 by the Committee on the Uniform Series. Printed in the U.S.A. All Scripture quotations, unless otherwise indicated, are taken from the *HOLY BIBLE, NEW INTERNATIONAL VERSION®. NIV®.* Copyright © 1973, 1978, 1984, 2011 by Biblica, Inc.™ Used by permission of Zondervan. All rights reserved. *King James Version* (KJV), public domain. The *New King James Version.* Copyright © 1982 by Thomas Nelson, Inc. *New American Standard Bible* (NASB), © The Lockman Foundation, 1960, 1962, 1963, 1968, 1971, 1972, 1973, 1975, 1977, 1995. Scripture quotations marked (*The Message*) are taken from *THE MESSAGE.* Copyright © by Eugene H. Peterson 1993, 1994, 1995, 1996, 2000, 2001, 2002. Used by permission of NavPress Publishing Group.

Resting in His Provision

So the people rested on the seventh day(Exodus 16:30).

Scripture: Exodus 16:22-30
Song: "Create in Me a Clean Heart"

Their marriage entered a mean season. He criticized. She snipped back. Her love for him withered . . . Then one day it occurred to her: God not only provided daily food for the Israelites in the desert, He preserved the perishable provision one extra day—the day they were not allowed to work. God's people got the rest they needed, and He provided the food they needed.

She wondered if God could help her love her husband again in the desert of her marriage. She wondered if somehow she could also obtain desperately needed mental and emotional rest in the meantime. "Lord," she prayed, "I no longer have a heart for my husband. Give me Your heart for him."

Day by week by month by year, she yielded more to the comfort and counsel of the Holy Spirit and less to the barbs of a critical spirit. Gradually, her peace returned. At length, from a position of rest, she was able to perceive her husband in a new light and to once again love him.

"As I committed to that prayer," she testified some years later, "I felt an immediate sense of relief. And even while our relationship was mending, I experienced the rest I so desperately needed." In time, her husband received a new heart for her too.

Lord, please give me Your heart for the one who is hurting me. If it's not Your will for me to leave, then give me all I need to stay, in peace. Through Christ, amen.

January 1–5. **Phyllis Beveridge Nissila** is a writer and instructor at Lane Community College in Eugene, Oregon. She is married and the mother of two daughters.

The Rest of the Story

The seventh day is the sabbath of the LORD thy God: in it thou shalt not do any work, thou, nor thy son, nor thy daughter, nor thy manservant, nor thy maidservant (Deuteronomy 5:14, *King James Version*).

Scripture: Deuteronomy 5:11-15
Song: "My Grandfather's Bible"

It's easy to think only of the "don't do that" part of God's commandments and rarely to consider the blessing part—the part where our obedience benefits not only our lives but the lives of others.

When we worship the true God, we don't fall into the deceptions of false gods, and we don't influence others to fall.

When we remain faithful in our marriage, we save our spouse and our children from anger and heartache, and we save another's loved ones from anger and heartache.

When we promote respect for what rightly belongs to people, we ensure that we, and others, retain the necessities of life.

When we tell the truth, we maintain our own dignity and honor, and we help preserve the dignity and honor of others.

When we choose life, we live, and so do others.

Today's verse gives us the fourth commandment, the Sabbath rest, and the benefits of observing that commandment are evident too. Not only is the immediate family of this household blessed, but so are all others in the house, including visitors.

Thank You, **Lord,** that the blessings of our obedience benefit not only us, but ripple outward to benefit our friends and relatives—and even those we may not know until eternity. Your goodness excels my comprehension! In Jesus' name, amen.

In Due Time

These are the feasts of the LORD, even holy convocations, which ye shall proclaim in their seasons (Leviticus 23:4, *King James Version*).

Scripture: Leviticus 23:1-8
Song: "In His Time"

One of God's gifts to mankind is timing. Timing helps us both anticipate and understand events. A baby takes nine months to gestate, for example, until its body parts and systems are complete. Timing also helps us believers comprehend God's plan for us, both historically and prophetically, as revealed in the feasts outlined in today's passage.

When Moses wrote Leviticus in the desert, the Israelites knew the historical import of the Feast of Passover. They understood it was a commemoration of their deliverance from the last plague visited upon Egypt. The blood of the sacrificial lamb, splashed on their doorposts, kept the angel of death away.

They also would have understood the historical significance of the Feast of Unleavened Bread. It commemorated that last week in slavery as well and the imminence of deliverance—no time for the yeast to rise!

Centuries later, we realize the prophetic import of those events too. Jesus is the spotless Passover lamb, who saves us from eternal destruction. Jesus is also the "unleavened bread," the yeast-free bread of life, who preserves us on our spiritual journey. In due time—God's time—all things come to pass.

Thank You, **Lord,** for Your perfect timing in fulfilling Your never-failing promises to Your people. In the precious name of Jesus, I offer my praise. Amen.

It All Starts Here

**They obeyed not, neither inclined their ear, but made their
neck stiff, that they might not hear, nor receive instruction**
(Jeremiah 17:23, *King James Version*).

Scripture: Jeremiah 17:19-27
Song: "I Choose Jesus"

When my daughters were young, they enjoyed a genre of
books that invited them to choose their own, individualized
adventures. When they got to page six, for example—the very
point at which a hero could choose between the path to a castle
on the right or the path to an enchanted forest on the left—the
author invited them to turn to a page corresponding to their
choice. The adventure shifted accordingly, and more exciting
options awaited.

In today's passage, God offered a choice to His people too.
The results of one of the choices, however, would be drastically
different than in the children's books.

If the Israelites chose to obey Him, starting with the Sabbath rest, further instruction awaited them. Good results would
ensue, as proclaimed by the prophet Jeremiah. If they chose,
however, to ignore His command to honor the day of rest—and
this, a command designed for their refreshment!—harm would
befall them, the details of which were also foretold by Jeremiah.

We too have a choice today: life abundant in Christ Jesus or
eternal separation from God's loving guidance and provision.

It all starts here.

Dear Father, help me choose Your will and Your way in all things today. Let me stop,
amidst my busyness, to hear Your still, small voice. Through Christ, amen.

Sabbath Eyes

He said unto them, That the Son of man is Lord also of the sabbath (Luke 6:5, *King James Version*).

Scripture: Luke 6:1-11
Song: "Give Me, O Lord, a Heart of Grace"

Recently, I discovered "computer glasses." These yellow-tinted reading glasses are designed to ease eye strain at the word processor. Every time I don them, the effect on my hardworking eyes is dramatic. Instantly, my eyes feel refreshed.

The religious leaders in today's passage had, you might say, a strained view of the Sabbath commandment. They focused only on what "work" couldn't be done on that day of rest. Their list of forbidden activities even included necessities such as gathering food and healing the sick.

Along came Jesus, on the Sabbath, eating corn picked in a field and healing a man's withered hand. The Pharisees were enraged. Jesus reminded them, however, that King David had gathered food on the Sabbath. The Savior even performed a miracle in their midst. But the religious leaders, focused on their own interpretation of the commandment, remained blinded to its true meaning.

It's easy to don the lens of legalism and miss the true rest that comes by keeping our eyes on Jesus. It's easy to forget He finished, on the cross, the only work that matters, so that all who believe can enter into the true rest (Hebrews 4:3).

Almighty and most merciful Father, teach me how to rest in Your Son's finished work on the cross. In Him, I have the peace that passes understanding—and I am thankful! In the name of the Father, the Son, and the Holy Spirit, I pray. Amen.

Facing Injustice?

Let the LORD judge the peoples. Vindicate me, LORD, according to my righteousness, according to my integrity, O Most High (Psalm 7:8).

Scripture: Psalm 7:7-17
Song: "Defend Us, Lord, from Every Ill"

When our son was falsely accused of dishonesty on his job, I became angry and wanted to tell his accusers a thing or two. One day in the grocery store, my anger reached a peak. *If I get a wobbly cart, I'll be mad,* I thought, jerking a cart from the racks.

As I pushed my cart down an aisle, two people blocked my way. *Can't they see I'm in a hurry?* One women moved and smiled an apology. I didn't smile back. As I reached into the dairy case, I sensed a voice saying, "Let it go. Let the anger and hurt go. That's not my way."

David, too, faced the pain of injustice when he was accused of trying to kill King Saul and seize the throne. It wasn't true, and he cried out to God. From his prayer, we gain insight into how we can react when falsely accused. Don't waste time brooding over false accusations or devising ways to get even. Instead, ask God to plead your case and restore your reputation. In His own time, in His own way, a just God promises to deal with unjust people and situations. (And remember the role of your own compassion: It's wounded people who wound others.)

Lord God, You are my defender. You will vindicate me and my loved ones in Your own good time. Thank You, through Christ my Lord. Amen.

January 6–12. **Jewell Johnson** lives in Arizona with her husband, LeRoy. They are parents to six children and grandparents to nine. Besides writing, Jewell enjoys walking, reading, and quilting.

God's Rescue Plan

The righteous person is rescued from trouble, and it falls on the wicked instead (Proverbs 11:8).

Scripture: Proverbs 11:3-11
Song: "A Mighty Fortress Is Our God"

When Jonathan Goforth went as a missionary to China in 1888, he had a difficult time learning the language. This was not a problem for fellow-missionary, Donald McGullivray, however, who arrived in China a year later than Goforth. "We don't understand you. Let McGullivray preach," the people told Goforth when he attempted to preach.

Goforth felt like a failure. Then one day something happened. He told his wife, "I began to speak, and the phrases and idioms that always eluded me came easily." He recorded the incident in his diary. Two months later a letter came from students attending a Canadian Bible college. At a prayer meeting, the students had been impressed to pray especially for Goforth.

The weapon of prayer—thrust at discouragement—had provided the breakthrough. When Goforth checked his diary, he saw that the day the students prayed corresponded with the time he began experiencing freedom with the Chinese language.

Difficulties confront believers and unbelievers alike, but Christians have spiritual weapons with which to overcome their problems. This week read Ephesians 6:10-18 and use God's defense plan often to rescue others—and yourself—from impossible circumstances.

Lord, I'm no match for the discouragements and inadequacies that often plague me. But with Your armor in place, I will confront them boldly today. Through Christ, amen.

Apply This Truth!

You have been set free from sin and have become slaves to righteousness (Romans 6:18).

Scripture: Romans 6:16-23
Song: "Shining for Jesus"

Margo is a beautician. She makes a living cutting and styling people's hair and giving manicures. But she does more than that.

When she felt led by the Lord to begin a women's prayer meeting in her church, she obeyed. Now every week she leads several ladies as they pray for world and local needs.

Then a desire grew in Margo's heart to learn sign language. Although there are presently no deaf people in her church, each week she practices the signs for the songs and accompanies the worship team. Margo could easily allow work, entertainment, and family to absorb her time and energy, but as a Christian, she walks in obedience to another voice.

Christians are no longer slaves to a wholly self-absorbed life. God has saved us to accomplish His purpose: To reach the world with the good news of Jesus. How He accomplishes the work through us will vary with each person. He may impress on us, His servants, a desire to learn a new skill, go on a mission trip, teach the church nursery children, or become involved in other outreach efforts.

"Saved to serve" isn't just a cliché. It's a down-to-earth biblical truth, ready for our personal, unique applications.

Speak, **Lord,** for Your servant is listening. Today I want to hear Your wisdom and guidance. How shall I use my gifts today? Where is the need? Who will be blessed? I pray this prayer in the name of Jesus, my Savior and Lord. Amen.

Make Beautiful Music

Live such good lives among the pagans that, though they accuse you of doing wrong, they may see your good deeds and glorify God on the day he visits us (1 Peter 2:12).

Scripture: 1 Peter 2:11-17
Song: "Take My Life and Let It Be"

Antonio Stradivari, Italian maker of stringed instruments in the eighteenth century, worked to perfect the violin and cello. The woods he used—maple, spruce, and willow—were carefully chosen and treated. He refused to sell an instrument until it was near perfect. "If my violins are defective, God's music will be spoiled," he said. He made over a thousand instruments in his lifetime. About 650 survive today and sell for a small fortune.

The apostle Peter wrote to believers scattered by persecution. Now they were enduring opposition from the Roman government under Nero. Yet Peter encouraged them to live their lives with the pagan population in mind. Even if these Christians were accused of wrongdoing, their good lives would speak loudly to onlookers.

As witnesses for Christ, we do not want "God's music" to be spoiled by a shoddy lifestyle. Yet, while we may avoid blatant sins, we might engage in more "acceptable" sins such as speaking critically of others or telling "little white lies." Not everyone reads the Bible, so our lives may be the only "Word" our neighbors and coworkers ever know. Let us play beautiful melodies to the watching world.

Almighty God, I long for my life to bear witness to Your goodness and grace. Reveal to me areas that may hinder my testimony. In Jesus' name, amen.

Forgive Quickly

"Lord, how many times shall I forgive my brother or sister who sins against me? Up to seven times?" Jesus answered, "I tell you, not seven times, but seventy-seven times" (Matthew 18:21, 22).

Scripture: Matthew 18:21-35
Song: "I Want to Be Like Jesus"

When our daughter Jenny auditioned for all-state chorus, I knew she'd be chosen. Why not? She read music easily and had a pleasant alto voice.

To my amazement, she was *not* the teacher's choice. Jenny accepted the decision, but I just couldn't. Day after day I entertained angry thoughts. In fact, I could hardly read my Bible for thinking of the injustice. "Just wait until the next parent-teacher conference," I told my husband. "I'll really give that teacher a piece of my mind."

Soon bitterness held me in its grip. Have you noticed that an unforgiving attitude has a way of taking over? No wonder Jesus told Peter to place no limits on the times we forgive.

Equally important is to forgive quickly after an offense. Harboring an unforgiving spirit produces a domino effect. We choose not to forgive, then we become bitter. Hatred is the next step on the downward spiral. Soon we may entertain violent thoughts toward the one who offended us.

So how do we forgive those who hurt us? We give our anger to God—once, twice, a hundred times a day, if necessary.

Lord, You willingly forgive my sins when I confess them. Now I offer the same forgiveness to those who have offended me. In the name of Jesus, amen.

Specks and Planks

First take the plank out of your eye, and then you will see clearly to remove the speck from your brother's eye (Luke 6:42).

Scripture: Luke 6:37-42
Song: "Search Me, O God"

Carla, a children's Sunday school teacher, was late for class almost every Sunday. Her students would sit in my classroom waiting for her to appear—which was usually 15 minutes after the bell rang. I became critical of Carla, not to her face, but in my spirit. *Why is she always tardy? Why does the superintendent allow her to teach when she can't be on time?*

Then I heard Carla had a chronic illness that caused her great discomfort. Although I never heard her complain, I learned that it was quite difficult for her to get moving in the morning. Perhaps she shouldn't be teaching, but I had no business finding fault with her.

My point: There are *reasons* for people's flaws and failures. And, because we do not know what another person is dealing with, let us not judge them by our imperfect standards. Often when we call attention to the faults of others, we are covering up similar shortcomings in ourselves.

When we set ourselves up as a judge, we take on the role of God. Our only obligation to those who seem "less than perfect" is to love them sincerely, just as we love our less-than-perfect selves.

Merciful God, forgive me for the habit of judging people. With Your help, I will enfold them with love as You enfold me, imperfect as I am. Through Christ I pray, amen.

Dealing with Our Enemies

Love your enemies, do good to those who hate you, bless those who curse you, pray for those who mistreat you (Luke 6:27, 28).

Scripture: Luke 6:12, 13, 17-31
Song: "Blest Are the Pure in Heart"

During the 1940s, Jewish people were targeted for extermination by the Nazis. Corrie ten Boom and her family hid Jews in their home in Holland during this era and because of their efforts, lives were spared. When their work became known to the Nazis, the ten Booms were imprisoned. Her father and sister died in concentration camps while Corrie survived and went on to preach in 60 countries.

After Corrie had preached at a meeting in Munich, a man extended his hand to her. Corrie recognized him as a former SS guard at Ravensbruck, the prison where her sister had died. Angry thoughts flooded Corrie's mind. Yet when she grasped his hand, a current seemed to pass between them. She couldn't forgive him, but Jesus in her could.

Our human reaction to "enemies" is to hold grudges and attempt to get even. In contrast, Jesus gave us a fourfold plan for dealing with those we'd prefer to curse: He said love these people, do good to them, bless them, and pray for them.

Each act mirrors the actions of our master. It is easy to wound others when we have been wounded. It takes Christ within us to respond as He did.

Heavenly Father, I do not feel love for persons who hurt me, but with Your help, I will show them Your love. In my merciful Savior's name I pray. Amen.

Save Me from Pride

How art thou fallen from heaven, O Lucifer, son of the morning! How art thou cut down to the ground, which didst weaken the nations! For thou hast said in thine heart, I will ascend into heaven (Isaiah 14:12, *King James Version*).

Scripture: Isaiah 14:12-20
Song: "Depth of Mercy"

For a number of years, I was a journalist in a small town with a big university. As the reporter who covered the university, I had access to many "important" people. When I would call the president of the university, he'd take my call. If I had a question, people would work to find answers. At the time, I didn't think all this was going to my head.

Then I left the newspaper. And, I discovered, I no longer mattered! When I ran into a high-ranking official of the school at a grocery store, he acted as if he'd never met me. A few months earlier, he would have treated me like an old friend. That stung.

The hurt I felt was my wounded pride, and this first of the deadly sins can easily infect our lives. Too often we find ourselves thinking too highly of ourselves, forgetting that every thing we have and are is a gift from God. When God knocks us back down to earth—as He did the prideful Lucifer—we should be grateful for the opportunity to live with a little more thankfulness. (Sadly, that didn't work with the son of the morning.)

Father, open my eyes to the ways I let pride get in the way of my love of You. Restore in me a grateful heart and a humble spirit. Through Christ I pray. Amen.

January 13–19. **John Meunier** is a part-time minister and a lecturer in Business Communication at Indiana University in Bloomington.

God on the Line

Humble yourselves before the Lord, and he will lift you up (James 4:10).

Scripture: James 4:7-12
Song: "Be Still, My Soul"

Andy was not a patient fisherman. He was only 10, so that was understandable. His impatience led to a theory. He decided that if he threw a rock into the lake—the bigger the better—the fish would get curious about what made the splash. They would come to investigate. So, Andy would throw a rock and then cast his line into the spot where the rock had hit the water.

Not a lot of people wanted to fish with Andy.

But how many of us treat our life with God the same way? We grow impatient. We chafe at the idea that God might deem it best to make us wait. We pick up rocks and throw them in the lake on the theory that our outbursts will get God's attention.

James teaches us what experienced anglers know. If you want to catch a fish, you must be humble enough to understand how a fish lives. You have to submit, let your actions and expectations grow out of the life of fish. (And fish certainly don't want rocks raining down on them!)

It is the same with God. When we humble ourselves to wait on God, to be patient for God, and to be attentive to God, that is when He shows up in His own time.

My soul can be so restless at times, **Father.** I want You to respond on my time. I want You to work on my schedule. Help me, Lord, to find the humility to wait on You. Let me stand before the still waters and wait for You. In the name of Jesus, who lives and reigns with You and the Holy Spirit, now and forever, amen.

Cast Your Cares upon Him

Cast all your anxiety on him because he cares for you (1 Peter 5:7).

Scripture: 1 Peter 5:1-7
Song: "Cares Chorus"

Anna prayed every day. She offered God her praise; she handed over her worries and cares—or most of them, anyway. When it came to her son, there were some things she just could not hand over. His alcoholism, his failed marriage, and his wandering away from the faith of his childhood—these were all too big to give over to God. She never said it this way, but a wise friend named it right: She thought these worries were too big for God. She would bear them instead.

You know what happened. The burden of those worries, her deep fears and anxieties, ground Anna down. It turned out that she was wrong. They were not too big for God. They were too big for her.

Can you relate? I know I can be like Anna. I hold back when God asks me for all of my anxieties and cares. I give him some, but I hold on to some, as well. Some of our fears just seem too big or too important or too close to our hearts to hand over to God.

Yet, I know: No pain, no fear, no worry, no anxiety of ours is too big for God. Nothing that we place on God's shoulders is worse than what He willingly took upon himself for our sake. Cast your cares upon Him.

Father, I know You ask me to give all my cares to You. I know, but my heart wants to hold on. Give me the courage and faith to let go today! In Jesus' name, amen.

More Than Just the News

The LORD builds up Jerusalem; he gathers the exiles of Israel (Psalm 147:2).

Scripture: Psalm 147:1-11
Song: "Battle Hymn of the Republic"

As Abraham Lincoln rose to give his second inaugural address in 1865, the end of the Civil War was in sight, but not yet reached. Bloody battle had cost the lives of thousands upon thousands. And it would demand many more. The president knew this as he spoke to a nation weary of war.

"Fondly do we hope—fervently do we pray—that this mighty scourge of war may speedily pass away. Yet, if God wills that it continue, until all the wealth piled by the bond-man's two hundred and fifty years of unrequited toil shall be sunk, and until every drop of blood drawn with the lash, shall be paid by another drawn with the sword, as was said three thousand years ago, so still it must be said 'the judgments of the Lord are true and righteous altogether.'"

God is not just a God for the quiet morning of our prayers and our worship on Sunday morning. He is the God of all. He is the God of our nation and world. When hardship comes to a nation, God is working. When prosperity comes, God is working. As God's people, we see Him at work where others see merely the news of the day. As it was in the days of ancient Israel, so it is today: The Lord builds up and gathers, in His sovereign wisdom.

God of wisdom and might, You rule the nations with truth and love. Help me to see in the news of this day Your hand at work, leading, judging, and loving Your world—or simply showing great and gracious restraint . . . for now. Through Christ, amen.

Enjoy Your Creator!

From the rising of the sun to the place where it sets, the name of the LORD is to be praised (Psalm 113:3).

Scripture: Psalm 113
Song: "For the Beauty of the Earth"

Joan loved the dirt. She loved to plant seeds in the ground and watch them grow. As a master gardener, she thrived on weeding and pruning. So, naturally, she took care of the plants on the church grounds and kept an eagle eye on the man the congregation had hired to mow the grass.

But Joan could be a bit of a tyrant when it came to the annual spring workday. She wouldn't tolerate a sloppy job as she watched volunteers spreading mulch or trimming spruce hedges. No one was immune to her wagging finger and knit brow when she thought the work wasn't up to par.

One fine spring day, an exasperated church member threw his trowel to the ground after one of Joan's mini-lectures. "Why do you make such a big deal about it?" he asked.

"George," she said. "God made that bush beautiful for us to look at and for all kinds of creatures to nest in. The least we can do is see that its feet stay warm."

Joan understood that every corner of God's creation is a testimony to His love. We who live in this beautiful earth are reminded to receive each and every piece of it as a gift. We praise the Lord when we care for it. (And Joan: relax, *enjoy!*)

Creator God, before there were nations and before You made us, You made this glorious world. Help me, Lord, to praise You for each gift, from the rising of the sun to its setting each day of my life. In Jesus' name, amen.

A Clean Heart

Because of your stubbornness and your unrepentant heart, you are storing up wrath against yourself for the day of God's wrath, when his righteous judgment will be revealed (Romans 2:5).

Scripture: Romans 2:1-11
Song: "And Can It Be?"

Doug didn't like his heart surgeon. The man was always giving him a hard time. Stop smoking. Stop eating cheeseburgers. Stop with the deep-fried foods. "If you keep on like this," he told Doug, "there won't be anything I can do for you."

"I'd rather live a happy life than a long one," Doug used to say. Sadly, he got his wish. Ten days short of his 61st birthday, the massive heart attack his doctor had been warning him about struck in the middle of his morning shower.

Too often we live as if our actions and our choices have no consequences. And we lash out with anger at anyone who points out the truth to us. Whether it is a doctor, a fellow Christian, or the apostle Paul, we turn a deaf ear. But the day of reckoning will arrive.

The good news is that we have a heart surgeon of another kind. Jesus Christ can clean the blockages in the vessels of our spirit and give us a renewed heart, if we will turn to Him. When the preacher reminds us of sin, it is the voice of Doug's heart surgeon calling him to lay down the smokes. He is warning us of the day to come and offering us a cure that never fails.

Father, You know my transgressions. You can purify my heart. By the blood of Your Son, my Savior, make me clean today. Through Christ I pray. Amen.

At the Table, Together

When you give a banquet, invite the poor, the crippled, the lame, the blind (Luke 14:13).

Scripture: Luke 14:7-18, 21-24
Song: "Come, Sinners, to the Gospel Feast"

Peter Storey was a bishop in South Africa during the height of apartheid. One night, visiting in a prison, he spoke with a black minister who had been arrested. As Storey prepared to offer the man communion, he turned to the white prison guard and invited him to join as well.

Storey said that it is a tradition that the least among us be served first, and so he offered the bread and cup to the black prisoner. He then offered them to the white guard.

The guard found himself suddenly torn. To drink after a black man would be an outrage to him. To refuse the cup of Christ would be an affront to God. After a moment of indecision, he drank. For a few moments, at least, the two men were brothers at the Lord's table.

Who we share a table with says a lot about us. Jesus taught His disciples always to include the poor, the disabled, and the suffering at the banquets of life.

It makes me wonder: Where in my life are the people whom God is inviting to fellowship with Him—and with me? If I will open my eyes to see them, I'll find many in need of food, of clean water, and of a genuine friendship. As God's people, I know I'm called to seek them out and bring them to the table with me.

Lord, open my eyes to see the hungry in the world around me. Open my heart so I might feed them out of the bounty You have given me. Through Christ, amen.

Open Your Hand

You shall open your hand wide to [the poor one] and willingly lend him sufficient for his need, whatever he needs (Deuteronomy 15:8, *New King James Version*).

Scripture: Deuteronomy 15:7-11
Song: "People Need the Lord"

The tiny hut sat in the center of an east African village. As the national host led us through the circle of thatched huts, an elderly woman burst through an open doorway and ran up the path toward us.

"Jambo," she cried in greeting, grasping our hands. The host told us that missionaries had never visited this village before. The woman was beside herself with joy at our presence.

It was a humbling experience, especially when the village people all began to bring gifts and lay them before us. Gifts given out of their poverty. And they each insisted that we lay a hand upon the head of each village child "to bless them."

It was my first of many trips to Kenya, each a soul-shaking experience that never failed to stir me. And today I am again reminded to open my heart and hands, not only in lands abroad, but on my own turf as well.

People need the Lord, and we need not fear giving too much. But like the Israelites in our Scripture, we must beware giving too little.

Father, please make me a vehicle of blessing to others; and may I be sensitive to respond to the needs around me. In Jesus' name, amen.

January 20–26. **Penny Smith,** freelance writer and speaker, has two married sons and lives in Harrisburg, Pennsylvania, with her two Bichon pups.

Caught in the Act

He need not further consider a man, that he should go before God in judgment (Job 34:23, *New King James Version*).

Scripture: Job 34:17-30
Song: "Freedom"

I never liked jury duty, but here I was again. The first case was easy: a shoplifter caught in the act. The second case, however, had been more challenging for the jurors. When a chunk of someone's future is in your hands, you feel as if you're swallowing an apple whole. (Gulp.)

We next carefully considered a drug case, and it brought back painful memories. I found it difficult to concentrate on the pro-and-con arguments in the jury room. My thoughts kept tugging me back to a prison cell where a close relative had served time for drug possession.

Job's comforters claimed that the Almighty hears the cry of the afflicted. From Job's perspective it didn't seem true. Yet Job had cried, "Though he slay me, yet will I hope in him" (Job 13:15). When problems escalate, will we yet believe in the goodness of God?

The drug addict was convicted of the charges against him. But the judge sent him to a drug rehabilitation program rather than to prison. He received another chance for a future.

In a sense, we have all been caught in the act. Yet we believers receive another chance because of Christ—because of the verdict that comes to us by His work on the cross: "Not guilty!"

Thank You, **Father,** for the liberating redemption won for me by the blood of Your Son! I can only respond with a life of humble gratitude. In Jesus' name, amen.

A Little Bit of Greed?

He said this, not because he was concerned about the poor, but because he was a thief, and as he had the money box, he used to pilfer what was put into it (John 12:6, *New American Standard Bible*).

Scripture: John 12:1-8
Song: "Loyalty to Christ"

The Gospel account is clear: Jesus knew the moment Judas betrayed him (see John 13:18-27). The dishonesty of Judas was like a disease that ate away at his character, as he walked the path of unrepentant sin . . . toward judgment.

Judgment is a fearsome thing, but salvation is a matter of choice, offered to all. That is the wonderful hope to which every Christian holds tightly. It is the same hope that Mary demonstrated when she poured out extravagant devotion at the feet of Jesus. Unknowingly, she prepared the Lord for the burial of His body on earth.

Likewise, our extravagant devotion to the Lord will keep us pure in heart. But let us always be aware that "sin crouching at the door" (Genesis 4:7) of our lives. It may start with just a little bit of greed—no doubt the way it crept into Judas's soul. His secret life led him to the brutality of robbery, even from the very poor. Whenever and wherever deception and dishonesty enter—whether in society or in the church—there the character of Judas is emerging.

My dear heavenly Father, help me to walk in Your ways with a true heart. Fill me with Your Spirit that I may reflect Your character for Your glory. In the name of the Father and of the Son and of the Holy Spirit, I pray. Amen.

Arrest His Attention!

Zacchaeus, make haste and come down, for today I must stay at your house (Luke 19:5, *New King James Version*).

Scripture: Luke 19:1-10
Song: "Visit Us"

The room was packed full, and with great detail I described the scene. I said, "Brother Zack was so short that the only way he could hope to see Jesus above the heads of the crowd was to climb a tree." As I was speaking, a gentleman entered the room, and seeing all the seats were taken, he ascended the open stairwell and sat on the top step. The irony of the situation is that the man was less than five feet tall. Show and tell!

Red-faced and stuttering—but realizing it was too late to back out—I continued: "Visitation is based on our desire to see Him," and the brother on the stairs beamed.

A "visitation of the Lord" is one way we might describe the spiritual release that comes when we determine to do whatever it takes to experience Him. Jesus chose to visit the home of Zacchaeus because of the man's obvious desire for such fellowship.

Even today, with us, the Lord comes close—and with a plan to stay, to abide (see John 15). But He also promises special "times of refreshing" from His presence (see Acts 3:10) that can break into our day at any time. That kind of "visitation" happens when we spend time in His Word and in prayer. We will arrest His attention when we give Him ours.

O gracious God, I turn from my insufficiency and crowded circumstances today, to see You at work in my life. Help me to be conscious of Your presence each hour of this day. In the name of Jesus, Lord and Savior of all, I pray. Amen.

Do We Get It?

The master commended the unjust steward because he had dealt shrewdly. For the sons of this world are more shrewd in their generation than the sons of light (Luke 16:8, *New King James Version*).

Scripture: Luke 16:1-9
Song: "Give Me Thy Heart"

The United States is probably the world's greatest offender when it comes to waste. We seem to have little concern for starving populations while we fill our dumpsters with edible food and usable materials.

The group of teens that accompanied me on a missionary trip to the hills of Haiti received a new perspective on stewardship and waste. They learned that not everyone has a soft bed—or even one meal a day. Drinking water had to be boiled, and there was very little of it for bathing. Travel accommodations inland were difficult, at best. Poverty surrounded us.

Our visit to an orphanage capped it. Small children slept on concrete floors and maybe ate one meal daily. In the overcrowded house, the children, faces smeared from running noses, raised their hands to be lifted. The teens obliged with tears streaking their own cheeks as they cuddled the children. Now they got it.

The team arrived home with a mission on their hearts. They now took seriously what Jesus had to say about giving and became faithful stewards of their allowances and earnings from part-time jobs. Bottom line: Stewardship replaced selfishness.

Lord, You have blessed me beyond measure. I want to be a wise steward, regardless of my circumstances. Immerse me in Your mercy, for Jesus' sake. Amen.

He Sees Inside

He said to them, "You are those who justify yourselves before men, but God knows your hearts. For what is highly esteemed among men is an abomination in the sight of God" (Luke 16:15, *New King James Version*).

Scripture: Luke 16:10-18
Song: "Purify My Heart"

After my message one of the missionaries approached me with a chuckle. "That's a nice broach you're wearing." Now I knew that I wore no jewelry because it happened to be taboo here. An evidence of regeneration among this particular tribe was the surrender of ornamental jewelry, and the missionaries honored the tribal custom (see 1 Corinthians 8:13).

The missionary pointed to my jacket lapel—and there sat a monstrous, colorful roach! He informed me that it had rested there throughout the entire message. Fortunately, I was completely unaware, or I would have added sound effects to the message.

Sometimes our view of ourselves is a far cry from what others see. We may either underestimate or overestimate ourselves. The Pharisees were in the latter group. Jesus "bumped their cup," but they would not acknowledge their greed and dishonesty. *The Message* translation of the Bible calls the Pharisees "a money-obsessed bunch." Jesus knew what was inside their hearts. And, as it is with us, when that "inner cup" is bumped, what's inside spills out for all to see.

Lord, I bless Your name for Your faithfulness. Help me to live with integrity of heart that I may be faithful in all my ways, by Your grace. Through Christ, amen.

Why Not Err on the Side of Mercy?

I beg you therefore, father, that you would send him to my father's house (Luke 16:27, *New King James Version*).

Scripture: Luke 16:19-31
Song: "Mercy Is Boundless and Free"

Our church is the first one listed in the yellow pages, and we receive many calls for financial help. We're only too anxious to assist with any legitimate need, yet people are disappointed when we give food or a gift card. You see, we're aware that cash will often be spent on tobacco, alcohol, or drugs.

One mother of three preschoolers was desperate. No food, no fuel, and definitely no fun. She had applied for government assistance, but the process was slow. She didn't know where to turn . . . when she finally looked in the yellow pages.

To ignore such need would be cold and heartless—acting as the rich man did in our Scripture today. So we helped the best we could.

This young mother then offered to pay back what we had contributed. Her heart was right. She also realized that she needed to identify with a local church and include God in her life. Soon she would have a whole family of supportive brothers and sisters in Christ.

The account in Luke may have turned out differently had the rich man extended mercy to Lazarus. No doubt they would have been enjoying the glories of Heaven together. If we are going to err, it is better to err on the side of mercy.

Blessed Lord, in these times of economic stress, help us not to withhold from others the mercy that You wish to extend through us. In the holy name of Jesus, amen.

Shame on You!

This is what the LORD Almighty, the God of Israel, says: Go ahead, add your burnt offerings to your other sacrifices and eat the meat yourselves! (Jeremiah 7:21).

Scripture: Jeremiah 7:21-28
Song: "Each Step I Take"

Did you notice the exclamation mark at the end of verse 21? To me, it's as if the Lord's telling the Israelites: Go ahead, do whatever you want. (But be ready for the consequences.)

Oh, the strong hand of discipline when we make unwise decisions. "I have been watching! declares the Lord," (Jeremiah 7:11). In my generation, it was all about the look. My dad was a man of few words, and the look usually sufficed when we kids needed a little settling down.

Mom, on the other hand, was sometimes a pushover. I truly believe she gleaned her favorite disciplinary words straight from the Bible. For instance, Mom: "How many times do I have to tell you?" God: "I spoke to you again and again, but you did not listen" (Jeremiah 7:13). Mom: "Behave yourself and you can go play." God: "Reform your ways and your actions, and I will let you live in this place" (Jeremiah 7:3). Mom: "Do what you want. You're only hurting yourself." God: "Are they not rather harming themselves, to their own shame?" (Jeremiah 7:19).

Abba, Father, I praise Your holy name. I know Your discipline is for my own good. Help me to reform and change my ways. Teach me to listen. I give thanks for the peace and blessing I will receive when I obey. In Jesus' name, amen.

January 27–January 31. **Shirley J. Conley** is a freelance writer living in Central Florida. She enjoys writing devotionals and creative nonfiction. Her hobbies are gardening and sewing.

His Love

As for God, his way is perfect: The LORD'S word is flawless; he shields all who take refuge in him (2 Samuel 22:31).

Scripture: 2 Samuel 22:26-31
Song: "Love Lifted Me"

I slid into my best shoes and grabbed my purse, Bible, and notebook. Then, rushing from the room, I stumbled . . . and stumbled again. I struggled to regain my balance, gripped my load tighter, and fought to retrieve my footing. *Who will pick me up?*

I live alone, and on occasion I've longed for someone to pick me up when my clumsiness got the better of me. Oh, how I wish I could see—as if on film—the fancy footwork that kept me from colliding with the hardwood floor that day! I think it would give me a good chuckle now.

As a Christian, I've often fallen short of what I believe God expects of me. When I think about that, a wave of self-pity can fill me. *Self-pity*—what an ugly word. And without a doubt it falls into the "flawed human being" category. I'm sure the Lord doesn't admire this trait in me.

On that day of my un-ballerina-like stumble, I rubbed my sprained foot and asked the Lord: "But who will pick me up next time?" I cried aloud as tears blurred my vision.

"I will," God gently whispered. And once more, I know I can rest assured in His promise: He will never leave me. (He even kept me from landing on the floor.)

O God, thank You for reminding me that You remain my shield. Your love lifts me up from my own faults when they threaten to drag me into the pit of self-pity. Thank You for never getting tired of picking me up when I stumble. Through Christ, amen.

Tell Them

Go near and listen to all that the LORD our God says. Then tell us whatever the LORD our God tells you. We will listen and obey (Deuteronomy 5:27).

Scripture: Deuteronomy 5:22-27
Song: "I Love to Tell the Story"

Evan dropped his grandmother's hand and came to stand in front of the lady on the workout machine beside me. His large brown eyes sparkled, and his grin magnified the dimples in his cherubic face. He looked into her eyes. With childlike confidence, he said, "When you die, you're going to Heaven." The lady to whom his prophecy was directed answered with a simple, "Thank you." Without another word, 3-year-old Evan returned to his grandmother's hand as he left the fitness center.

What prompted the child to speak those words to his chosen woman? Is he a modern-day prophet? Is it something he learned in church, and it continued to dwell on his mind? And what made him choose this *particular* lady? (This started me wondering whether Jesus was like Evan at the age of 3.)

In Mark 10:15, Jesus said, "Truly I tell you, anyone who will not receive the kingdom of God like a little child will never enter it." Scripture tells us to listen to the Lord and spread the good news to all the people. We adults should exhibit the courage to approach strangers with words of hope in our struggling world.

O God, the king of glory, teach me to listen and obey. Give me the boldness to go into a sometimes hostile world with Your words of hope and love. Help me to leave fear behind and go forward in faith, so others will know the wonders of Your love. I pray this prayer in the name of Jesus, my merciful Savior and Lord. Amen.

Teach the Children

Do not forget the things your eyes have seen or let them fade from your heart as long as you live. Teach them to your children and to their children after them (Deuteronomy 4:9).

Scripture: Deuteronomy 4:1-10
Song: "Everything Is Beautiful"

"My baby just pee-peed on the potty!" Pride and excitement resonated through the text message sent by my granddaughter, Savannah. I laughed when I saw the accompanying photo of 19-month-old Alexis; her grin reflected her mama's glee.

This started me thinking about what we teach our children—the basics: to walk and talk, to feed and dress themselves, and of course, the potty training. But how much do we teach them about God? (How pleased I was when my granddaughter, Shelby, at the age of 12, recited the books of the Bible.)

As a young child I said the prayer, "Now I lay me down to sleep." I later learned John 3:16, the Lord's Prayer, the 23rd Psalm, and the Ten Commandments. But I still can't recite the books of the Bible.

Now I'm a great-grandmother, and I've returned to Scripture to find out what I should teach the children. On my smartphone, I searched for "teach the children" and came up with 15 Scriptures. All but one was about teaching our children to love and obey God and His laws. However, my personal favorite is Proverbs 22:6, "Start children off on the way they should go, and even when they are old they will not turn from it."

Father, let Your Spirit overflow in me. I want to be a light shining for You in the lives of the little children You've placed in my life. I pray in Jesus' name. Amen.

Hungry for More

They claim to know God, but by their actions they deny him (Titus 1:16).

Scripture: Titus 1:10-16
Song: "Anywhere with Jesus"

"Good morning, Sweetpea," a middle-aged, stout and balding gentleman greeted me at the entrance to the church. *Sweetpea?* I've been called many things, but this was a first. Not sure how to respond, I smiled and accepted his hand. Would this greeting fit with the essential qualities Charles Swindoll included in his article, "How to Recognize a Healthy Church?" I wondered about it as I entered this place of worship for the first time.

My deep desire to let the Holy Spirit have more influence in my life had led me to visit a number of churches. I wanted to expand my biblical knowledge while serving the community. Even more, I needed a church where my soul would be fed as I worshipped in awe of God.

I found that most churches have kept up with technology, making some of them seem impersonal. For example, in this church I never actually met the minister, though I received a welcoming "form letter" by e-mail later in the week. Consequently, I browsed the church's website to discover its core values. As a result, I attended this church for many months—and although some of my needs were met, I never quite felt as if I belonged. I've never been part of planting a church, but my journey has helped me understand the struggles Titus faced.

Lord, I ask for Your guidance and wisdom as You lead me on this journey. May I never lose the love of the Holy Spirit planted in my heart. In Jesus' name, amen.

DEVOTIONS®

February

This is how we know what love is: Jesus Christ laid
down his life for us.

—1 John 3:16

Gary Wilde, Editor   **Margaret Williams,** Project Editor   Photo iStockphoto | Thinkstock®

DEVOTIONS® is published quarterly by Standard Publishing, Cincinnati, Ohio, www.standardpub.com.
© 2012 by Standard Publishing. All rights reserved. Topics based on the Home Daily Bible Readings,
International Sunday School Lessons. © 2010 by the Committee on the Uniform Series. Printed in
the U.S.A. All Scripture quotations, unless otherwise indicated, are taken from the *HOLY BIBLE,
NEW INTERNATIONAL VERSION®. NIV®.* Copyright © 1973, 1978, 1984, 2011 by Biblica, Inc.™
Used by permission of Zondervan. All rights reserved. *The New King James Version.* Copyright ©
1982 by Thomas Nelson, Inc.

Heart Love

This is how we know what love is: Jesus Christ laid down his life for us (1 John 3:16).

Scripture: 1 John 3:14-20
Song: "Lord of Our Life and God of Our Salvation"

It's been said that music is a window to the soul. "How He Loves," written by songwriter John Mark McMillan, certainly touches my soul. It's been my message from God—like a trail of bread crumbs leading me to where He wants me.

My hunger—to let the indwelling Holy Spirit have more of me—persuaded me to search for another church. I never dreamed it would be so difficult. I'd entered this quest the first time I heard "How He Loves," and I thought *Surely this is the church for me.* It wasn't.

After many prayers, I attended another church and joined a women's Bible study that included a Christ-centered exercise and stretching class. During a period of meditation, music softly played in the background . . . God spoke to me through the words of the song.

Not knowing the name of the song, fragments of lyrics spun through my mind until I could no longer stand it. Needing to know the words, I searched iTunes until . . . yes! . . . I found it. Over and over I listened—and worshipped from the heart.

Father God, sometimes I forget, during the hurricanes of life, how much You love me. You gave Your life for me, and I give my life to You. In Jesus' name, amen.

February 1, 2. **Shirley J. Conley** is a freelance writer living in Central Florida. She enjoys writing devotionals and creative nonfiction. Her hobbies are gardening and sewing.

The Implanted Word

Do not merely listen to the word, and so deceive yourselves. Do what it says (James 1:22).

Scripture: James 1:19-27
Song: "Who Keepeth Not God's Word"

The Bible: a precious treasure to some, unimportant to others. A minister once asked several people what one hand-carried item they would take with them if they were exiled to a deserted island. The answers varied from a Boy-Scout knife to matches. Without hesitation, one woman answered, "My Bible. It would entertain me, teach me, bring comfort through the lonely days and nights, and remind me that I'm not alone."

I thought about this some years later when I truly took notice of a homeless man. Each day as I left the parking garage on my way to work, I saw him huddled in a doorway, an island unto himself. His wrinkled shirt hung sloppily below a dirty green jacket. A sweat-stained baseball cap kept his long, dirty hair from his eyes, while a straggly beard covered his face. The shopping bag beside him held his worldly possessions.

What drew my attention to this man? What made him stand out from the many homeless people wandering the streets by day and sleeping in doorways of the city at night? It was the Bible he hovered over. I could tell it wasn't just a Bible like we often give to those in need, but a well-worn personal book. He held the Bible in his lap and humbly received the Word of God.

Gracious Heavenly Father, let me receive Your Word in the same manner as those who cling to the Bible as their only and most treasured possession. I pray that the Holy Spirit will implant the Word in my heart. In the name of Jesus. Amen.

Anybody Here Indispensable?

How can I alone bear your problems and burdens and your complaints? (Deuteronomy 1:12, *New King James Version*).

Scripture: Deuteronomy 1:9-18
Song: "Just a Closer Walk with Thee"

Sadly, power plays are all too common in Christian fellowships. Some people want to be "in the spotlight" at any price. They don't like sharing the work; they become a one-man band.

Moses, in his dawning wisdom, eventually realized that God's work must be shared. As the Jewish nation grew, difficulties increased. Troubles multiplied and had to be sorted out. Growing populations always produce more problems, so Moses needed to find the best and wisest among the tribes to contribute their diplomatic skills for the benefit of the nation. Moses most certainly was not a loner at that point.

God's work is for sharing, and no one is to "lord it over" another. As seventeenth-century Bible commentator Matthew Henry said: "We must not grudge that God's work be done by other hands than ours, provided it be done by good hands."

And none of us is indispensable, of course, in spite of the reports! When it comes to God's work, it's crucial that we work well with others. Why? For the glory of God. But also in order to give all believers the blessed opportunity to exercise their spiritual gifts in kingdom service.

Thank You, **Father,** for giving me the ability to share. Help me to share Your work with others so they may also minister in Your church. Through Christ, amen.

February 3, 5–9. **David R. Nicholas** is a minister and writer who lives with his wife, Judith, in New South Wales, Australia. His interests are history, stamp-collecting, and photography.

Decide for Yourself

Nevertheless good things are found in you, in that you have removed the wooden images from the land, and have prepared your heart to seek God (2 Chronicles 19:3, New King James Version).

Scripture: 2 Chronicles 19:1-7
Song: "All to Jesus"

Brothers Christopher and Peter Hitchens had a similar upbringing but took very different paths in life. Christopher was a member of the "New Atheists" who believed that the concept of a supreme being destroys individual freedom. In his book *God Is Not Great*, he wrote on atheism and the supposed negative effects of religion. Peter, on the other hand, became an active member of the Church of England. He advocates for moral virtues based on the Christian faith. His 2010 book, *The Rage Against God*, tells his own journey to faith and argues against the reasons that people use to reject God.

Father and son Asa and Jehoshaphat also took two very different approaches to faith in God. As king of Judah, Asa refused to seek God's will or obey His laws. Jehoshaphat was not a perfect king, but he did try to seek God's guidance and worked to remove idols from the land. Because he had "prepared [his] heart to seek God," the Lord blessed his reign.

Those who sincerely seek the true God will find him. We just need to prepare our hearts and head toward the Lord.

Father, thank You for offering us the freedom to make our own decisions to follow You. Give us hearts that are able to respond to Your call on our lives. In Jesus' name, amen.

February 4. **Cheryl J. Frey** is a professional proofreader living in Rochester, New York.

Justice and Mercy

Defend the poor and fatherless; Do justice to the afflicted and needy (Psalm 82:3, *New King James Version*).

Scripture: Psalm 82
Song: "Help Somebody Today"

Charles Spurgeon, the great English preacher of the 1800s, speaking on Psalm 82, told of Francis I of France. A woman knelt before him and begged for justice. The king said, "Justice I owe you, and justice you shall have. But if you *beg* anything of me, let it be mercy."

Our psalm tells us the poor and fatherless were at the mercy of judges. They were without money and without friends to help them. Such needed defending.

Times have changed but similar situations abound, as many still deal unkindly with the needy. The psalmist knew full well the need for mercy in human existence. While our verse calls for justice, we may also recall Micah 6:8, "What does the Lord require of you but to do justly, to love mercy, and to walk humbly with your God?"

Sometimes we miss opportunities to reach out and help others because we're so caught up with our own problems and difficulties. We have "I" trouble and fail to see those struggling right next to us. So today I'm asking the Lord to help me remember: when I help others I unwittingly help myself. I take one more step toward becoming a person characterized by a compassionate heart.

Gracious Lord, may I have the wisdom to extend mercy to those in need in my world. After all, how merciful You have been to me! In Jesus' name, amen.

Wealth and Wings

A man with an evil eye hastens after riches, And does not consider that poverty will come upon him (Proverbs 28:22, *New King James Version*).

Scripture: Proverbs 28:18-22
Song: "The Gift of Love"

A multimillionaire I knew fell sick and died. Then, of course, all his wealth was of little use to him. Further, after his death his family squabbled over what he had left behind. Even they found little comfort in riches.

Wealth comes; wealth goes. There's no certainty in it for, as the Bible says, "Riches certainly make themselves wings; they fly away like an eagle toward heaven" (Proverbs 23:5). Our verse provides a strong warning against the dangers that come with riches. Ironically, so often, some form of poverty tends to follow wealth.

Our western civilization is largely a consumer society, a sign of much riches. Yet personal debt is on the rise, and government spending seems to know no bounds. Nevertheless, a settled joy and happiness go undiscovered among the populace at large. No doubt the apostle James holds the key: "Every good gift and every perfect gift is from above, and comes down from the Father of lights" (1:17). When we recognize and understand this wonderful fact, we're able to keep riches in perspective and live for God's glory.

Dear Lord, I know that You are not so much concerned about how much money I give, but how much I consider to be purely my own. Remind me that all I have is on loan from You. Help me to be a good steward of Your riches! Through Christ, amen.

Judgment Is Coming

To Him all the prophets witness that, through His name, whoever believes in Him will receive remission of sins (Acts 10:43, *New King James Version*).

Scripture: Acts 10:34-43
Song: "Judge Me, O Lord, and Prove My Ways"

In the days of slavery in America, slaves would sing, "My Lord sees all you do, my Lord hears all you say, and my Lord keeps a writin' all the time." Such a song made plantation owners tremble, for it spoke of coming judgment. Indeed, the task of the Holy Spirit, down through the centuries, is to "convict the world of sin, and of righteousness, and of judgment" (John 16:8).

These days we hear little of judgment, so we do well to heed the words of Paul in Acts 10. Sin is our problem. Jesus, however, came into this world and dealt with that sin. When we enter the waters of baptism, we receive remission of our sins. Moreover, the Holy Spirit comes to dwell within us—and starts the lifelong process of making us holy (i.e., like Jesus). God has always had His witnesses and, all the while, He's creating new ones.

Isn't it wonderful to know that you are no longer separated from God, but rather joined to Him in Christ? Whenever we become aware of this great truth, we become strong ambassadors for Christ. Then when people look at us, they see Christ in us as their "hope of glory" (Colossians 1:27).

Thank You, **Almighty God and Father,** that Your Son has paid the price of all my sin. Now help me live a life of thanksgiving and praise until the day I stand before You with joy! In the precious name of Jesus my Savior. Amen.

Armored with the Word

The night is far spent, the day is at hand. Therefore let us cast off the works of darkness, and let us put on the armor of light (Romans 13:12, *New King James Version*).

Scripture: Romans 13:8-14
Song: "Labor On"

Lowell Mason's hymn arrangement puts it well, "Work, for the night is coming, work through the sunny noon; Fill brightest hours with labor, Rest comes sure and soon. Give every flying minute, something to keep in store."

Our verse today reflects a strong biblical theme that runs throughout the Scripture: the theme of darkness versus light, night versus day. And what a vast difference there is between the works of darkness and the works of light! So here's a firm challenge from the apostle Paul for us to throw off dark works and put on the armor of light, a call to change our way of living. The devil seeks to pull us down, but the Lord desires to build us up. The two ways are worlds apart and lead to very different places.

True love is the result of living in the light and walking in the light, even as Christ is the light of the world. It's night, but dawn is on the way. Therefore, we're wise when we use the armor God has provided—His Word. Will you join me in reading it today?

Father, today help me remember that the Christian walk means a constant conflict with the powers of darkness. I know that when I'm armed with Your Word, the works of darkness cannot harm me. You have given Your children the best—and ultimate—protection against all temptations. Thank You, through Christ my Lord. Amen.

No Favorites

If you show partiality, you commit sin, and are convicted by the law as transgressors (James 2:9, *New King James Version*).

Scripture: James 2:1-13
Song: "Earthly Pleasures Vainly Call Me"

When I lived in Melbourne, I discovered that the Nicholas family, makers of aspirin, were very wealthy (but I was not related). When I moved to Sydney, I began attending a Bible study there. A stranger approached me and said, "You're from Melbourne, so are you one of the Nicholas family?"

When I said, "No," he turned away and never spoke to me again, even though I saw him every week.

With ease we play favorites, an attitude to others that will quickly reveal our attitude to God. Here's what I mean: Show me how a person lives, and I'll tell you what they think of God.

Clearly, our text reminds us that we must not play favorites. It becomes easier to do if we'll stop and ask ourselves: *How can I compare the riches of Christ with the riches of this world?*

There is no comparison, yet we often give place to someone because they're rich in this world's goods. I want to remember today that I possess unsearchable riches in Christ (see Ephesians 3:8). True, the things of the world can bedazzle me at times. But they are so temporary, and the face of Christ, my Lord, shines so much more brightly, even than gold. He it is who will fill my vision throughout eternity.

Heavenly Father, help me see everyone as equal in Your sight. Remind me that, at the foot of the cross, the ground is completely level! In Jesus' name, amen.

Increasing Faith

We ought always to thank God for you . . . because your faith is growing more and more, and the love all of you have for one another is increasing (2 Thessalonians 1:3).

Scripture: 2 Thessalonians 1:3-12
Song: "Growing Dearer Each Day"

I am an online missionary, inviting people to know more of Christ through the Internet. About six months ago, Mike wrote in and committed his life to the Lord. I answer dozens of e-mails from people like him who have expressed faith in Jesus Christ, but Mike's story touched me.

Mike is paralyzed. When he first contacted me, Mike asked questions about why he was paralyzed, wondering whether God loved him. Over several months, I shared my faith and helped him realize that having a disability isn't the end of the world. My friend was eventually baptized. And he sometimes says: "I can see how my disability is actually a gift."

Today's verse encourages me. Not only am I blessed to minister to folks like Mike, but my faith and love increase as I do so. I learn more about the Lord when I research a question, and my prayer life deepens as I intercede for a new believer.

What are you doing today to increase your faith and deepen your prayer life? Could you send an encouraging Scripture to a friend or pray for the person in front of you at the store?

Lord, help me find new ways to increase my faith and show my love today. May I be creative in the ways I do it. In the name of Jesus, amen.

February 10–16. **Tait Berge**, living in Colorado Springs, is the Church Relations Director at Mephibosheth Ministry. When not working, he enjoys sports, especially hockey and golf.

Want to Be Skillful for Christ?

Fight the good fight of the faith. Take hold of the eternal life to which you were called when you made your good confession in the presence of many witnesses (1 Timothy 6:12).

Scripture: 1 Timothy 6:6-12
Song: "Weary, Burdened Wanderer"

I'm tired. My body aches. I don't want to do this anymore. *I quit, Lord!*

That has been my attitude for the last couple of weeks. The Lord feels far away. The words aren't coming out for my writing projects, and typing with bad hands and shoulders is painful at best. I wonder if anyone I've ministered to recently really accepts the message of the good news of God's love. Bottom line: Does my work in the kingdom of God really matter?

Then I read today's verse, and I remember—the last time I felt near the Lord, the last time I received positive feedback on my writing, and an encouraging note from someone I've discipled. Most of all, I remember the time when I first said "yes" to Christ's call to ministry.

Today's verse is a good reminder for me as I battle my discouragement. I must remember to fight the good fight of my faith. How about you? Will you join me in fighting the good fight of faith in times of discouragement? Our times of spiritual dryness and all our adversities are working to make us stronger. As one African proverb puts it: "Smooth seas do not make skillful sailors."

Father, help me to battle my discouragement and to fight the good fight of faith, no matter the circumstances. You are sufficient in all things! Through Christ, amen.

The Power of Prayer

May the Lord make your love increase and overflow for each other and for everyone else, just as ours does for you (1 Thessalonians 3:12).

Scripture: 1 Thessalonians 3:4-13
Song: "Let Us Love and Sing and Wonder"

Sometimes I don't know where to begin to pray. I stumble on words, and names refuse to come to mind.

The other day, sitting in worship, I started to pray for everyone that came to mind. I prayed for the worship leader. I prayed for my brother's family, and I lifted my brother before the Lord, that he might receive the good news and become a Christian. I also prayed for my mom and my fiancée.

I looked up when I finished. I couldn't believe where the time had gone.

My brothers live in other states, and I haven't seen them for a long time, yet my prayers for them helped me realize how much God is concerned for them. My prayers for my mother's health helped me realize that she is God's child too. When I prayed for my fiancée, I realized in a deeper way how much she means to me.

My love for the people I prayed for increased that day. Each person is close to me, and I saw each of them through the Lord's eyes. I am newly aware of the power of prayer. Our love increases as we pray for everyone on our prayer lists.

Lord, I want to pray more during my days! Help me to see that this is never time wasted, but that it is at the heart of Your will for me. So, increase my love as I pray for my family, my friends, strangers, and even my enemies. Through Christ, amen.

Why Not?

When Jesus heard this, he was amazed at him, and turning to the crowd following him, he said, "I tell you, I have not found such great faith even in Israel" (Luke 7:9).

Scripture: Luke 7:1-10
Song: "Faith Is a Living Power from Heaven"

Have you ever thought about amazing Jesus? Is it even possible? After all, Jesus is all-powerful and all-knowing, the Alpha and Omega . . . the very Son of God.

According to Scripture, a certain man amazed our Lord. It was a Gentile, a commander in the Roman army, and his servant was sick. But he came to a Jewish rabbi, believing this humble preacher could heal his servant. In the commander's view, Jesus wouldn't even need to come to the place where the sick one lay. Just saying a few words would suffice; healing would follow.

What faith! Luke tells us that Jesus was amazed. Was it because the soldier was a Roman—yet still believed? Was it because the entire religious culture of the day would naturally deny such a possibility? (After all, some of the religious folks thought Jesus' healings were actually from the devil!)

Let us learn from this soldier's outlook on the miraculous. Do we believe Jesus still heals? I know that I would like to amaze Jesus with a powerful depth of faith—that He might accomplish marvelous things in and through me as I seek to do His will. Today I may even ask Jesus to do something impossible, something only He could do. Why not?

Lord, give me the boldness to ask for the impossible from You. Give me the insight, as well, to make sure it conforms to Your kingdom plans! In Jesus' name, amen.

Valentine for Jesus

As she stood behind him at his feet weeping, she began to wet his feet with her tears. Then she wiped them with her hair, kissed them and poured perfume on them (Luke 7:38).

Scripture: Luke 7:36-50
Song: "Merciful Savior, Come and Be My Comfort"

Today is Valentine's Day, a day when we show "sweet" love to the special people in our lives. Typically we give cards or chocolate, but sometimes our gifts are more extravagant—like perfume. Jesus received a jar of perfume one day, and it changed a woman's life.

We know the story well. Jesus is dining at Simon's house when a woman starts kissing His feet and wiping them with her hair. She pours perfume on them.

This is a beautiful scene, marred only by one sad fact: Everyone knew who this woman was—a prostitute. But outweighing everything is this happy, blessed fact: Jesus showed mercy, extended compassion, forgave her sins.

Isn't it interesting that the woman gave her gift *before* Jesus forgave her? She took a risk in extending herself, letting down and being vulnerable. With this opening of her heart lay the chance that she might be severely scolded and sent away—or worse.

What can you and I give to Jesus on this Valentine's Day? The same thing this woman gave: an open, sweet heart.

Heavenly Father, on this Valentine Day, I give You my best gift: willingly, I give You my whole self. And thank You for Your greater gift to me—forgiveness and unconditional love through the merits of Your Son, in whom I pray. Amen.

Don't Compare

So then, just as you received Christ Jesus as Lord, continue to live your lives in him, rooted and built up in him, strengthened in the faith as you were taught, and overflowing with thankfulness (Colossians 2:6, 7).

Scripture: Colossians 2:1-7
Song: "Ten Thousand Thanks to Jesus"

Lately I've felt that my ministry borders on the meaningless. I sit down to hammer out a devotional or two or write an encouraging e-mail to a friend, and I wonder if my effort is worth it. *Do my words mean anything? Am I making any difference in people's lives?*

To make matters worse, I came across a story about someone who is—clearly, and obvious to all—making a real difference. This person is speaking, traveling, and writing books. People follow her on twitter. Compared to my small ministry, it seems the Lord is using her so much more than He is using me.

Today's verse helps me reverse my thinking. I've received Christ as my Lord and accepted His calling on my life. I have been built up in Christ. I am being strengthened in my faith. Instead of envying another's ministry, perhaps I could use this verse as an encouragement to renew my thinking—and approach each new day of work with the joy of the Lord. Yes, this verse helps me understand that my calling is unique to me. So why should I ever compare myself to others?

Almighty and most merciful God, each day help me live in the truth that Your calling is designed especially and uniquely for each of Your servants. Forgive my jealousy toward the ministries of other brothers and sisters in the body of Christ. Help me to be grateful for all that You pour into my life. In the name of Jesus, amen.

Why Hold Anything Back?

Was not our father Abraham considered righteous for what he did when he offered his son Isaac on the altar? . . . His faith was made complete by what he did (James 2:21, 22).

Scripture: James 2:14-26
Song: "Faith of Our Fathers"

My faith was tested when I met a woman with whom I envisioned spending the rest of my life. Before we could marry, however, we discovered obstacles in our way. We both used wheelchairs and needed a big enough place to live. Our finances wouldn't meet our needs, and friends warned me to be careful.

Still, I was convinced that God would provide for us, and I went forward, planning a new life with my fiancée. I did everything to try and make this work—including being willing to give up everything I had.

As I think back to that time, I rejoice in the many ways my faith grew amidst my increasing willingness to obey the Lord. He may have indeed asked me to marry, but he eventually pulled me back from giving up everything. Like Abraham, I believe that God tested my love for Him, bringing me to the brink of making life-changing decisions.

Is God asking you to do something difficult? Do you love Him enough to give it all up? Remember that His "tests" are always for the purpose of displaying our genuine faith. As the severely tested Job proclaimed: "He knows the way that I take; when he has tested me, I will come forth as gold" (Job 23:10).

Lord, amidst my trials, help me remember to ask: "How will He use this to grow my faith?" In other words, help me turn my faith into action! In Jesus' name, amen.

Already There

"Because the poor are plundered and the needy groan, I will now arise," says the LORD. **"I will protect them"** (Psalm 12:5).

Scripture: Psalm 12
Song: "Rescue the Perishing"

A few years ago, I took a group of teenagers on a mission trip to Juarez, Mexico. In the months leading up to the trip, our team met together on a regular basis for training and preparation. After a few sessions, I realized that team members seemed to have a skewed perspective on the importance of our ministry to the Mexican people. I sensed a subtle arrogance, for example, about how we were going to take the hope of Jesus to "those poor, suffering people."

As I prayed during the next week, I began to realize that these people weren't just sitting around waiting on us to come to them! The Lord showed me that they were not without hope. He also convinced me that we were not taking Jesus to Mexico—because He was already there among the poor. We were simply going to *join Him in His work,* in order to win the hearts of those He already deeply loved.

Here in this psalm, God declares that He will arise and protect the weak and needy. Wherever we find poverty and suffering, there we will find God.

Heavenly Father, You are there in the midst of humanity's pain, just as You were centuries ago, when Jesus took on flesh and dwelt among us. In His name, amen.

February 17–23. **Mark Williams** is an associate minister, college professor, and freelance writer who lives with his wife, Kelley, and their seven children near Nashville, Tennessee.

Victory in the Valley

The Philistines occupied one hill and the Israelites another, with the valley between them (1 Samuel 17:3).

Scripture: 1 Samuel 17:1-11
Song: "How Great Is Our God"

As a child I played basketball each year in a league run by the local YMCA. My older brother was the undisputed star of the team, while I kept the bench warm for him during the games.

At the end of one season, our team had progressed to the championship game, and the score was very close as we headed to the end of the fourth quarter. The game was exciting, friends and family were cheering, and my stomach was in knots.

At a decisive point—in the final seconds—one of our players fouled out. As the coach turned toward our bench, I heard my voice say, "Please don't put me in, Coach." I was afraid I'd make a mistake and be the reason our team lost the game.

Ouch. Today, I am still embarrassed at my cowardice in that moment. All the glory and excitement were out on that floor, but I settled for the view from the bench on the sidelines.

As Goliath came out from his camp each morning, the Israelites watched from the sidelines as well. Fear and discouragement ran through their ranks as he shouted out his threats each day. The victory was there for the taking, but the Israelite army just sat on the bench.

O God my Father, today give me the courage to get off the sidelines and find victory in the valley with You! Help me to remember that You and I, working for the advance of Your kingdom, are always an overwhelming offensive threat! In the name of Jesus, who lives and reigns with You and the Holy Spirit, amen.

Just One Sacrifice

At that time they sacrificed to the LORD seven hundred head of cattle and seven thousand sheep and goats from the plunder they had brought back (2 Chronicles 15:11).

Scripture: 2 Chronicles 15:1-12
Song: "Nothing but the Blood"

I once helped an elderly relative with two different eyedrops: one went in the left eye four times a day and the other in both eyes three times a day—but not at the same time as the other drops. How I wished there were drops that worked with just one dose a day!

In the Old Testament, the sacrificial system was also complicated. It demanded that different animals be sacrificed for the forgiveness of the sins of the people. In this passage, thousands of animals were slaughtered as an atoning sacrifice.

Can you imagine how long it would take to slaughter 7,000 sheep and goats or 700 head of cattle? Can you see the river of blood that would flow from the altar as the throats were slit? Can you smell the stench of death, see the pile of carcasses? It would be hard to stomach . . . so much blood . . . constantly repeated.

Yet, on the cross, we find an eternally effective bloodletting, putting an end to the old way. As the writer of Hebrews put it: "It is impossible for the blood of bulls and goats to take away sins. Therefore . . . we have been made holy through the sacrifice of the body of Jesus Christ once for all" (10:4, 5, 10).

Dear Father in Heaven, I rejoice and give thanks for the perfect lamb of God, the once-for-all sacrifice for sin. In His victory over death, I am victorious in life. Help me to remember His cross today and live in His power. Through Jesus' name, amen.

Hearing When He Speaks

When I heard these things, I sat down and wept. For some days I mourned and fasted and prayed (Nehemiah 1:4).

Scripture: Nehemiah 1
Song: "Sweet Hour of Prayer"

Back in my early days of ministry, I served as a youth minister for a larger church in eastern Tennessee. One year, as high school graduation approached, I was asked if I would like to preach in our main services on the Sunday morning that we honored our high school graduates. As I had never preached in a Sunday morning service before, I was both excited and terrified.

Even though I was nervous, I sensed the presence of the Holy Spirit with me as I prayed for inspiration in my preaching. I was reminded of how Nehemiah fasted and prayed when he heard about the condition of his people, and I sensed that God was calling me to fast and pray as well.

I started my fast on Monday morning and felt that God was calling me to fast for five days. Each day, I read the Scriptures and prayed for His guidance. Slowly, as the week progressed, the sermon God had planned for me became clear. When I stepped to that pulpit on Sunday morning, I was confident that God had a message for our graduates and their families. That sermon, "Advice for the Ages," is still tucked away in my files in my office . . . as a reminder that God speaks when I listen.

Almighty and everlasting God, when I face tough decisions or need a word from You, remind me that You will speak when I seek You with prayer and fasting. In the name of Jesus, Lord and Savior of all, I pray. Amen.

A Need . . . or a Greed?

Before I finished praying in my heart, Rebekah came out, with her jar on her shoulder. She went down to the spring and drew water, and I said to her, "Please give me a drink" (Genesis 24:45).

Scripture: Genesis 24:42-52
Song: "God Is Able"

I dread taking my younger children to the grocery store because of the checkout aisle. Our shopping usually goes fairly well until we come to this treasure trove of goodies, all exactly positioned at eye level in a child's world. It's here that they start begging me to buy something for them. "Daddy, can I please get some candy? *Please?*" Sometimes I give in (especially to my 3-year-old daughter) and let them each pick one thing. At other times, with more resolve, I refuse.

Either way, it's a good teachable moment where I remind them that they don't actually *need* what they are asking for, they simply *want* it. I am standing with a basketful of needs: milk, bread, fruit, cereal . . . to carry us through the week.

God in His generosity has always provided for our family. He is faithful to take care of our needs, both spiritually and physically, but not always as quick to give us our wants on demand.

As in our Scripture passage, God is working to provide our needs before the prayer passes our lips. Why? Because these things are in His will for us and are good for our growth and development.

O Lord God, thank You for providing all of my needs according to Your will for me. Help me also to want the things You want for me. In Jesus' name, amen.

It's All in the Name

The name of the LORD is a fortified tower; the righteous run to it and are safe (Proverbs 18:10).

Scripture: Proverbs 18:2-13
Song: "Blessed Be Your Name"

Part of good marketing is to sell not only your product but also your name. Companies spend millions each year trying to help us remember their brand and become loyal customers of that name. For example, as I was growing up, my father always encouraged me to buy a certain brand of appliance "because the name meant quality." Now, as an adult, I have a tendency to look for this product because I've come to believe it's higher quality, based entirely on the name.

The ancient Israelites knew God by a special name. When we see the word *LORD* capitalized in Scripture, it refers to the Hebrew name *Jehovah*. This name was, and is, so holy among Jews that many won't say it aloud even today. (They say *Adonai* in its place.)

Instead of being known by an image or a form, the God of Israel chose to be known by His name. And this name is more than just some letters across the front of a shirt; it is pregnant with meaning. This name means love, faithfulness, and strength. It means that God is a refuge in a time of trouble. He is our redemption. He is the LORD, and we are His people walking together with Him.

Lord, today may I truly come to understand that You alone are my refuge and strength. With each problem I face in the days ahead, remind me that I can trust in You to carry me through. In Jesus' name, amen.

Sticks and Stones

Out of the same mouth come praise and cursing. My brothers and sisters, this should not be (James 3:10).

Scripture: James 3:1-12
Song: "They'll Know We Are Christians by Our Love"

"Sticks and stones may break my bones, but words can never hurt me!" As children, we chanted this rhyme at recess to other children who were being mean or making fun of us. As a young child, I took it at face value; as an adult, I believe it to be an unadulterated lie.

In reality, it has been my experience that sticks and stones can *only* break your bones, while words can damage and scar your heart for a lifetime. Broken bones heal in a matter of months; broken hearts sometimes never heal.

Having worked in church ministry for over 20 years, I am amazed by the number of people who carry deep wounds because of things that were said to them by their parents, spouses, children, friends, or fellow church members. These memories can affect a person's self worth, their view of God, and their ability to love others.

The tongue can be a "fire" and a "world of evil," but it can also be something much more powerful. Words of love and forgiveness can save a marriage; words of compassion can heal a friendship; words of praise and encouragement can lift the spirits of a child. As followers of Christ, our words should reflect the love we have for one another.

Holy Spirit, fill my mouth today with words that build others up and bring You glory! In the name of Jesus, my Savior, I pray. Amen.

Stronger Than the Surf

Your statutes, LORD, stand firm; holiness adorns your house for endless days (Psalm 93:5).

Scripture: Psalm 93
Song: "He Wills That I Should Holy Be"

Living in the corner of Kansas, our trips to the ocean are rare. So it was with tremendous anticipation that my wife and I visited the coast of northern Oregon some years ago. Its rugged, rocky beauty did not disappoint us!

As we stood on the rocks, it was impossible not to feel some sense of awe as the waves crashed in, again and again and again. How could anything withstand such power? Surely, in another ten thousand years, every block and boulder would be ground to sand. The constant pounding of the waves and the wind could eventually send even the hardest rock into the beach. And yet, the coastline still holds, the beaches still stand. The ocean is still held in check.

Of how much greater power is the Word of God! Through the centuries it has withstood the bitterest attacks. Even though the enemies of truth still seek to silence the Scriptures, the revelation of the Lord through His prophets and apostles, through the Son himself, still guides, still stands firm. Against the relentless attacks of the enemy, the statutes of the Lord provide us with a solid anchor for life and for living.

O God, though the winds of life beat against me, sustain me by the power of Your Word. Let my feet be firmly anchored on the truth of Christ. In His name, amen.

February 24–28. **Doc Arnett** is the director of Institutional Research at Highland Community College and minister of New Life Church in Blair, Kansas.

A Sure Refuge

Kiss his son, or he will be angry and your way will lead to your destruction, for his wrath can flare up in a moment. Blessed are all who take refuge in him (Psalm 2:12).

Scripture: Psalm 2
Song: "Rest in Jesus"

My wife and I live in an old farmhouse in northeastern Kansas. Our gravel driveway runs straight up from the highway to our backdoor. Down near the road, just at the end of the small horse paddock, was an old evergreen shrub. Over the years it had spread out to nearly 20 feet wide. Many of the branches had died and turned brown and ugly. So I decided to get rid of it.

As I'd hoped, my little utility tractor with its hydraulic bucket loader made short work of the project. As I raised the tangled mass of roots and branches up from the ground, I saw a rabbit shoot out from underneath, streaking toward the tree line a few hundred feet away. The cottontail had held to its hiding place throughout the upheavals of the tractor's work. I chuckled as I imagined the rabbit's astonishment as its dense, sheltering cover had been plucked up into the sky!

When we take refuge in the Son of God, we do not have to worry that one day our true shelter will be destroyed. There is no force on Heaven or earth that can overcome Him who protects us. While all else might be shaken and removed, those who hide their souls in Him need never fear.

I thank You, **Lord,** and give You praise, that You have provided me with the refuge of Your arms. Keep me safe, I pray, in the name of Jesus. Amen.

The Right Blend

In your majesty ride forth victoriously in the cause of truth, humility and justice; let your right hand achieve awesome deeds (Psalm 45:4).

Scripture: Psalm 45:1-9
Song: "Majesty"

Although my cooking experiments usually turn out to be edible, they don't always turn out to be desirable. One reason is that I'm not at all reluctant to substitute and experiment.

Recently, I wanted to make some cookies. Since we didn't have any graham cracker crumbs on hand, I substituted some crushed cinnamon squares cereal. Dark brown molasses filled in for light corn syrup. Seems like there was another substitution or two as well. Anyway . . . to make a short story shorter, the experiment was less than amazingly successful. Too many strong flavors competing for limited taste capacity, I suppose.

Just as we need balance in our favorite recipes, we need balance in our battles for hearts and souls. So often, we see people on different sides of some issue rip one another apart like piranhas in a feeding frenzy. When we're so convinced of the justice of our cause and the truth of our claims that we forget humility, we depart from the example and spirit of Christ.

I remember something I heard an old preacher say years ago: "Christianity doesn't make someone mean." If even the cause of Christ should be pursued by "speaking the truth in love," shouldn't all of our lesser causes also be pursued in humility?

Dear Lord in Heaven, help me to remain humble, even when fighting for truth and justice. I pray through my deliverer, Jesus. Amen.

Righteous Judgment

Judgment will again be founded on righteousness, and all the upright in heart will follow it (Psalm 94:15).

Scripture: Psalm 94:8-15
Song: "Judge Eternal, Throned in Splendor"

As an administrator and teacher at a small community college, I sometimes have the opportunity to do some informal counseling. Recently, a young man sat in my office and poured out his heart. "I think I'm cursed," he confided. With little prompting, he shared some of the episodes from his young life.

After a while, I started to probe a little bit, asking him for details of one thing and another. Soon, I was able to show the young man that in every one of these episodes, he'd demonstrated a pattern of making decisions without getting the required information—or just ignoring the available information.

I've found, in my own life, and seen frequently in the lives of others, that most of the blame for bad situations rests ultimately on the decisions that we have made for ourselves. Either we use a faulty foundation or we ignore truth and righteousness. That's when we begin paying a high price for our bad choices.

I suppose it seems easier to blame God for the messes we find ourselves in—or to chalk it up to "being cursed" (or just having a run of bad luck). It's easier than to accept that responsibility ourselves. But to choose and use righteousness as the foundation of our decisions brings life and blessing.

Dear Lord, help us all, whether young or old, to make righteousness the bedrock of our judgments. Before taking important steps may I immerse the decision in prayer and get the information I need. In Jesus' name, amen.

The Applause of Earth

Let the rivers clap their hands, let the mountains sing together for joy (Psalm 98:8).

Scripture: Psalm 98
Song: "Come, O Creator Spirit Blest"

I have been fascinated by water since I was a little kid. Whether wading in the tiny creek that ran through the woods on our Kentucky farm or standing on an ocean beach, I have always been captivated. Because of their beauty, power, and sparkling reflections, the waters of the world draw me to contemplation, admiration, and appreciation for our maker.

The rivers are my favorites, especially the rock-bed streams of the mountain regions. I love the feel of cold, smooth stone against my feet as I wade cautiously. I love the smell and feel of the spray at the base of a waterfall. Whether running the rapids in a canoe or just sitting on a huge boulder and feeling the fall sun on my face, I love the experience.

It is easy in the surging sounds of the waterfall and the rapids to sense that the rivers are, indeed, clapping their hands. For the believer, the thunderous applause becomes an expression of admiration for the creator.

Yes, the rushing waters of the earth applaud Heaven for the joy of their being. So how much more fitting it is for us to shout for the joy of our salvation.

O God, Creator of Heaven and earth, with all of my being, I applaud You for the beauty of Your creation and for the joy of the salvation You have given the world through Christ Jesus. When I look at the glories of this universe, let me lift my voice to You in praise. Through Christ my precious Lord, amen.

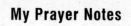

My Prayer Notes

_____
_____
_____
_____
_____
_____
_____
_____
_____
_____
_____
_____
_____
_____
_____
_____
_____
_____
_____
_____
_____
_____
_____
_____
_____
_____

My Prayer Notes

_____

_____

_____

_____

_____

_____

_____

_____

_____

_____

_____

_____

_____

_____

_____

_____

_____

_____

_____

_____

_____

_____

My Prayer Notes

DEVOTIONS®

March

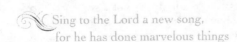

Sing to the Lord a new song,
for he has done marvelous things

—*Psalm 98:1*

Gary Wilde, Editor | **Margaret Williams,** Project Editor   Photo by Brand X Pictures | Thinkstock®

Volume 57   No. 2

DEVOTIONS® is published quarterly by Standard Publishing, Cincinnati, Ohio, www.standardpub.com.
© 2013 by Standard Publishing. All rights reserved. Topics based on the Home Daily Bible Readings,
International Sunday School Lessons. © 2010 by the Committee on the Uniform Series. Printed in
the U.S.A. All Scripture quotations, unless otherwise indicated, are taken from the *HOLY BIBLE,
NEW INTERNATIONAL VERSION®. NIV®.* Copyright © 1973, 1978, 1984, 2011 by Biblica Inc™.
Used by permission of Zondervan. All rights reserved. *King James Version (KJV),* public domain.
New American Standard Bible (NASB), © The Lockman Foundation, 1960, 1962, 1963, 1968,
1971, 1972, 1973, 1975, 1977, 1995.

A Day Is Coming

The time has come for judging the dead, and for rewarding your servants the prophets and your people who revere your name, both great and small—and for destroying those who destroy the earth (Revelation 11:18).

Scripture: Revelation 11:15-19
Song: "We Will Ride"

Even though I try hard to keep peace in my heart, I have to admit there's something about those old Clint Eastwood movies that attracts me. Is it the ancient aching of humans to see justice done, to see the wicked punished for their deeds? Yet there's a part of me that has to admit: It's not always easy to see the white-hatted cowboy as being so different from the villains.

I often grow weary of seeing the powerful abuse the weak, of seeing the influential gain advantage over the powerless. I think all of us long for that reckoning of justice over injustice, to see the ultimate triumph of good over evil.

In order to embrace the great day of reckoning, let us also reckon with what might need purifying in our own hearts. Thankfully, we can, daily, cooperate with the Holy Spirit in guarding our hearts from the ever-present inclination toward sin. As we continue in our vigilance, persevere in our submission to God's will for our lives, and increase in reverence for Him, we grow in anticipation of our reward on that wonderful day!

Lord, let me never yield to the deceit of my own desires, but ever submit to Your judgment and Your will. In Jesus' name, amen.

March 1, 2. **Harold "Doc" Arnett** directs institutional research at the oldest college in Kansas (Highland Community College). He and his wife, Randa, live in Blair, Kansas.

An Eternal Throne

Your house and your kingdom will endure forever before me; your throne will be established forever (2 Samuel 7:16).

Scripture: 2 Samuel 7:4-16
Song: "Our God Reigns"

Over the last 40 years or so, I have done eight major house remodelings. During these years, I've invested multiple thousands of dollars and hundreds of hours. The results have been pretty impressive from one point of view; I've created beautiful kitchens, lovely bedrooms, and bath areas that are attractive and functional.

From another perspective, though, all this work could be seen as a complete waste of time. Every one of those houses will one day rot or burn or be torn down. They cannot endure forever.

So it is with every nation, every dynasty, and every power on earth. All kings and kingdoms, all realms and rulers, all nations and notions will one day fail and fall. All . . . with only one exception: the kingdom of Christ, Son of David.

When Jesus promised Peter, "I will build my church, and the gates of Hades will not overcome it" (Matthew 16:18), He served notice that the throne of David would be finally established forever, just as God had promised the shepherd king.

Though everything of this world that I have put my hand to will one day perish, not even a drop of cold water that I have given in His name will lose its eternal significance. Thus, I'm thankful to know that God always keeps His promises.

Lord, do not let me be deceived by the cares of this world, but let me rather store up treasure in Heaven. Through Christ I pray. Amen.

Taking It on Faith

[Joseph] did what the angel of the Lord had commanded him and took Mary home as his wife (Matthew 1:24).

Scripture: Matthew 1:22-25
Song: "Faith of Our Fathers"

When it comes to trusting the Lord, it's hard to beat George Mueller. He's perhaps the nineteenth-century's premier example of what it means to walk in faith. Mueller lived most of his 92 years in England, where he founded five large orphanages that ministered to more than 10,000 orphans during his lifetime. He never asked anyone directly for money, he never took on debt, he never received a salary, and his orphans never went hungry.

When asked why he opened orphanages, his answer took people by surprise. It wasn't primarily to feed, clothe, and house children, or even to expose them to God's saving grace, though that was certainly high on his priority list. The real reason, he claimed, was to showcase God's faithfulness to those willing to put Him to the test. Mueller's mantra was one word: *faith*.

Centuries earlier, Joseph demonstrated faith on an even greater scale. Engaged to Mary, he found himself in an embarrassing bind. Mary was expecting a child, and he had nothing to do with it. But an angel appeared to Joseph in a dream, assuaged his fears, and informed him that the baby would one day "save his people from their sins" (v. 21). Joseph took God at His word.

Lord God, like the father of the demon-possessed son in Mark 9, I confess, "I do believe; help me overcome my unbelief!" In Jesus' name, amen.

March 3–9. **Paul Tatham** has been a Christian school administrator and teacher for more than 40 years and is currently serving at the First Academy in Orlando, Florida.

The Bible Is Basically a Myth?

After Jesus was born in Bethlehem in Judea (Matthew 2:1).

Scripture: Matthew 2:1-6
Song: "The B-I-B-L-E"

I was talking with a man about what the Bible has to say about Jesus. After I pointed him to several verses, he said, "Well, it seems you've made a pretty good case. But the problem is that I really have doubts about the Bible. In fact, isn't it just a lot of fanciful myths?" His reply raised the discussion to a whole new level. For many people, verse-quoting carries no clout whatsoever, because they don't believe the Bible is authoritative in the first place.

One reason we Christians believe the Bible to be divine revelation is because of its fulfilled prophecies. Daniel accurately predicted four coming world empires. Isaiah named the Persian king Cyrus a full 200 years before Cyrus was even born. Isaiah had foretold the Babylonian captivity 100 years earlier, while Ezekiel prophesied the destruction of the city of Tyre 250 years before its final demise under Alexander the Great.

And Micah, 700 years prior, pinpointed not only Bethlehem as the coming Messiah's birthplace but specified it as *Ephrathah*, the ancient name of the Bethlehem in Judea, and not another town by the same name in northern Israel.

Bottom line: the Word of God is reliable. We need not hesitate in taking a stand upon it.

Dear Father in Heaven, what an encouragement it is to realize that my faith is not groundless but, rather, rooted in heavenly truth. In Jesus' name I pray. Amen.

Don't Get Sidetracked!

He healed all who were ill. He warned them not to tell others about him (Matthew 12:15, 16).

Scripture: Matthew 12:15-23
Song: "I Shall Not Be Moved"

Flushed with his successes in Western Europe during World War II, Adolf Hitler turned his attention to the east. He recklessly rolled the logistical dice and invaded his most formidable enemy, the Soviet Union. When he launched his forces in June 1941, they quickly overran the ill-prepared Russians. One of his three-pronged spearheads headed north, another south, and another toward Moscow, the capital in the center.

When German troops had pushed to within sight of the city, Hitler unexpectedly diverted them to bolster Army Group South in meeting its objective—capturing Stalingrad. The reason for the move? Was it simply that the city bore the name of Hitler's ideological and military nemesis, Joseph Stalin?

Because of this strategic blunder, German forces lost the crucial time needed to take Moscow before the grip of a bitter Russian winter made it impossible. Had Moscow fallen, it likely would have dramatically altered modern world history. But it didn't—and only because Hitler got sidetracked.

During Christ's earthly ministry, He often told those who had been healed not to broadcast their joy to others. He refused to be pressured into becoming a revolutionary activist, sidetracking Him from His true mission.

Lord, You tell us that if we resist the devil he'll flee from us (see James 4:7). May I remember this the next time I'm distracted from fulfilling my purpose in life. Amen.

The Power of Praise

From the lips of children and infants you, Lord, have called forth your praise (Matthew 21:16).

Scripture: Matthew 21:12-17
Song: "Praise Him! Praise Him!"

One of the most bizarre battle plans in all of world history unfolded back in Bible times. Jehoshaphat, one of the few godly kings of Judah, was threatened by an imposing alliance of foreign forces. With an attack imminent, Jehoshaphat cries out to the Lord. The response: Not to worry; those aligned against you will self-destruct, and your only job will be to gather the spoils (see 2 Chronicles 20:15).

Confidently—some would say brazenly—the king takes God at His word and places his praise singers to lead his troops into battle. Weaponless, without armor, and dressed in mere choir robes, they march confidently forward while singing praises to the Lord at the top of their lungs. Pleased with Jehoshaphat's unabashed trust, God snaps His fingers, and the enemy threat implodes. The once vaunted "great horde" (see Ezekiel 38:15-22) turns upon itself, instead of the army of Judah, and leaves God's people awestruck.

There's something strange about praise. It's *powerful!* In today's passage, when the children gathered with their parents at Jerusalem's temple and began to praise God, Jesus quoted Psalm 8:2. But He substituted the word *praise* for *strength*, thus equating the two. In other words, when we praise our Savior, we're strengthened—and things happen.

O Lord, how majestic is Your name in all the earth! I stand amazed at Your power as You go before me. Praise to You, through Christ. Amen.

But You Don't Know What It's Like!

The Lord said to my Lord: "Sit at my right hand until I put your enemies under your feet" (Matthew 22:44).

Scripture: Matthew 22:41-45
Song: "Does Jesus Care When My Heart Is Pained?"

I hurried from the school office to my classroom. I wanted everything ready when my students entered their first-period class, and only 10 minutes remained before the bell.

But before I could get there, a heated hallway discussion caught my attention. One of the students was arguing with her father over his disapproval of her boyfriend. "He's not bad, Dad," she implored. "Besides, you don't know what things are like in this day and age!"

Her point, of course, was that her father was out of touch and just couldn't identify with her modern world. And how could he possibly relate to her teenage struggles?

Do we sometimes view God the same way? How could God even begin to relate to us, since He lives in Heaven while we have to cope in "the real world"?

In today's Scripture passage, Jesus sparred with the Pharisees. When He quoted the psalmist, "The Lord said to my Lord," He was referring to the fact that He was *both* David's Messiah and David's physical son. The coming Savior was to be both God and man—dual natured. Otherwise, we could argue, He could not truly relate to us mere mortals.

So, God does feel our pain. He lived it.

O God, I confess to You that I am prone to excuse sin by claiming that You couldn't possibly understand my circumstances. Forgive me, in Jesus' name I ask. Amen.

I Give Up!

He began to shout, "Jesus, Son of David, have mercy on me!" Many rebuked him and told him to be quiet, but he shouted all the more (Mark 10:47, 48).

Scripture: Mark 10:46-52
Song: "Follow On"

She arrived amidst much fanfare. After all, we'd never had a full-time school nurse in our Christian school in the Bahamas. As I drove her to the school from the airport, she excitedly pointed to the pristine beaches and tropical landscape. And she talked of her plans to make an impact on young lives.

After unpacking her luggage, we sat down to outline her duties. As I explained her health-care responsibilities, her excitement for her new ministry began to wane. She had reservations about some of our procedures and even began to question their legality. I assured her that our health laws differed from those stateside and that she need not worry. But it was to no avail. Finally, she stood up, declared that she could not work under such circumstances, and stormed out of the office. The next day, she abruptly caught a flight home.

What an absolute shame, I thought. This lady had little clue of the extent God wanted to use her in our school. As far as I could tell, she had quit before God could even start.

Doubtless, the reason blind Bartimaeus got what he asked for was because of his persistence. He was no quitter.

Dear Lord, I've learned from Your Word the value You place upon persistence. Yet I confess that I too often throw in the towel before giving You a chance. Grant me the power to stick to the task and delight in Your blessing upon it. In Jesus' name, amen.

What's Your Word Worth?

Once for all, I have sworn by my holiness — and I will not lie to David (Psalms 89:35).

Scripture: Psalm 89:35-37
Song: "Standing on the Promises"

Prior to the kings ruling over ancient Israel, the nation's leadership fell to a series of judges. Called by God, these 13 individuals were more like military leaders than political figures, and their exploits have been the staple of untold Sunday school lessons. Who hasn't thrilled to Deborah's triumph over Sisera amidst a driving rainstorm on the slopes of Mount Tabor? or Gideon's routing of the Midianites with a mere handful of warriors armed only with trumpets, jars, and torches? or Samson's one-man harassment of the Philistines?

But one judge of ancient Israel is often overlooked and relatively unknown — Jephthah. God's charge to him was to rid Israel of their long-standing enemy, the Ammonites. As part of his battle preparations, Jephthah sought Heaven's help but made a rash promise in return that cost him his own daughter. The take-away is that this judge was a man of his word, despite its alarming price tag.

Our Lord puts a high premium on keeping one's word, even though such expectations stand in contrast to the glib promises so prevalent today. In today's passage, God repeats His promise to David that his line would endure forever. His promises were absolutely trustworthy. How about yours and mine?

Heavenly Father, I must admit that too many of my promises are shallow and only partially fulfilled. Help me in this area, I pray in the name of Jesus. Amen.

Caution: Other Gods

Those who run after other gods will suffer more and more. I will not pour out libations of blood to such gods or take up their names on my lips (Psalm 16:4).

Scripture: Psalm 16:1-6
Song: "How Great Thou Art"

We see it too often. A person with great potential gets addicted to drugs and ends up fighting for her life. Another person's life is ravaged by gambling, or a career becomes an overwhelming passion that leaves family and friends behind. The gods of this world can be devastating.

In the Bible David had observed the lives of those who served other gods, and he didn't want to have anything to do with them. We too shake our heads at the Philistines for worshipping idols—but aren't we tempted to worship "idols" that differ only in name and apparent sophistication?

Many of us will avoid the blatant pitfalls of drugs and gambling while falling prey to more "acceptable" diversions. We work late, skip lunch, or take on more than we can handle, all the time telling ourselves we are doing it for the family. Yet we find that success can be fleeting, and our personal relationships grow more and more strained.

David's advice is still good today: Stay away from those who ignore the true God. Their troubles just keep increasing.

Dear God, what is pulling my time and attention away from prayer today? Let my mind stay focused on You. In Jesus' name, amen.

March 10–16. **Danny Woodall,** of Port Neches, Texas, has written numerous articles and devotions for Christian publications. She also directs the Texas Christian Writer's Conference.

He Loves Us Anyway

I have set the LORD** continually before me; because He is at my right hand, I will not be shaken** (Psalm 16:8, *New American Standard Bible*).
Scripture: Psalm 16:7-11
Song: "Rock of Ages"

Earthquakes and hurricanes can devastate an area. Only buildings with the proper foundations survive. For King David, that foundation was the Lord. He had learned, through long experience, that with God the life he'd built could survive the storms of life; there was nothing to fear.

But think of the challenges he faced. He fought wild animals, a giant, and an angry king. That's for starters. He dealt with family squabbles and political intrigue. Yet he faced his battles head on, knowing God was on his side.

You might say the only battle that David lost was the onslaught on his own self-control. He fell to temptation, and his life began spinning out of control. Still, in his darkest hour, he turned to God for mercy.

He learned a lesson we need to remember: if we are right or wrong, God is still on our side. After all, this sinner ultimately became known as "the man after God's heart" (see Acts 13:22).

The world has a "what have you done for me lately" attitude. Mess up and you're replaced. Thankfully, God doesn't see us that way. He knows we aren't perfect; He loves us anyway.

Father, thank You for being the solid rock in my life. When the storms of life come, You are the anchor that holds. And thank You for Your mercy and the forgiveness that comes to me by the cross of Your Son. I praise You in His name. Amen.

No One Understands Like Jesus

Since He Himself was tempted in that which He has suffered, He is able to come to the aid of those who are tempted
(Hebrews 2:18, *New American Standard Bible*).

Scripture: Hebrews 2:14-18
Song: "What a Friend We Have in Jesus"

"You don't understand!" It's a cry for help from those who
feel lost and alone. When we're down to our last chance, we
want someone who's dealt with the same situation. We want a
battle-worn veteran, not a fresh rookie.

The writer of Hebrews reminds us that Jesus understands
what we're going through, because He came to earth and lived
as we live. He too suffered heartaches and disappointments.

For starters, the king tried to kill Him when He was a toddler.
No doubt, there were whispers about His mother's pregnancy
and, approaching his teen years, His parents didn't understand
Him. After His baptism, He went into the wilderness for 40 days
without food. In one week, He went from hosannas to crucifixion. His brothers didn't understand until He rose from the dead.

My point: Jesus did not have an easy life! He overcame
death—and everything else the world dealt Him. Because He
was victorious, we also can win in life. Christians don't worship
dusty pages of dogma or a worn-out creed, as valuable as they
may be. We serve a risen Savior who's faced the storms of life.
He not only cares, He understands as well.

Dear Father, help me to remember that Your Son faced the heaviest human trials and
temptations, and He knows what is best for me. When I'm going through trials, He is
clearly my best option. Come to my aid this day, and always! In Jesus' name, amen.

Who Needs Whom?

May [I] be found in Him, not having a righteousness of my own derived from the Law, but that which is through faith in Christ, the righteousness which comes from God on the basis of faith (Philippians 3:9, *New American Standard Bible*).

Scripture: Philippians 3:7-11
Song: "Spirit of Faith, Come Down"

I unpack the new computer and look at the wires, considering the connections. This goes here, this over there, check this cord. OK . . . ready. Click. The computer doesn't make a sound. *Now what?* Thirty minutes later, I'm still switching wires and cords: no Internet. *OK, let me look at the directions.*

Without Christ, our lives are still unplugged from God. The apostle Paul is an excellent example. He lived by the law, trying to prove his goodness. His attitude was: "Look at me, God." He was apparently convinced that God needed him in order to defeat those pesky, heretical followers of "the Way." But once Paul met Christ, his life's ambition changed: "What can I do for You, Lord?"

The law shows us our need for a Savior—and can help show us how to live for Him—but we have a way of turning it into a checklist for spiritual success. *I go to church. I pray. I read my Bible. I give my tithe. I'm worthy.*

Paul finally figured it out. If we want to make a difference in our world, our lives must reflect an indwelling Christ. (And we need Him more than He needs us.)

Father, help the world see Christ in my life, and not my own efforts at trying to please You. In the name of Your Son, my Savior, I pray. Amen.

He Stayed on Track

I press on toward the goal to win the prize for which God has called me heavenward in Christ Jesus (Philippians 3:14).

Scripture: Philippians 3:12-16
Song: "Higher Ground"

In 1925, 20 mushers and 150 dogs braved the Alaskan winter to bring a diphtheria antitoxin serum to the city of Nome. The teams covered almost 700 miles in five and a half days, a record that still stands. The "Great Race of Mercy" prevented an epidemic from spreading through Nome and the surrounding communities. Balto, the lead sled dog on the final stretch into Nome, became a famous canine celebrity. In fact, his statue is a popular tourist attraction in New York City's Central Park.

As if he were running a race, Paul pressed toward the goal — the "finish line" of his own resurrection — as he shared the gospel during his time on earth. In a sense, he carried the antitoxin for sin along with him, the message of the cross, as he traveled through Asia Minor and southern Europe.

There were plenty of distractions, of course, and no doubt there were times when he wanted to give up. Yet, he pressed on, with one thing in mind: to tell others about Christ.

He kept pressing upwards, and so should we. Today there are plenty of distractions; even good things can become hindrances to ministry and mission. But when we keep Christ as the focus of our lives, we won't get off track.

Almighty and everlasting God, help me hear Your call and press on until the day I stand before You with joy. Help me avoid the daily distractions that would deter me from witnessing for You. In the name of Jesus I pray. Amen.

The Mulligan Gospel

Let all the house of Israel know for certain that God has made Him both Lord and Christ—this Jesus whom you crucified (Acts 2:36, *New American Standard Bible*).

Scripture: Acts 2:33-36
Song: "Show Pity, Lord, O Lord, Forgive"

In golf a "mulligan" is simply a do-over, a second chance. Hit a bad shot? No problem; take a mulligan and try again. On the Day of Pentecost, Peter preached a mulligan sermon to the house of Israel.

The "house of Israel" refers to the religious class in that culture. Peter's sermon makes it clear that they had made a mistake by rejecting Jesus as the messiah they sought. The Pharisees had done an excellent job in protecting their religion from the pagan influences of the Greeks and Romans. However, when God came down from Heaven and walked among them, they missed Him.

Can we make the same mistake today? Certainly we can become so intent on protecting our faith from worldly influences that we shut out the ones we are supposed to reach. If we look around our churches and see more empty pews than people, we might be protecting our church rather than opening it, like a hospital, to a wounded and hurting world.

As we read the Gospels, the message of Jesus will stay fresh in our hearts and minds. There we see a "doctor" who healed the sick and brokenhearted, a Lord of second chances.

Father, help me to remember that the world needs Your grace so much more than religious rules. And may I, personally, convey that grace today! Through Christ, amen.

Final Score: God Wins

Sit at My right hand until I make Your enemies a footstool for Your feet (Psalm 110:1, *New American Standard Bible*).

Scripture: Psalm 110:1-4
Song: "Days of Elijah"

In the eighth grade, our school held an intramural basketball tournament. Those of us who were the last ones cut from the varsity formed one of the teams. At halftime of the first game, my team had a choice: to run up the score or just go for a shut-out. We played defense and delivered the goose egg. We easily won the tournament.

David reminds us throughout the psalms that God is in control. Theologians call these psalms "Messianic Psalms"; I call them little self-stick notes of how God is always sovereign in our world. From time to time, don't we need these reminders?

Look at today's headlines. Unrest throughout the world, continual fighting, and economic upheavals: it's easy to see why some may wonder whether random chaos is our only reality. Even our personal lives sometimes seem to swirl in utter turmoil. A job loss, a sudden death, or a scary diagnosis can suddenly thrust us into doubt.

But take heart today through David the psalmist. A frequent fugitive, a man betrayed by friends and family, knew that no matter what happened, God was in control. In tough times, let us remember: The score may be close, but in the end God wins.

O God, king of glory, thank You for the day ahead when You will correct all wrong, and Your will shall indeed be done on earth as it is in Heaven! In the name of Jesus, who lives and reigns with You and the Holy Spirit, one God, now and forever, amen.

Lots of Little Rogers

Jesus called his twelve disciples to him and gave them authority to drive out impure spirits and to heal every disease and sickness (Matthew 10:1).

Scripture: Matthew 9:35–10:1
Song: "Great Is Thy Faithfulness"

When my husband, Roger, and I travel to India, we often visit remote villages. After the songs have been sung and the message given, there are always long lines of men, women, and children waiting for prayer. They crave a personal touch and a specific prayer offered on their behalf. Their needs are great.

My husband has wonderful faith for healing and has prayed over many women who could not bear children. He lays his hand on their bowed heads and prays that next time he visits their village God will have given them a child. And, sure enough, he's seen many of those women the following year wearing smiles on their faces and holding babies on their hips. (We know of at least three little boys who thus carry my husband's name!)

I often wonder why we see so few healings in America. I only know the Indian poor are desperate for healing and put their entire faith in prayers sent up by an obedient servant to our Father in Heaven. As today's disciples our task is to pray faithfully and then wait upon the Lord's gracious answers. And may our hearts be just as desperate for a healing touch from the Lord.

Lord, I want the faith You gave the Twelve to go into the world and minister to the needy. May my perseverance in faith-filled praying please You. Through Christ, amen.

March 17–23. **Jan Pierce** lives in the beautiful Pacific Northwest with her husband of 45 years. They travel to India annually to do mission work with house churches, schools, and orphanages.

Grafted In

You transplanted a vine from Egypt; you drove out the nations and planted it. You cleared the ground for it, and it took root and filled the land (Psalm 80:8, 9).

Scripture: Psalm 80:8-19
Song: "We Plough the Fields and Scatter"

So many biblical illustrations relate to plant life: the vineyards, the fig tree, the seed cast here and there on various soils. God must know that we learn best from lessons we can see and touch in our daily lives.

Our Lord transplanted His people from their home in Egypt to the choice land He'd selected for them. He "cleared the ground" for them as they obeyed His commands, and then the people blossomed and flourished. When they forgot Jehovah and, in stark rebellion, worshipped before other gods, they faced the "pruning" of divine displeasure.

The Lord has seen fit to graft Gentiles into the vine. He's opened up His miracle of life to all who will be grafted into Jesus, the true vine. But just as the Israelites triumphed only when they obeyed and lived under God's protection, so we too will thrive and grow only when we stay near to Him and worship Him only.

What is the secret to a happy, healthy life in the Lord? It's the same message, given over and over again to the Israelites—love the Lord God with all our hearts and obey His commands. When we do that, our roots will go deep, we'll thrive, and we'll bear fruit.

Father, give me eyes to see and ears to hear Your messages for me. I want to live in the rich soil of Your Word and bear good fruit in the kingdom. Through Christ, amen.

What We Need

Ask the LORD for rain in the springtime; it is the LORD who sends the thunderstorms. He gives showers of rain to all people, and plants of the field to everyone (Zechariah 10:1).

Scripture: Zechariah 10:1-5
Song: "O God, Your Constant Care and Love"

Those of us who live in the Pacific Northwest know all about rain. It drizzles, it mists, it sprinkles, and it pours. We learn to buy coats with hoods and are too proud to carry umbrellas. Most of us have a love/hate relationship with rain; we tolerate it because we love the glorious green vegetation it produces. But even the staunchest Northwesterner gets fed up when spring turns to summer, and the rains are still with us. Then we complain.

God's rains are life-giving and life-sustaining. We are directed to ask for them. When we do, we'll receive the blessings we need for a full and healthy life in Him. God alone is the source of the life-giving waters we need to live and grow and stay vibrant.

Along with the rains we may also experience some gray skies and gloomy times. That is to be expected, but the good things that come from God's rains are worth a few clouds in the sky.

Yes, He sends both the thunderstorms and the spring rains. But when we ask the Lord to provide for our needs and trust Him to keep His promises, rest assured, He'll provide all that's necessary for life and health.

Almighty and most merciful God, You are the source of all that is good. You provide the things I need for life and health. Help me remember to look to You for my provision and for my joy in life. I pray through my deliverer, Jesus. Amen.

Not Home Yet!

The heavens receded like a scroll being rolled up, and every mountain and island was removed from its place (Revelation 6:14).

Scripture: Revelation 6:12-17
Song: "He's Got the Whole World in His Hands"

The natural world we live in is an absolute wonder. It's filled with plants and animals and places of sublime beauty. The deep canyons, the ocean shores, the hidden valleys—its complexity and intricacy are beyond our comprehension.

It's also temporary. The world is like a prisoner with a death sentence. Why? Because the created world, lovely as it is, is not eternal. The Bible tells us it will be destroyed one day—rolled up, removed, burned, gone.

God has given us beauty and goodness to enjoy while we live on this good earth. He's also encouraged us to live with our eyes set on eternity, becoming familiar with our future hope and storing up our treasures in relationships rather than possessions. We're to trust in things we can't yet see, believing by faith.

No one knows the hour and the day these things will take place. But we know that God's Word is true. So for now we're free to thoroughly enjoy the world God created for us. And when life on this earth disappoints, as it surely will, we can rest in the knowledge that we're not home yet.

O God, eternity remains after You roll up the heavens and the earth—a forever to spend with You, my Father. Give me eyes to see beyond life on earth to my eternal home. But also help me to focus on the things that will bring honor to You while I'm here, that I may rejoice in Your Son's coming. In the name of Jesus I pray. Amen.

A Member of the Choir

Before me was a great multitude that no one could count, from every nation, tribe, people and language, standing before the throne and before the Lamb (Revelation 7:9).

Scripture: Revelation 7:9-12
Song: "Praise, My Soul, the King of Heaven"

When I first trusted Jesus to be my Savior, I was much more interested in my life here on earth than I was in eternity in Heaven. I needed God to help me live a better life *here*. I was young, and old age seemed impossibly far off in the future. And Heaven—well, what did I care for sitting around in a white robe singing musty hymns?

I'm older now. I've lived long enough to see that life on earth really is just a finger-snap of time before it's finished. My picture of Heaven has changed too. Now I imagine all those who have ever loved God, finally in His presence, in absolute awe, worshipping Him in unity. All the Old Testament prophets will be there. All the members of the early church and the faithful throughout the ages will come together. All the martyrs and every quiet saint from every nation who heard and responded to the message of Jesus will sing His praises.

I know that any picture of Heaven is wildly incomplete and impossibly limited by the finite mind to mere analogy. But its untold beauty is drawing me now, holding promise for an eternity filled with joy. What a privilege it will be to join that choir!

Lord Jesus, one day I'll be in Your presence, standing before the throne with the great multitude too large to count. I look forward to that day with all my heart. Through Christ I pray. Amen.

Modern Martyrs

The Lamb at the center of the throne will be their shepherd; he will lead them to springs of living water. And God will wipe away every tear from their eyes (Revelation 7:17).

Scripture: Revelation 7:13-17
Song: "Father, Let Thy Kingdom Come"

In 1999, in the North India state of Orissa, missionary Graham Staines and his two young sons were burned to death while sleeping in their station wagon. Their family had traveled to a village to conduct outdoor meetings amongst the tribal people of the area, but they were attacked by members of a Hindu radical group known as the Bajrang Dal. This group opposes any conversion from Hinduism, fearing potential political influence. So a mob of young men poured gasoline over the vehicle, set it afire, and blocked the doors to watch it burn.

Staines was from Australia and had treated lepers in India for over 30 years. His wife, Gladys, and daughter, Esther, publicly forgave the violent mob who killed their loved ones, thus spreading the love of Jesus throughout the area. The very acts meant to stamp out Christianity served instead to strengthen it.

Graham Staines's faithful service both to God and to the poor of India was rewarded on earth with a brutal, fiery death. How wonderful to know that immediately upon giving up his life, he and his children met the Lamb at the throne. There he found springs of joy, and every tear was wiped from his eyes.

Heavenly Father, I thank You for those who have gone before me to serve You, even at the cost of their lives. Give me courage to speak out, even amidst intense opposition. In the name of Jesus I pray. Amen.

What a Deal!

With your blood you purchased for God persons from every tribe and language and people and nation (Revelation 5:9)

Scripture: Revelation 5:5-13
Song: "Are You Washed in the Blood?"

She held a cloth in her hands, and her eyes were filled with tears. But she had a task to attend to. She moved to the pools of blood coloring the stone courtyard in red and carefully blotted each place, soaking up as much as she could. It was precious blood—the blood of her son, Jesus, who had just been scourged unmercifully and was now being led up the hill to Golgotha.

That graphic image, a scene from the movie *The Passion of the Christ,* caught me by surprise on the day I viewed it. Did Mary understand the exchange taking place? Did she know her Son's blood would be traded for the lives of generations of sinners?

Certainly she understood something of the ministry He'd accepted as the Father's will. She knew He was laying down His life through no guilt of His own.

Generations of disciples continue to tell the remarkable story of God's own Son, Jesus, who shed His blood to buy eternity for peoples from every tongue and tribe and nation. Yes, He poured out His life that we might have life. He was buried in a tomb that couldn't hold Him that we might be buried in life-giving waters of baptism—to rise up and serve Him. What an exchange. What a Savior!

Lord, I can never thank You enough for giving yourself to death for my sins. I pray that my life will honor You and that Your name will be known far and wide for the loving, kind God that You are. I praise You, in Christ's holy name. Amen.

Put in Some Practice Time

Ascribe to the LORD, O sons of the mighty, Ascribe to the LORD glory and strength. Ascribe to the LORD the glory due to His name; worship the LORD in holy array (Psalm 29:1, 2, *New American Standard Bible*).

Scripture: Psalm 29
Song: "Come and Sing Praises"

"Ascribe to the Lord" means: give to the Lord the honor He deserves. Our challenge may come in knowing *how* to ascribe. But consider some of the ways we can tell of His greatness.

We can sing with a congregation, lifting our voices in praise to God. Surely that honors Him.

We can read His Word and revel in how far beyond us is His holiness. Yet, He tells us to seek holiness too, for without it no one will see the Lord. Giving our entire lives—every corner of our hearts—to His perfect will surely honor Him.

We can pray with an open heart each day—or "pray the Bible" by simply reading passages as prayers. Spending time like that with God brings honor to Him.

Clearly, "ascribing" requires diligence and planning on our part. But if we are to spend an eternity giving glory to God in the heavenly realms, why shouldn't we put in some serious practice time here on earth?

Lord God Almighty, today lead me into creative ways to honor You. Quiet my heart and still my mind, so I can focus on Your will and Your ways, as I ascribe glory to Your name. Through Christ the Lord, amen.

March 24–30. **Margaret Steinacker,** of Winamac, Indiana, belongs to The Writing Academy and is part of the poetry exchange in that organization. She and her husband are retired worship leaders.

Out of the Waterless Pit

As for you also, because of the blood of My covenant with you, I have set your prisoners free from the waterless pit. Return to the stronghold, O prisoners who have the hope; this very day I am declaring that I will restore double to you (Zechariah 9:11, 12, *New American Standard Bible*).

Scripture: Zechariah 9:10-15
Song: "He Brought Me Out"

Maybe the pit Zechariah describes is like the one we envision as we read about Joseph's brothers throwing him into an old well. Can't you just imagine that dried-up pit in the desert? No doubt it swarmed with scorpions, insects, and snakes. Being dropped into a waterless pit could make even the strongest man's heart fill with fear and gloom. And the panic would increase with hunger and thirst.

In Zechariah's day, empty wells became makeshift prisons. As the ropes lowered the prisoner, he soon realized he was entering a living grave. No water to drink, nothing to eat, and a large rock sealing the pit—what total hopelessness!

Until we find Christ, who came to free us from the pit of sin and death, we're no better off than pit-fallen prisoners. We wallow in self-centeredness and pride, full of ourselves and sinful. Unlike the waterless pit dwellers, though, we can come to our senses. We can confess our sins and ask for forgiveness. Then Christ offers us hope and restores our inmost being. He pulls us up into a kingdom of light, filled with every good thing.

Lord, I praise You for who You are and for the freedom You offer through Your Son's atoning death on the cross. In His precious name I pray. Amen.

Follow the Signs

Now this I know: The LORD gives victory to his anointed. . . .
Some trust in chariots and some in horses, but we trust in the
name of the LORD our God (Psalm 20:6, 7).

Scripture: Psalm 20
Song: "'Tis So Sweet to Trust in Jesus"

Recently I attended a presentation where the importance of
quilts used for the Underground Railroad became clear. If the
escaping slaves saw certain quilt blocks, they knew to go north
or not to stop at a certain station. If a warning quilt hung in the
window of the house, they knew to follow the flying geese or to
fill their baskets for a long journey to the next station.

At least 15 different quilt blocks appear in documented history. (Apparently one block was used as encouragement alone,
for it was called "Jesus, the Carpenter.") The slaves memorized
the blocks and trusted their messages.

And many of the slaves sang of their trust in the Lord while
working. The Scripture shows us that we are to trust in the
Lord alone, not in horses or chariots (vehicles, houses, things,
etc.), but in the victory promised to His anointed. When we
acknowledge Him as our Savior, His anointing rests on us (see
1 John 2:20, 27). As we memorize His Word, we prepare ourselves for signs of stopping or not stopping along our Christian
journey.

Almighty and most merciful God, I pray You will help me always remember the
importance of keeping Your Word in my heart. And prompt me to carefully read the
signs You give me along the way—and then give me courage to follow that path! In
the name of Jesus, who lives and reigns with You and the Holy Spirit, one God, now
and forever, amen.

The 5 W's of Praise

Clap your hands, all you nations; shout to God with cries of joy. For the LORD Most High is awesome (Psalm 47:1, 2).

Scripture: Psalm 47
Song: "Praise to the Lord, the Almighty"

As a GED teacher for 30 years, I taught in community class-rooms as well as in two county jails. The GED required test-takers to write a short essay. To help students practice, I often referred to the 5-Ws way of writing articles, a method that answers these questions: Who, What, Why, When, Where. For me, Psalm 47 stands out as giving answers to almost any question we might have about the nature of praise.

The "Who" is twofold: we are to praise *God*, who is the audience, and *we* are the ones doing the praising. Yet it's all about Him, not about us.

"What" are we to do? Singing, shouting, clapping, and praising all line up as possibilities. But don't worry, even one of these actions pleases God. They can be done individually or corporately, but the "why" is simple: He deserves it!

"When?" We can praise him at any time, of course, and the "Where" needs only one word: *anywhere*.

Anyone can praise God at any time, in any way, anywhere. He loves us with an unfailing love and is worthy of our best offerings of praise. How will you honor Him today?

Lord, as I praise You, I give thanks for who You are. Help me continue to lift Your name at all times, in every place, so others may come to know of Your greatness and praise You too. Through Christ, amen.

Post Those Signs

Pass through, pass through the gates! Prepare the way for the people. Build up, build up the highway! Remove the stones. Raise a banner for the nations. (Isaiah 62:10).

Scripture: Isaiah 62:8-12
Song: "Make Me a Blessing"

Ever-present roadwork causes more than slowed traffic in our cities and towns. Detours add miles and time to commutes. On most highways, road departments warn us with signs, alerting us to the work ahead, the detour to come, or the possibility of stopped traffic. We may not like the inconvenience, but because of the warnings, we can get to our destination safely.

Isaiah's instructions, in several passages, tell us to make a straight road, to build up the highway, to remove the stones, and to put up a banner for the people. In our daily lives, this means we strive to stay on the "straight and narrow" pathway God chooses for us.

How to do that? We can make every effort to avoid being a stumbling block to others. We can attempt to build up others in the faith. Finally, we can post signs pointing to God's way—through our words and deeds. As King David said, "You have given a banner to those who fear You, that it may be displayed because of the truth" (Psalm 60:4, *NASB*). If we can do this kind of "road work" to keep our Christian witness clear and flowing, we'll enjoy the journey to our ultimate destination.

Dear Heavenly Father, I thank You for the instructions and warnings You give in Scripture. Help me to see the stones on my path and clear the way for close fellowship with You today. In Jesus' name, amen.

All the Thanks He Deserves

I will give you thanks, for you answered me; you have become my salvation. . . . Blessed is he who comes in the name of the LORD (Psalm 118:21, 26).

Scripture: Psalm 118: 21-29
Song: "There Is None Like You"

Following the horrible terrorist attacks of 9/11, many stories surfaced about the marvelous rescues the police, firefighters, and volunteers of New York City accomplished. Families of the rescued still sing the praises of these brave men and women who gave them back their loved ones. Although thanks have been given publicly and privately, these grateful people continue to say "thank you" in a variety of ways.

But is there ever a way we can *fully* thank someone for saving our lives? I think of the lines in Elizabeth Barrett Browning's sonnet: "How do I love thee? Let me count the ways." If you are so inclined, take her poem as an example, rewrite it, turning it into your praise to God. It's a rewarding exercise.

God sent Jesus, His only Son, to be the sacrifice for our sins. Christ's death on the cross provided the blood needed to forgive our sins. He offers, to as many as will receive it, the gift of eternal life. He blots out our confessed sins, never to be remembered again. With that in mind, how can we not give Him all the thanks He deserves?

Lord, keep my heart open and my voice busy giving You thanks and acknowledging Your grace in my life. I know my praise will never be enough, yet the more I offer thanks, the closer my relationship with You grows. There is none like You, Lord. Please accept my sacrifice of thanksgiving and praise, in Christ's name. Amen.

The Humble King

Rejoice greatly, Daughter Zion! Shout, Daughter Jerusalem! See, your king comes to you, righteous and victorious, lowly and riding on a donkey, on a colt, the foal of a donkey (Zechariah 9:9, 10)

Scripture: Zechariah 9:9, 10
Song: "Rejoice, the Lord Is King"

Imagine telling your children, "The king is coming. As soon as the temple musicians march by, you'll see him. He'll be riding on a donkey." The sudden fulfillment of Zechariah's prophecy, written 550 years before Christ, must have startled the crowd. They would have expected a king to ride in on a war horse, perhaps a white stallion. They could hardly imagine a king on a donkey! That would have been too lowly. But Christ was to come in that way to show humility and grace, for He would soon offer himself as our sin sacrifice.

Today we glory in the coming of Jesus, and as we give our lives to Him, He shows us opportunities to be His hands and feet in our world. We do it by modeling our lives after the humility He portrayed on that great day of Palm Sunday.

But if we put on humility, will we somehow lose out on the good things of life? I love the way Louisa May Alcott saw the matter: "Conceit spoils the finest genius. There is not much danger that real talent or goodness will be overlooked long; even if it is, the consciousness of possessing and using it well should satisfy one, and the great charm of all power is modesty."

Dear Father, I seek a genuine humility in my life. Help me to see that my future is in Your hands. Having "died in you," I have no "me" to defend! In Jesus' name, amen.

How Will You Use That Breath?

Woe to him who says to wood, "Come to life!" Or to lifeless stone, "Wake up!" Can it give guidance? It is covered with gold and silver; there is no breath in it (Habakkuk 2:19).

Scripture: Habakkuk 2:18-20
Song: "Breathe on Me, Breath of God"

I hate emphysema. I remember the many years my father struggled with it prior to his death. He had grown up on a farm — and then became a farmer — and that translates into many years of breathing in dust and moldy crops. Of course, years of smoking didn't help either. I was sad for him as he struggled to get enough air into his lungs as he grew older, especially after any physical exertion. He spent the last 18 months of his life breathing with the help of an oxygen tank.

Do you take breathing for granted? Sit back, relax, and take a really deep breath . . . now slowly let it out. According to Askpedia.com, the average person at rest takes 25 breaths per minute; 1,500 breaths per hour; and 36,000 breaths per day. That is amazing! In the beginning, we're told, God breathed the breath of life into Adam, and he became a living being (Genesis 2:7). He became a living being because of the breath of God.

Praise be to our life-giving Lord, who gives us each of those 36,000 daily breaths. Let us use some of them for a most worthy purpose: to praise Him and bring Him glory.

Lord, praise You for being my life-breathing Creator, Redeemer, and Sustainer, now and forever. Help me always look to You for my every need. In Jesus' name, amen.

March 31. **Maralee Parker** is a wife, mother, and grandmother living in Elgin, Illinois. She has written curriculum and devotionals and loves investing in people through social media.

DEVOTIONS®

April

The LORD is the stronghold of my life —
of whom shall I be afraid?

— Psalm 27:1

Gary Wilde, Editor   **Margaret Williams,** Project Editor   Photo: Brand X Pictures | Thinkstock®

DEVOTIONS® is published quarterly by Standard Publishing, Cincinnati, Ohio, www.standardpub.com.
© 2013 by Standard Publishing. All rights reserved. Topics based on the Home Daily Bible Readings,
International Sunday School Lessons. © 2010 by the Committee on the Uniform Series. Printed in
the U.S.A. All Scripture quotations, unless otherwise indicated, are taken from the *HOLY BIBLE,
NEW INTERNATIONAL VERSION*®. *NIV*®. Copyright © 1973, 1978, 1984, 2011 by Biblica Inc™.
Used by permission of Zondervan. All rights reserved. *King James Version* (*KJV*), public domain.
Holy Bible, *New Living Translation* (*NLT*), © 1996, 2004, 2007. Tyndale House Publishers. *The New
King James Version*. Copyright © 1982 by Thomas Nelson, Inc.

His Sheltering Hand

In the day of trouble he will keep me safe in his dwelling; he will hide me in the shelter of his sacred tent and set me high upon a rock (Psalm 27:5).

Scripture: Psalm 27:1-5
Song: "Hiding Place"

How thankful I am to know that I have a hiding place, a shelter, a tent of safety. My life can be extremely stressful. Our adult daughter is bipolar and autistic, and she has friends who suffer from mental illness as well. Recently, one such friend suffered a psychotic break and physically attacked a young woman he knew, along with her young child. It was shocking, like something from a horror movie, and we could barely process it when we heard it. In fact, it took days to comprehend the reality of what had happened.

In my times of trouble I come crawling to the Lord, seeking comfort, strength, guidance, and encouragement. I whimper with pain and exhaustion, but I also feel His strong arms around me, soothing my injured soul.

I know there is no better place to be, sheltered from the winds and waves that could destroy me. I may be tossed about by the storms of life, but ultimately, I know I am safe in His arms.

Where can I go, **Lord,** when the pressures of life seem too great? I just want You to make it all go away. But I choose to trust You, my faithful and merciful Lord, when I can't make sense of my life's circumstances. Please hold me tight today! I pray these things in Jesus' strong name. Amen.

April 1–6. **Maralee Parker** is a wife, mother, and grandmother living in Elgin, Illinois. She has written curriculum and devotionals and loves investing in people through social media.

He's Waiting for Your Call

In my distress I called to the LORD; I cried to my God for help. From his temple he heard my voice; my cry came before him, into his ears (Psalm 18:6).

Scripture: Psalm 18:1-6
Song: "Cry Out to Jesus"

Animals can be so therapeutic. Thus, over the years we've had a virtual zoo in my house. My daughter recently purchased a "fancy corn snake," although I have no idea how snakes can be fancy. I am not a snake lover, but I chose to allow it for her benefit.

We purchased the reptile tank with the special top that said "escape proof." That made me feel somewhat better until Beth phoned and told me the snake had escaped. I was having coffee with an old friend and really didn't want to rush home. However, I could tell my daughter was freaking out, so my friend and I said our good-byes, and I started for home.

A song on the Christian radio station included lyrics about peace, and I immediately started praying that Beth would find the snake, so she could have peace. When she was at peace, then I could be at peace too. Literally, at the moment I finished my prayer, my cell phone rang: she had found the snake.

Such times of immediate response from my Lord make me cry for joy. That's when I clearly see that He hears my cries and answers . . . because He loves me.

Father, how amazing it is that I can call upon You, the Alpha and Omega, the great I AM, at any hour, with any request. I can't comprehend the magnitude of that privilege. It humbles me and makes me so grateful. Thank You, in Christ's name. Amen.

On Second Thought—Yes, Lord!

From inside the fish Jonah prayed to the LORD his God (Jonah 2:1).

Scripture: Jonah 2:1-9
Song: "I Surrender All"

Ever felt thoroughly trapped and terrified? It happened to me as a teenager when I first began driving. I pulled my old car out on a very busy road at night, and the motor quit, right in the middle of the road. I was petrified, knowing that semi trucks zoomed down that road and around the bend—right where I was. They wouldn't be able to see me until they were on top of me. For a few seconds, which seemed to last an eternity, I prayed, "Lord, *help!*" Would He answer? He definitely had my full attention.

I'm happy to report that the car did start again, and I was able to drive away. But I will never forget that feeling of complete terror and helplessness. For a moment, I was in a situation where I just couldn't escape by my own wits.

God has a way of getting our attention, as Jonah learned. If we won't listen the first time, He may have to take away some distractions in our lives in order to redirect our focus.

Today, I'd rather try to listen and obey that sweet, small voice of the Holy Spirit within me. Perhaps, then, the Lord won't have to use a more direct approach—the Jonah method!—to lead me in the way He wants me to go.

So, **Lord,** I have learned that Your way is always the best route to take. Help me discern the straight and narrow road that's often hidden by life's broader, seemingly more attractive options. I want to choose Your path, Lord. In Christ, amen.

What Does Jesus Want from Me?

If you had known what these words mean, "I desire mercy, not sacrifice," you would not have condemned the innocent (Matthew 12:7).

Scripture: Matthew 12:1-8
Song: "All About Love"

Most of the time, I am a rule follower. I feel that rules provide boundaries and expectations. (They help people with different worldviews live alongside one another without killing each other, for example!) It's my belief that if people break rules, they deserve the consequences. Otherwise, what will encourage them to obey the rules the next time?

Because that type of thinking comes naturally to me, today's Bible verse isn't easy to hear. I confess that I also wrestle with the story of Martha tidying up the house while Mary gets the fun part: welcoming Jesus (see Luke 10:38-42). I also identify with the older brother as the prodigal son returns home to a party in his honor (see Luke 15:21-32).

I flinch a bit at these Bible stories, but also cherish them, because I know they are given to us from God for our learning. They clearly teach us that loving people is the most important thing we can do and that it pleases God. Following the rules, keeping our homes clean and tidy, and being highly respected, responsible citizens are good things, but not what God demands. He wants us to love people. It was a long time coming, but I think I get it now.

Heavenly Father, please help me get over myself. Nothing I can do will ever make You love me more than You already do. In Jesus' name, amen.

Christ for All!

He himself is our peace, who has made the two groups one and has destroyed the barrier, the dividing wall of hostility (Ephesians 2:14).

Scripture: Ephesians 2:11-22
Song: "Jesus Messiah"

Today is election day. I haven't yet voted, but I will, for it's a privilege to live in a free country where democracy prevails. It's also interesting, considering today's Bible verse, that five minutes ago I received a prerecorded political call that began "I am Joe, and I am a Jew." Then a woman's voice said, "I am Ruth, and I am a Christian." They went on to say how they both supported a particular candidate because of his political stand. They explained that they came together, despite their religious differences, in unity, to support this man.

I thought it was a fitting illustration for today's verse. However, in Ephesians, the two religious groups didn't just *agree* to work together nicely; they actually blended into one—in Jesus. Gentiles are blessed indeed that God saw fit to open the door of eternal life to them after He had already offered the gift of salvation to His chosen people.

The apostle tells us of such a great truth: We are all redeemed through the shed blood of Jesus Christ. There is no barrier any longer; Christ has eliminated it. In Him we are His body, His presence of goodness and light on the earth.

Jesus, it's all about You. It's only about You. You're the one who paid the price so all peoples—black, white, red, brown; Jew and Gentile—everyone can be born again and be redeemed for all eternity. Thank You, loving Lord! Amen.

What's Your Main Thing?

Teachers of the law heard this and began looking for a way to kill him, for they feared him, because the whole crowd was amazed at his teaching (Mark 11:18).

Scripture: Mark 11:15-19
Song: "One Pure and Holy Passion"

Steven R. Covey is the popular author of *The 7 Habits of Highly Effective People*, among his many other works. One of Covey's more famous quotes says: "The main thing is keeping the main thing the main thing." It sounds simple, but it's not easy. You must first come to terms with what you think your "main thing" is.

Jesus had no doubt as to what the main thing was as He entered the temple courts. He was dismayed and very strongly proclaimed, based on Scripture, that the temple and its courts were to be a sacred place of prayer for all peoples. This wasn't to be a retail outlet for the latest Jerusalem merchandise. That was the main thing!

How are you doing at keeping the main thing the main thing in your life? It's so easy to get caught up with our worries, fears, and countless little emergencies through the day. But the main thing, we're told in Matthew 22:37, 39, is to love the Lord your God with all your heart, soul, and mind, and your neighbor as yourself. All of the rest falls into place under that main thing.

Father God, please help me remember to seek You first in all things, to love You more than anything or anyone, and to keep my focus wholly on Your kingdom. Please give me discernment concerning any distractions that may be keeping me from fully living my life for Your glory. In Jesus' name, amen.

God Has a Place for You

I go and prepare a place for you (John 14:3).

Scripture: 1 Chronicles 17:7-14
Song: "Here Am I, Send Me"

In today's Scripture passage, David is concerned over the fact that God and His followers do not have a place in which to dwell. But God instructs the prophet Nathan to tell David, "I will provide a place for my people" (v. 9).

An elderly friend told me one day, "My church has no place for me anymore. They just put us old people on the shelf." I've heard the same complaint from teens—"They think we're too young to do anything" and from physically disabled people—"Because I'm in a wheelchair, I feel useless."

When I hear such words, I think of the older people at the church I attend, many of them winter visitors—affectionately referred to as snowbirds or northern lights. You can find these prime-timers everywhere: rocking babies in the nursery, folding bulletins, and visiting shut-ins.

Others who may have health issues are sending out birthday and get-well cards or heading up telephone prayer chains. The teens at our church are often busy painting various classrooms, mowing lawns, and going on mission trips. Whatever your age or physical condition, God has a place for you to serve in His kingdom—if you have a place for Him in your heart.

Lord, take away any thoughts that I've been put on a shelf. Show me something I can do to help one of Your children today. In Christ I pray. Amen.

April 7–13. **Donna Clark Goodrich** lives in Mesa, Arizona, with her husband Gary. Founder of the annual Arizona Christian Writers conference, she holds writers' workshops around the country.

Jesus Understands Temptations

Because he himself suffered when he was tempted, he is able to help those who are being tempted (Hebrews 2:18).

Scripture: Matthew 4:12-17
Song: "Yield Not to Temptation"

The first word of Matthew 4:1, *Then*, holds a special meaning, signifying that something had happened before. To find out what, we need to return to chapter 3, where we see that Jesus was baptized and began His earthly ministry. *Then*—we don't have a time span, but we can assume almost immediately—Satan began tempting Jesus.

Didn't it happen to you too after you became a Christian? You confessed your sins and made a new beginning, thinking everything would be easygoing from that point on. *Then* the temptations began—perhaps more powerful than ever before.

You pray for help to break a bad habit, but *then* the temptation grows stronger. Perhaps you return from a spiritual retreat where you felt God's presence in a special way, but *then* everything falls apart when you come home. So what do you do?

One thing to remember: Jesus understands. His temptations were real. In His human nature, He experienced the same weaknesses, doubts, fears, and wishes that we have. His temptations were real, but He overcame by using the Word of God. Find a Scripture verse today that helps you. Memorize it, and post it in your home, car, or workplace. It will remind you that help is only a prayer away.

Lord, I know Satan doesn't bother much with those who are already his. Help me today to fight my temptations as Jesus did—with Your Word. Amen.

Bank on This!

Jesus looked at them and said, "With man this is impossible, but with God all things are possible" (Matthew 19:26).

Scripture: Matthew 19:23-30
Song: "Follow, I Will Follow Thee"

Americans own a lot of stuff. According to the Self-Storage Association, self-storage has been the fastest growing sector of U.S. commercial real estate for the last 30 years, growing into a $220 billion industry. We pay thousands just to store treasures we never use.

A Christian magazine reported that a songbook had a misprint in one line of the hymn "Guide Me, O Thou Great Jehovah." Instead of "Land me safe on Canaan's shore," it read, "Land my safe on Canaan's shore." But neither my safe, nor any of my belongings, will accompany me to the promised land.

In today's passage of Scripture, Jesus met with a rich young ruler who, from all appearances, had what it took to be a follower. "What do I still lack?" he asked the young rabbi. When Jesus commanded him to sell everything he had and give to the poor, "He went away sad, because he had great wealth" (Matthew 19:22). This story makes me wonder: Is any of my stuff becoming a hindrance to my following Christ today?

Jesus later told His disciples that it was difficult for a rich person to enter Heaven, "But with God all things are possible." I'm certainly banking on that possibility.

O Eternal Lord God, may I refuse to depend on my possessions to bring the peace that only You can give. Help me to remember that I never really possess anything until I give it away. Through my Lord Jesus Christ I pray. Amen.

Pray Without Ceasing

For this reason, since the day we heard about you, we have not stopped praying for you (Colossians 1:9).

Scripture: Colossians 1:9-14
Song: "For You I Am Praying"

"We pray for you every day." I paused in reading an annual Christmas letter from longtime friends. Every day? We had seen them only twice since moving away 46 years before, and they still pray for us every day!

In looking up a song for today's devotional, I saw the title of a familiar hymn, "Sweet Hour of Prayer." It is said that John Wesley prayed for two hours every morning, but if he knew he had an especially hard day ahead, he prayed for three hours.

I find it hard to pray for an hour at a time, but I do realize that I can maintain an attitude of prayer, an awareness of God's presence, all through the day. I do this by:

• praying over the phone when someone shares a need.
• praying in a church foyer with a friend.
• praying for a person as I address a birthday, anniversary, or get-well card.
• praying when I read an e-mail or Facebook posting.
• praying when I see emergency vehicles hurrying down the street or hear a siren.

Paul says that he had not stopped praying for the church at Colossae since he first heard of them. Can we say that to our friends today?

Lord, help me pray without ceasing today, in contemplation and intercession. Bring to my mind those who need Your special touch right now. In Jesus' name, amen.

Our High Priest Forever

At that moment the curtain of the temple was torn in two from top to bottom (Matthew 27:51).

Scripture: Hebrews 7:11-19
Song: "The Unveiled Christ"

The verse for today is one of my favorite portions of Scripture. One evening when our choir was rehearsing the hymn "The Unveiled Christ," with little or no expression, I stopped them. "Are you even listening to the words you're singing?" I asked.

I reminded them that before Jesus came, no one but the high priest could go into the Holy of Holies and confess the people's sins—and then only once per year. Everyone else was separated from the mercy seat by a curtain, or veil, weighing approximately four tons. No one could go directly to God.

But on Good Friday, as soon as Jesus breathed His last breath, the curtain was torn in two from top to bottom. We no longer need a priest to intercede for us once a year as we now have a great high priest who takes us into the very presence of God, the one who is holy and blameless.

And unlike the Old Testament priests, we don't need the sacrifice of lambs. Jesus—both priest and victim, the Lamb of God—paid the sacrifice, once and for all. Thus, as the great hymn reminds us: "Lo! He is the mighty conqueror, since He rent the veil in two."

Dear Father in Heaven, thank You for the priestly work of Jesus on my behalf. By His atoning work, He made it possible for me to come directly to You. May I always cherish this marvelous fellowship! Through Christ my Savior I pray. Amen.

Our Coming Judge

This will happen when the Lord Jesus is revealed from heaven in blazing fire with his powerful angels. He will punish those who do not know God and do not obey the gospel of our Lord Jesus (2 Thessalonians 1:7, 8).

Scripture: Revelation 19:11-16
Song: "Our Lord's Return to Earth Again"

A young man, getting ready to cross a street, didn't see the car rapidly approaching. As he stepped off the curb, a man standing nearby darted out and grabbed him, just before the car whizzed by. The young man thanked the stranger profusely.

A few years later, this same young man was arrested for burglary. Arriving in court and seeing the robed person behind the desk, he was relieved to see it was the same man who had saved his life several years earlier. Thus, he was shocked when the judge issued a harsh sentence.

"Don't you remember me?" he asked, reminding the magistrate of the earlier occasion.

"I do," the judge replied. "But then I was your savior. Now I am your judge."

During Jesus' ministry, He healed many, raised some from the dead, and preached repentance. Many followed Him, others didn't. On the coming Day of Judgment, when those who rejected Him stand before Him, they will say, "Don't You remember me? You often tried to rescue me on earth." And He will respond, "Then I could have been your savior. Now I am your judge."

Lord, I accept You today as my Savior. I want to be ready to meet You on that day and hear You say, "Well done, good and faithful servant." Through Christ, amen.

Our Faultless Savior

Once more Pilate came out and said to the Jews gathered there, "Look, I am bringing him out to you to let you know that I find no basis for a charge against him" (John 19:4).

Scripture: John 19:1-5
Song: "I Find No Fault in Him"

A recent broadcast of *48 Hours* told of an innocent man who'd been on death row in Texas for 18 years for the murder of six people. Before the trial, the actual killer had told the prosecutor that the other man had nothing to do with it. Yet the prosecutor didn't convey this to the defendant's lawyers.

Twelve years later a journalism professor chose this case as a class project. After months of interviewing old witnesses and digging up new evidence, they presented all their data to a new prosecutor. This woman looked over the updated information and told the judge, "I can't find a shred of evidence that this man was involved in these murders." The prison doors were opened, and the death-row inmate walked free.

Jesus stood on death row, awaiting Pilate's decision. And while Pilate was "sitting on the judge's seat, his wife sent him this message: 'Don't have anything to do with that innocent man, for I have suffered a great deal today in a dream because of him'" (Matthew 27:19).

But Pilate listened to the crowd who cried, "Crucify him!" They nailed Jesus to the cross, and He breathed His last. Our prison doors were opened—and we walked free.

Jesus, even though You were innocent of all the charges, You willingly went to the cross so I could be free. I am eternally thankful. In Your name, amen.

Where Are You, God?

I cry out to you, God, but you do not answer; I stand up, but you merely look at me (Job 30:20).

Scripture: Job 30:20-31
Song: "Holy Father, Hear My Cry"

I awoke slowly from a deep sleep, confused. *Where am I?* The dim light over my bed revealed the electronic equipment surrounding me, and the tubes attached to my arm reminded me: I'd undergone knee surgery yesterday.

My knee throbbed with pain. I reached for the nurse's call button and knocked it to the floor. I tried to pull it back up with its cord, but as I tried to roll over to reach it, I realized my leg was secured in a vise-type cast.

I prayed to God that He would send me some help. After awhile I cried out, "Help me, please!" I thought of Job who couldn't understand why God didn't answer his cries.

Finally, a nurse walked into the room. She looked at me and said, "You need help, don't you? Sorry, but I checked about an hour ago, and you were asleep." She refilled my IV, gave me some pain medicine, straightened the bed, and secured the call button to my pillow.

What seemed forever had only been an hour. And isn't that how it is with our prayers? We expect an instant answer—and God answers in His time.

O God, may I never forget that You hear and answer my prayers. Give me the patience to trust You, whether You say, "Yes, No, or Wait." Through Christ I pray. Amen.

April 14–20. **Jean Pitts** is a retired banker, originally from Virginia, who now lives in Florida. She has been published in numerous magazines.

God's Treasure Chest

They trust in their wealth and boast of great riches. Yet they cannot redeem themselves from death by paying a ransom to God (Psalm 49:6, 7, *New Living Translation*).

Scripture: Psalm 49:5-15
Song: "I'd Rather Have Jesus"

I was becoming disenchanted with the lifestyles of the rich and famous that I kept seeing on television. So it was refreshing and a blessing to meet Mr. and Mrs. Brown. My husband and I were new Christians when someone knocked on our door one day. There stood a lovely gray-haired lady, who said, "Good morning, I'm Iva Brown, from the church you and your family have been attending. May I come in?"

We sat and talked for a long time, and then, as she prepared to leave, she said, " I'll be looking to see you on Sunday." I replied, " Yes, but I want to buy a hat first." (In those days women wore hats to church). She hugged me and left. The next day she returned carrying a hat box with three beautiful hats in it. That was the beginning of a lifelong friendship.

Yes, the Browns were very rich. They lived in a grand farmhouse and owned a big trucking business. But they gave much of their wealth to God's work and to needy people—and they gave freely of themselves in Christian service. They believed that to lay up treasure for themselves in Heaven they must first lay down treasures on earth to be used for the kingdom of God.

Dear Lord, help me to be content with all I have in Christ, and forgive me any envy of those who have more of the luxuries of life. May I be willing to share all I have in time, money, and service for Your kingdom. In Jesus' name, amen.

My Lifeguard

I still belong to you; you hold my right hand. You guide me with your counsel, leading me to a glorious destiny (Psalm 73:23, 24, *New Living Translation*).

Scripture: Psalm 73:16-28
Song: "Jesus, Hold My Hand"

Frequently, when I need to make a quick trip to the store or get to an important appointment, the school near our house is either beginning or ending its day. And it was one of those mornings! As I approached the school, I saw the flashing caution sign and the school guards holding up their red stop signs.

Traffic was now coming to a standstill. I looked at my watch, sighed, and felt my face getting red. Then the thought came to me: Doesn't God send His stop sign, the Holy Spirit, to keep us safe along the dangerous roads of life?

I watched several of the guards firmly holding the hands of the younger children. I reminded myself of God's promise never to leave or forsake us. He will hold my hand along the way. He simply looks for obedience, asking me to follow the counsel of His Word.

The school personnel will watch over the children until they are safely headed towards home. God not only stays with us on the road of life, but takes us to His home in glory when our life is over.

Heavenly Father, what a blessing to remind myself that we who know Your Son will go to Your heavenly home when this journey of life is over. It is comforting to know that You will always be with me. Thank You for sending the Holy Spirit to indwell me and to guide and direct in His gentle way. Through Christ I pray. Amen.

Fresh Beginning

He said to me, "Speak a prophetic message to these bones and say, 'Dry bones, listen to the word of the LORD! This is what the Sovereign LORD says: Look! I am going to put breath into you and make you live again!'" (Ezekiel 37:4, 5, *New Living Translation*).

Scripture: Ezekiel 37:1-14
Song: "I'll Have a New Life"

Spring is the prettiest season in Virginia. Everything growing is getting a new life. The grass and trees are greener, and the flowers are blossoming. One morning I was going to a meeting some miles from where I lived. I looked out the window and was amazed to see the ground covered with a heavy white snow and icicles hanging from the trees.

I walked cautiously down the two-lane narrow road. All along the sides were pink and white dogwood, redbud, and yellow forsythia—all coated with ice. I thought they were surely dead. However, the next morning when I came back up the road, those lovely flowers were still alive with beautiful blossoms.

Can you imagine Ezekiel's dismay when God showed him the vision of dry, white bones? Then God told him to prophesy; those bones would live again!

We Christians were made "alive with Christ even when we were dead in transgressions" (Ephesians 2:5). God is able to bring life to dry, dead bones. And by the Spirit and through the Word, He is able to bring life to the deadest of sinners.

Father God, I realize that You are Almighty and that nothing is too hard for You. I praise You for the new life I have in Christ. Through Him I pray. Amen.

Nice but Lost?

Are you not in error because you do not know the Scriptures or the power of God? (Mark 12:24).

Scripture: Mark 12:18-27
Song: "Holy Bible, Book Divine"

The Sadducees didn't believe in immortality, angels, or evil spirits. In other words, not seeing was not believing.

Scoffers, critics of all things spiritual, fill our world. They shut their eyes and close their ears to God's truth. Recently I asked a lady to come with me to a Christmas program at my church. She replied with a smile, "I don't want anything to do with church!" On another occasion, I spoke to a nice lady who had just moved into our neighborhood and invited her to come to a Bible study. She answered politely, "Sorry, but I don't believe in the Bible."

There are a lot of nice but lost people all around us—and they hovered around Jesus too. He told the Sadducees, "You do not know the Scriptures or the power of God!"

Our world has the same problem today as it had in Jesus' time: People everywhere looking for something to guide them through life, something or someone to give them peace—but let it not be the Lord! Yet Jesus still calls out to every seeking soul: "Come to me, all you who are weary and burdened, and I will give you rest" (Matthew 11:28).

Lord God, put Your hands on my eyes that I may see the world as You see it. Give me compassion to reach out to those who don't know yet how much they long for You. May I live that my neighbors may see You in me, and may I speak the words of grace with all gentleness, just as You have spoken them to me. Through Christ, amen.

Empty Tomb or Olympics?

If Christ has not been raised, then your faith is useless and you are still guilty of your sins (1 Corinthians 15:17, *New Living Translation*).

Scripture: 1 Corinthians 15:12-20
Song: "He Is Risen!"

God has written the promise of resurrection not in the Bible alone but in every green leaf and blooming flower of springtime. Spring means pushing away the cold of winter to experience the warmth of a brighter sun. We scatter dry, cold leaves and look for the green sprouts of daffodils, crocuses, jonquils and other heralds of new life. These little bulbs and seeds lay dormant and dead in the ground, but they are now pushing their little colorful blossoms up and saying, "Here I am. Look! I am alive!" They died to live so their resurrected beauty could live for us.

After her questions about the death of Lazarus, Martha heard reassuring words from Jesus: "I am the resurrection and the life. The one who believes in me will live, even though they die" (John 11:25).

After the dark night of the crucifixion and the placing of the stone in front of the tomb, how glorious was the shout of Mary proclaiming, "He is risen!" The tomb was empty.

This was the great message of the apostle Paul to the Greeks so long ago. Paul told those church members that everything hinges on that empty tomb. Without it, they might as well close up the church, throw the hymnals away, and spend Sunday watching the Olympics.

Father, by Your omnipotent power You raised Jesus from the tomb. I believe it, I willingly stake my life on it. In the name of the risen Lord, amen.

Hitting Bottom: a Beginning

Come, let us return to the LORD. He has torn us to pieces but he will heal us; he has injured us but he will bind up our wounds (Hosea 6:1).

Scripture: Hosea 6:1-3
Song: "Lord, I'm Coming Home"

I know from experience how a parent grieves when one of their children strays from home and from God. When my son was a teenager, he chose some unsavory friends. Soon he was into drugs and alcohol, and addictive habits continued through his early adult life. He had professed Christ in his early years. But he changed completely when these addictions so thoroughly possessed him.

We, his parents, seemed to have no influence with him. Yet we prayed for him, year after year. Finally, on a night I will never forget, he called and said, "Mom, I need help."

A miracle truly happened. He entered a Christian rehab center for several months. Through much prayer and the Word of God, our son came home and is now living for the Lord.

I know how God suffers when one of His children walk away from Him. I also know the joy He feels when one of His flock says, "I'm coming home." It's just as one anonymous alcoholic once said: "At bottom is the best soil to sow and grow something new again. In that sense, hitting bottom, while extremely painful, is also the sowing ground."

Precious Father, thank You for answers to prayer. You know our hurts and feel our pain. Help me to live each day for You that I may be a child You can be proud of. Make me worthy of Your great, unfailing love. In Jesus' name, amen.

Where Is God?

Oh, that I knew where I might find Him, that I might come to His seat! (Job 23:3, *New King James Version*).

Scripture: Job 23:1-7
Song: "I Want to Know You"

Have you ever played hide-and-seek with a toddler? Young children love to "hide" by putting a blanket over their heads. Though still in plain sight, because their eyes are shielded, they assume they can't be seen.

Don't we sometimes act that way with God? When things are going well, it's easy to see God's presence in our lives. However, when times are difficult and God seems silent, sometimes we assume God isn't there—that He's more distant than He was back in the good times.

Does God hide? No. He has promised never to leave us or forsake us. But during those times when our circumstances cloak us, covering us and surrounding us, we should never assume that because we cannot see God, He must not be there.

In our Scripture today, Job wishes he could find where God is so he can tell Him how lousy his circumstances were. We know, though, that every word of Job's was recorded, that God was listening and working out a great and eternal purpose. And remember how Job's faith grew by leaps and bounds. Before his death he said: "I know that You can do everything" (Job 42:2, *NKJV*).

Lord, give me the faith to trust You, even when it feels as if You are far away. And please send me a reminder of Your presence today. In Jesus' name, amen.

April 21–27. **Kimberly Rae** has lived in several countries as a missionary. She now lives in North Carolina with her husband and two young children.

Going Through the Fire?

He knows the way that I take; when He has tested me, I shall come forth as gold (Job 23:10, *New King James Version*).

Scripture: Job 23:8-14
Song: "It Is Well with My Soul"

Brian worked at a funeral home, and one of his jobs was to cremate bodies. He would put the body into the fire, and then, after a set time, pull out the ashes. Flesh does not withstand fire. But at times he would find metal among the ashes: gold teeth or steel joints placed into the body during surgery.

Isn't it wonderful that God's way is the exact opposite! When He allows us to go through the "fire"—tough times that try our faith—His purifying presence, in a sense, burns up the things in our life that matter very little. Yet those are the things that often keep us from walking closely with Him. This testing tends to burn away the useless things, the distracting things, the harmful things. Then after a time, He leads us out of the fire, and we, His children, come forth as gold.

Going through a fiery trial in your life? You need not fear being destroyed by it. God's purpose in these times is always to strengthen our faith and show it to be solid and genuine, like a pure, precious metal. Cling to Him, allowing the fire to refine who you are and how you live. There is no other way to grow patience and endurance than to be tested by waiting amidst pain.

Almighty and everlasting God, help me remember that the trials of life can work a deeper faith in my soul. My job is not to ask why it is happening, but to consider how You might use it in my growth to maturity. So please keep me from fearing the tough times, knowing You are working right there for the good. In Jesus' name, amen.

So Great a Love

He is despised and rejected of men; a man of sorrows, and acquainted with grief: and we hid as it were our faces from him; he was despised, and we esteemed him not (Isaiah 53:3, *King James Version*).

Scripture: Isaiah 52:13–53:4
Song: "How Deep the Father's Love for Us"

"Ryan, look!" Davy bent over the anthill. "There must be thousands of ants in there." The boy stomped his foot, grinning as hundreds of ants responded to their home being destroyed.

"Your turn, Ryan . . . Ryan? What are you doing?"

Ryan was watching the ants. "I was reading my Bible today about God coming down to earth from Heaven to save us," he murmured.

"Yeah. What's that got to do with ants?"

"I was just thinking, most of the time, I like playing with ants or messing up their hills. I sure would never love them, not enough to shrink myself down to become one of them—and especially not if I knew they were going to hate me and make fun of me and even kill me!"

Davy sat on the ground near the hill. "Me neither, but who would?"

"Jesus did even more than that."

Davy looked at the tiny, insignificant insects at his feet. "Wow, that would take a lot of love."

Ryan nodded. "A whole lot."

Lord God, thank You for loving me enough to become incarnate in Your Son, so I could know You. May I never forget Your great mercy! In Jesus' name, amen.

Whose Life Is It?

Whosoever will save his life shall lose it: and whosoever will lose his life for my sake shall find it (Matthew 16:25, *King James Version*).

Scripture: Matthew 16:21-28
Song: "I Need Thee Every Hour"

Missionary Jim Elliot once said, "He is no fool who gives what he cannot keep to gain that which he cannot lose." At the time, he had no idea how those words would be tested.

Jim and four other men risked everything to take the gospel to the remote and dangerous Auca Indians in Equador. However, before getting the chance to fully share the good news of salvation, every man was killed.

It looked like a tragic failure, a terrible waste. But time told the true story. In years to come, Jim Elliot's wife would live among the Aucas, giving years of her life to the very people who killed her husband. Today, the Aucas are not a dangerous people who know nothing of Jesus. Quite the opposite.

And they were not the only ones affected. As a result of the five missionaries' deaths, many others committed their own lives to become missionaries—many more than five.

Most of us will not be asked to die for Christ, but all of us are asked to live for Him—to give our whole lives as living sacrifices (see Romans 12:1).

Will we spend our lives trying to save our lives? Or will we offer them up to God for whatever He has planned for us?

Lord, I hand over my life to You for whatever You want, whatever You choose for me. I am Yours. Through Christ I pray. Amen.

Approaching the King

They did not understand this saying, and were afraid to ask Him (Mark 9:32, *New King James Version*).

Scripture: Mark 9:30-37
Song: "The Power of Your Love"

In the movie *Anna and the King,* there's a scene where the majestic king's subjects have prostrated themselves at his feet. Into this intimidating setting comes a young child, the king's daughter. She sidesteps the kowtowing subjects and scampers up to the throne, where she climbs into the king's lap. He is the king, but to that child, he is also Daddy.

In today's passage, Jesus tells His disciples a hard truth. They did not understand what He was saying, but they were too afraid to ask about it. They missed an important lesson out of fear, unwilling to admit their lack of understanding. Yet they were soon arguing amongst themselves about which of them was the greatest.

Today, instead of trying to prove ourselves great, let's set aside our pride and just be God's children, coming to Him as a child would. Let's take the time to sit in the king's lap and ask Him our questions. He doesn't mind us asking about things we don't understand. For God is not just King of kings and Lord of lords. He is also our loving Father.

Almighty and most merciful God, thank You for being more than God, more than king. Thank You for being my Father. Knowing that You love me and care for me gives me confidence to come to You with my every need. So remind me, at special quiet moments in the day ahead, that You are ever so close. In the name of Jesus, who lives and reigns with You and the Holy Spirit, one God, now and forever, amen.

Enough Grace

Of His fullness we have all received, and grace for grace (John 1:16, *New King James Version*).

Scripture: John 1:10-18
Song: "He Giveth More Grace"

As a little girl, Corrie ten Boom once told her father, "I am afraid that I will never be strong enough to be a martyr for Jesus Christ."

Her father responded, "When you take a train trip to Amsterdam, when do I give you the money for the ticket? Three weeks before?"

"No, Daddy, you give me the money for the ticket just before we get on the train."

"That is right," her father replied, "and so it is with God's strength. . . . He will supply all you need—just in time."

This truth proved true when Corrie, her sister, and her father were taken from their home and forced into a Nazi concentration camp. Day after horrible day, God gave enough grace, enough strength. As their destinies played out, God gave Corrie's sister and father the grace to die and to Corrie He gave the grace to live—and also to forgive.

If you worry about receiving bad news about a loved one; if you fear death; if you are anxious over an upcoming medical procedure or major life change, know that God has sufficient grace ready to give you—just when you need it.

Thank You, **Heavenly Father,** for being greater than anything I will face in my life today. Help me to rest in You, and fill me with Your grace and strength to live for You. In the precious name of Jesus I pray. Amen.

Whipping Boy

He was wounded for our transgressions, he was bruised for our iniquities: the chastisement of our peace was upon him; and with his stripes we are healed (Isaiah 53:5, *King James Version*).

Scripture: Isaiah 53:5-8
Song: "In Christ Alone"

In England during the monarchies of the fifteenth and sixteenth centuries, when a prince was still a child and needed to be disciplined, a "whipping boy" would be called forth. This lad would take the punishment for the young king, who could not be spanked.

It is possible to conceive of such a task being forced upon someone who has no choice in the matter. But it's hard to imagine someone taking it on by choice.

Yet this is exactly what Jesus Christ did for us. We deserved punishment, death, and Hell. Jesus took it for us. The pain of that must have been infinitely greater than the *physical* pain of the lashes, the thorns, or even the nails. For an infinite God, who knew all the glories of Heaven, would surely suffer beyond any human comprehension in "emptying" himself on our behalf.

But Jesus suffered so we would not. He endured pain and death so we could live. By His stripes—those painful wounds made by angry whips—we are healed and can live forgiven and free. May we never forget, and never take for granted, the sacrifice Jesus made out of love for us.

Christ, my Lord, I don't deserve the love that was displayed to the universe so magnificently at the cross. I will ever be grateful that You humbled yourself—the Almighty God—to be the "whipping boy" for me. Praise to You! In Your name, amen.

On Waiting and Wandering

Remember how the LORD your God led you all the way in the wilderness these forty years, to humble and test you in order to know what was in your heart (Deuteronomy 8:2).

Scripture: Deuteronomy 8:1-11
Song: "All the Way My Savior Leads Me"

When my husband and I became empty-nesters, I cried a lot. I missed my daughter. But I missed my grandson too. We had spent every day together for five years, while my daughter went to college and work.

My husband desperately tried to encourage me. When he suggested that this was the time for me to do whatever I wanted to do, I decided to write full time. All of a sudden, my life had purpose again. I wanted to glorify God with my writing.

God blessed me immediately. I received regular writing assignments and had several manuscripts published. But then the assignments stopped coming. Every article I sent out came back to me, rejected. For a full year, my well went dry.

I began to question my decision to write. I cried out to God for direction. As the months dragged on, God began to do a work in my heart. He humbled me. He showed me sins where I thought there were none. If God had blessed me with another year of success, I'm certain I'd still be living with those sins.

Almighty God, You humbled the Israelites by letting them wander. Perhaps my times of waiting and wandering are divine appointments for my instruction. I know they draw me nearer to You, Lord. So, thank You! In Jesus' name, amen.

April 28–30. **Kathy Hardee** likes riding her motorcycle, fishing with her husband, and writing about her great God. She and her husband of 35 years live in Mendota, Illinois.

Temptation Away!

Watch and pray so that you will not fall into temptation. The spirit is willing, but the flesh is weak (Matthew 26:41).

Scripture: Matthew 26:36-41
Song: "What a Wonderful Savior!"

Have you noticed that being a Christian doesn't make you immune to temptation? Here are a few things I struggle with. Maybe you can relate.

Anger: When someone says something critical of me, vengeful anger is the first emotion to arrive on the scene.

Gossip: A friendly conversation can turn negative in a flash.

Worry: It seems easier to fret than to trust God.

Unthankfulness: I don't always remember to thank God for the blessings He has given.

Pride: As soon as I overcome pride in one area, it pops up in another.

Selfishness: A desire to have things my own way happens more often than I'd like to admit.

So how do we gain the victory over sin, when even the apostle Paul said, "I have the desire to do what is good, but I cannot carry it out" (Romans 7:18)?

The answer is simple. We run to the one who conquered sin for us, Jesus our Savior. Just as Jesus told the sleepy disciples to watch and pray, we are encouraged to go to Him for the help we need. The one who saved us from our sins is able to keep us from falling back into them!

Lord, open my eyes to the sins I commit every day. Forgive me, please, and give me strength to overcome temptation this day. In Christ's name I pray. Amen.

Help Needed

Brothers and sisters, if someone is caught in a sin, you who live by the Spirit should restore that person gently (Galatians 6:1).

Scripture: Galatians 6:1-5
Song: "Gentle Shepherd"

A few years ago, I decided to give motorcycle riding a try. So I signed up for a three-day basic rider course. If I passed, I'd get my license without any further testing by the state.

The instructor was a big man. He yelled a lot. His favorite expression was, "Trust me! I'm the professional!"

One of my riding-mates asked, "What happens if it rains?"

He hollered, "You'll get wet!"

The man was intimidating. And, sadly, I failed the final evaluation. But to my surprise I really enjoyed riding. So my husband picked up my training where the rider course left off.

Every evening Bob came home from work eager for my daily practice. He watched me do U-turns, quick stops, and daunting cone weaves. And he patiently explained how I could improve.

On October 7, 2011, we made the trip to the Illinois Department of Motor Vehicles—and I passed the test! Bob picked me up and spun me around right there in the parking lot.

Bob's patience with me reminds me of how we should treat those who stumble into sin. We never give up on them. We give helpful instruction and gently encourage. Then, when the victory is won, we rejoice together.

Lord, help me be quick to offer Your love and encouragement to those who struggle with sin. Give me a gentleness that inspires their endurance. In Jesus' name, amen.

My Prayer Notes

_____

_____

_____

_____

_____

_____

_____

_____

_____

_____

_____

_____

_____

_____

_____

_____

_____

_____

_____

_____

_____

_____

DEVOTIONS®

May

Whoever dwells in the shelter of the Most High
Will rest in the shadow of the Almighty.

—Psalm 91:1

Gary Wilde, Editor   **Margaret Williams,** Project Editor   Photo: Hemera | Thinkstock®

Don't Run Ahead

Give us today our daily bread (Matthew 6:11).

Scripture: Matthew 6:9-13
Song: "Day by Day"

We've already considered a story about our marvelous sister in Christ, Corrie ten Boom. Here's another snippet from her life: When she was a little girl, she and her mother visited the home of a family whose baby had died. "I stood staring at the tiny unmoving form with my heart thudding strangely against my ribs," Corrie wrote of the experience.

That evening, when her father tucked her in bed for the night, she burst into tears. Fearful that her dad would one day die, she sobbed, "I need you! You can't die! You can't!"

Her father sat on the edge of her bed and spoke to her of God's gracious provision. "Don't run out ahead of Him, Corrie," he said.

It's *daily* bread that God gives us. So we've got to trust Him with our future. And that can be difficult. (There are so many things that could go wrong!) But we can find comfort in today's Scripture and in Corrie ten Boom's story. Our heavenly Father will give us exactly what we need, at exactly the right time. Of that we can be confident.

O God, Creator of Heaven and earth, You hold the whole cosmos in Your hands, so I know You can take care of me, day by day. Thank You for your faithfulness to give me the strength I need for each day. Help me to trust You completely with all of my tomorrows. In the name of Jesus my Lord. Amen.

May 1–4. **Kathy Hardee** likes riding her motorcycle, fishing with her husband, and writing about her great God. She and her husband of 35 years live in Mendota, Illinois.

Open Doors

I know your deeds. See, I have placed before you an open door that no one can shut. I know that you have little strength, yet you have kept my word and have not denied my name (Revelation 3:8).

Scripture: Revelation 3:8-13
Song: "I Will Serve Thee"

I write a blog. The daily posts take about one minute to read, but they often take me several hours to write.

Every day, as I read my Bible, I ask God for a little nugget of gold. Like a treasure hunter digging for jewels, I search for new insights about God. And I scour through Scripture for promises I may have missed the first time around.

God told Jeremiah: "Call to me and I will answer you and tell you great and unsearchable things you do not know" (Jeremiah 33:3). I ask God to teach me new and wonderful things too.
You see, there's a longing in my heart to share God's goodness with my little corner of the world. So, I record my thoughts in a journal, and then on my blog. Once in a while, readers give me feedback, but usually not. Sometimes I wonder if my efforts benefit anyone, or if I should be doing something else.

Today's Scripture reminds us that God is the one who opens doors of service for us. We need not concern ourselves with the outcome or significance of our labors. Our job is to keep God's Word, proclaim His name, and walk through the doors of opportunity as He opens them to us.

O Lord, keep me faithful where You have already placed me, with the work You've set before me. I want to bloom for You where I'm planted! In Jesus name, amen.

He's Mine

I will say of the LORD, "He is my refuge and my fortress, my God, in whom I trust" (Psalm 91:2).

Scripture: Psalm 91:1-12
Song: "My Jesus, I Love Thee"

There are websites galore on how to raise unselfish children. According to many of them, selfishness is normal, but it must be corrected. One website gave this helpful advice: be a good role model, encourage sharing, teach empathy, promote serving, and give your child responsibility. Helping our children get over that horrible *mine* stage is crucial for their social development.

However, in the Psalms David often refers to a personal God who truly is his very own. For example, I love David's boldness in Psalm 23, where he says: "The Lord is *my* shepherd." And my ears perk up every time the Psalms include statements such as: "Lord, *my* God," or "You are *my* Lord," or "I cried to *my* God for help," or "The Lord is *my* light and *my* salvation," or "Exalted be God *my* Savior!" (See Psalms 7, 16, 18, 27.) Need I go on?

In Psalm 18:2, David displays the *God-is-mine* attitude eight times. Eight times in one verse! And in today's verse, Moses proclaims, "He is *my* refuge and *my* fortress, *my* God, in whom I trust."

Aren't you glad we have a personal God like that? He wants us to claim Him as our very own Lord. And He loves to call us *His* very own children.

Dear Father in Heaven, I am so thankful that You are my God, my hope, my strength, and my salvation. I am thrilled to be Your beloved child. In the holy name of Jesus, my Lord and Savior, I pray. Amen.

No "What If's"

Do not put the LORD your God to the test as you did at Massah (Deuteronomy 6:16).

Scripture: Deuteronomy 6:13-16
Song: "Great Is Thy Faithfulness"

I've been experiencing shortness of breath, so the doctor ran me through a series of tests. I was hoping they would reveal the problem. But every result came back normal. So, more doctor appointments have been scheduled.

A part of me wants to panic. What if this feeling gets worse? What if I pass out from lack of oxygen? What if I have cancer? *What if …?*

The Israelites faced nagging fears after finding no water in the desert. Perhaps they wondered: *What if we never find water? What if we die of thirst in this wilderness? What if the Lord isn't with us? What if …?*

They tested God by blaming Moses for their predicament and were about to stone their great leader. Imagine their surprise when God intervened by bringing them water from a rock!

I sometimes wonder how the Israelites could have been so forgetful, considering their miracle-laden past. But then I consider how quickly I forget about God's faithfulness to me. I would like to begin to look at each trial as one more opportunity to trust God. After all, He is most pleased with us when we have confidence in Him (see Hebrews 11:6).

Lord God, help me to trust You at the first sign of trouble, rather than waiting until you deliver me from it. And may I ever look back over my history with You and be comforted and encouraged by Your past faithfulness. In Jesus' name, amen.

Puzzling Prose

Though I have been speaking figuratively, a time is coming when I will no longer use this kind of language but will tell you plainly about my Father (John 16:25).

Scripture: John 16:25-33
Song: "Sanctuary"

I really enjoy the whimsy of the 1971 movie *Willy Wonka and the Chocolate Factory,* starring Gene Wilder. But amidst the vibrant colors and candy-filled scenery, the dialogue is often complex and creative. It makes the audience listen closely to discern clues as to what might happen next. The Oompa Loompas sing songs that include the words "I've got another puzzle for you." And Willy often speaks philosophically with such lines as "Where is fancy bred? In the heart, or in the head?"

During His short ministry, Jesus often spoke in parables that His listeners may or may not have understood. However, He assures the disciples that plain talk was forthcoming.

God does not want us to be confused about His ways, and time spent reading the Bible will be clearer when we pray for the Holy Spirit to join us as we delve into the Word. On the other hand, the Scriptures will be nothing to us but puzzling prose if we attempt to understand them on our own accord.

Holy Father, I thank You that Your Word is full of grace and truth. May Your Spirit illuminate the Scriptures to me that I may gain heavenly wisdom and understanding. Guide me as I seek to know Your will for my life, and help me speak to others about Your wonderful ways. In Jesus' name, amen.

May 5–11. **Sharon Vance** lives in Mattoon, Illinois, where she is active in her church and enjoys reading, writing, cooking, and walking.

Eternal Flame

My Father's will is that everyone who looks to the Son and believes in him shall have eternal life, and I will raise them up at the last day (John 6:40).

Scripture: John 6:35-40
Song: "Shine, Jesus, Shine"

I don't know how anyone can go to a memorial spot and not be moved. By definition, memorials are constructed to evoke memories—often symbolized by a perpetual flame somewhere on the grounds.

That single flicker has always amazed me, as it seems logical to me that fire should be extinguishable. Through the wonders of science and engineering, though, such flames remain aglow. Usually, a constantly flashing electric spark near the tip of its nozzle relights the gas if the flame is accidentally extinguished. That nozzle is connected to a dedicated fuel source. That's how, for example, the flame at the John F. Kennedy grave site in Arlington National Cemetery continues to stay alight.

Christians are also fueled by a dedicated line—God himself. Believing in Christ's sacrifice for our sins is the spark that allows the fuel—the sanctifying grace of God—to continue pumping into our daily lives. Stormy gales and pounding rains can threaten to extinguish that flame of God's love within us. But let us continue to look to the Son. The blaze of glory will warm our hearts and draw others to take comfort in the glow.

Almighty God, You alone can promise eternity for our souls, and You alone can keep the flame of faith lit. Thank You for the sacrifice of Jesus that provided the spark for Your unending love for me. In His precious name I pray. Amen.

Spitting Image

The one who looks at me is seeing the one who sent me (John 12:45).

Scripture: John 12:44-50
Song: "Have Thine Own Way, Lord"

I proudly display a portrait of my parents, taken somewhere around their 40th wedding anniversary. It's a wonderful picture of the two of them, and friends who come to visit see it and often ask, "Are these your parents?"

Once I responded that my mother always said I took after my father's side of the family. But my friend replied, "I can see *both* of them in you."

Truth be told, there has never been any doubt that I am my mother's daughter. Along with all my sisters, I have the crooked little toes and pinky fingers we inherited from her. With a look at our hands and feet, Mom told the doctor in the hospital that there was no doubt which babies were hers.

Jesus told those listening to Him at the Passover festival that He is "the spitting image" of His heavenly Father. Christ came to earth so people could see God the Father in human flesh. And though He said what His Father commanded Him to say, He wasn't just some spokesman reciting a well-rehearsed script. He was the full image of God, living on this earth so we could truly see and know our Creator.

Open my eyes today, **Lord,** that I may truly see You. Thank You for sending Jesus, the spitting image of yourself, to this earth that we may see You and know You more fully. Help me, Father, to become more like You and Your Son, Jesus, in whose matchless name I pray. Amen.

Go to the Source

"Is that your own idea," Jesus asked, **"or did others talk to you about me?"** (John 18:34).

Scripture: John 18:33-38
Song: "O God, Our Help in Ages Past"

As a journalism major in college, I found my professors to be excellent at drilling key principles into the minds of future reporters. The importance of timeliness of the story, relevance to the reader, and the significance of answering all the questions (who, what, when, where, why, and how) were all stressed in nearly every class.

Early on, the professors lectured on how reporters need to avoid basing stories on hearsay or secondhand information. In short, they told us we need to *go to the source to get the story*. This prompted me to post a saying over my desk: "In God we trust—everything else we check."

When Jesus was interrogated by Pilate, He questioned whether the Roman governor had his facts in order or whether he was just relying on hearsay. Then Jesus set the record straight: "In fact, the reason I was born and came into the world is to testify to the truth."

Just as Christ testified truthfully about himself before the authorities, He continues to be our source of truth today. As we go directly to the source, we'll find that He has perfect timing, is relevant to our situation, and has the answers to life's questions.

Father, I acknowledge that Christ alone is the source of truth. I know that I am not always able to trust others, but I can fully place my trust in You. I come to You today for guidance, wisdom, and a renewed filling of your Spirit. In Jesus' name, amen.

This Is the Night

Now my soul is troubled, and what shall I say? "Father, save me from this hour"? No, it was for this very reason I came to this hour (John 12:27).

Scripture: John 12:27-32
Song: "My Jesus, As Thou Wilt!"

My son, Derrick, has always enjoyed performing, and his musical and theatrical talents flow naturally from him. Because of that, early on he assumed everyone in a production was just as excited about it as he was.

The night of our church's children's Christmas program, when he was in elementary school, Derrick was with the other kids as they donned their costumes and makeup and collected their props. At one point, in the midst of the flurry of preparations, Derrick spoke some encouragement to his fellow performers: "All right, everyone – this is the night we've been waiting for!"

Derrick felt it was important to remind the other children that all the preparation had been done to bring them to that specific hour. Just days before His death, Jesus admitted that His soul was troubled at the coming suffering. Yet, He was sent to earth for a specific purpose, and the appointed time to fulfill that purpose had come. He could glorify God at the prospect.

In His human nature, Jesus didn't want to die. But He set aside all reservations to become my Savior and yours—just what we'd been waiting for. We too can glorify God for that.

God of glory, there is no way I will ever be able to praise You enough for sending Jesus to be my Savior. Thank You for Christ's example of obedience, even in the midst of a very human fear and sorrow. In Jesus' name, amen.

No Need to Stray

They will never follow a stranger; in fact, they will run away from him because they do not recognize a stranger's voice (John 10:5)

Scripture: John 10:1-10
Song: "Savior, Like a Shepherd Lead Us"

When I was young, my father decided to fulfill his long-time dream of raising sheep. We lived on 23 acres, which was mostly pasture, so Dad saw no reason why we couldn't have about a dozen sheep to go with our three horses and small herd of cattle. Once we got the sheep, they had very different ideas about our wonderful farm. Several times we received a phone call in the middle of the night from a neighbor, informing us that our sheep had gone astray—again. We would all get up and get dressed to herd the sheep back to our pastures. The problem is, we were as new to the sheep as they were to us. We hadn't had a chance to know each other. Because of that, herding the sheep was a real challenge.

Jesus reminds us that sheep, by nature, will *follow* their shepherd because that's who raised them; it's who they know. Christ is the good shepherd, so we, as His sheep, can joyfully follow Him. However, let us spend time with our shepherd so we can know His voice when He calls us. There's just no need to wander around, fearful and without direction.

Gentle Shepherd, thank You for always being willing to lead me, even when I wander off and go astray. Help me to take time today to listen for Your voice. I need Your protection this day too, from an influence that might seek to rob my joy. In Your precious name I pray. Amen.

New Wardrobe

Provide for those who grieve . . . a garment of praise instead of a spirit of despair (Isaiah 61:3).

Scripture: Isaiah 61:1-3
Song: "Change My Heart, O God"

Two wonderful ladies in my church both have new wardrobes, but for completely different reasons. Kim worked very hard for a long time to shed many, many pounds, so her clothes no longer fit her. Kim beams when people tell her how great she looks, and she's thankful for all those who supported her. Tina lost all of her clothes in a Saturday morning fire that quickly consumed her home. She initially shared clothes with her daughter-in-law. But one day Tina's sisters surprised her with several outfits they'd bought for her.

It's great to be able to change for the better what's on the outside of us. But God's love can change us from the inside out. And only the Lord can make those drastic inner changes that Isaiah proclaims: a heartfelt willingness to offer comfort for those who mourn, a crown of beauty instead of ashes, the oil of joy instead of mourning, and a garment of praise in place of a spirit of despair.

We all have different circumstances that bring us to a saving knowledge of God. But our Father welcomes each one and clothes us with a new wardrobe of righteousness that can be classified as "one size fits all."

Father, I confess that change isn't easy for me. But I am thankful for Your infinite patience with me and how You gave me a new wardrobe that's a perfect fit: the robe of Christ's righteousness. In His holy name I pray. Amen.

Breaking Through the Fog

In that day the deaf will hear the words of the scroll, and out of gloom and darkness the eyes of the blind will see (Isaiah 29:18).

Scripture: Isaiah 29:17-19
Song: "Through the Night of Doubt and Sorrow"

Dense fog surrounded me as I drove to work early one morning. Visibility was limited to a few hundred feet. I couldn't see all the homes and businesses I knew I was passing, and I squinted to see car lights ahead. *How far will I have to drive like this?*

As suddenly as the fog enveloped me, it left. Blue sky broke through, and sunshine warmed and cheered me. I continued to my destination with confidence and arrived on time safely.

Are you in dark or foggy times? Many of us have felt confused, unable to see which way to turn. Sometimes we're afraid because we can't see the future, and we wonder how long we can endure. In our confusion, we may make poor choices, put our faith in dubious people, or seek help from the wrong places.

Throughout the Old Testament, prophets cajoled the people to turn back to God. This passage from Isaiah reminds us that God loves us and wants to "wow" us. In response, we worship Him with sincere hearts. In dark times, He promises to break through our fog, lighting the way to the next step. We who were blind can now see, thanks to God's love.

Awesome God, forgive me for doubting You when the fog of life gets thick. Remind me of Your presence even in the dark. In Jesus' name, amen.

May 12–18. **Jane Heitman Healy,** a librarian and former teacher, writes for Christian and education publications from her home in Sioux Falls, South Dakota.

A Real Treat

Honor your father and your mother, so that you may live long in the land the LORD your God is giving you (Exodus 20:12).

Scripture: Exodus 20:12-20
Song: "Teach Me, O Lord, Thy Way of Truth"

A home health nurse interviewed my elderly mother to determine what level of care she needed. "Who gets your groceries?" the nurse asked.

"She does," Mom said, pointing to me. "She gets me what I ask for, and sometimes she brings a little treat too."

"Just like you used to do for her," the nurse said.

Bringing Mom groceries is one way to honor her. I delight in choosing treats for her so I can see her surprised smile. Honoring my mother is a commandment a privilege, and a joy—most of the time. Sometimes it is a burden and an inconvenience. Because it's a commandment and because I love my mother, I assist her whether I feel joyful or burdened.

I wonder if God gave us the Ten Commandments to help us do right, even when we don't feel like it. Emotions are fleeting and circumstances change. God's love and words to His people are constant. And though the commandments are often cast negatively, known for "Thou shalt not," the results of following them are overwhelmingly positive In following them we show love and respect for God and others, a real treat indeed.

Almighty God, thank You for loving me enough to give me the guidance of the Ten Commandments. Forgive me for disobeying and misunderstanding them. Help me keep them in love for You and love for others. In Jesus' name, amen.

We're in It Together

All are justified freely by his grace through the redemption that came by Christ Jesus (Romans 3:24).

Scripture: Romans 3:21-26
Song: "There's a Wideness in God's Mercy"

Heavy snowfalls and spring rains caused flooding along riverbanks last spring. Townspeople came together, aided by the National Guard and nonprofit disaster relief agencies. Neighbors and strangers filled and placed sandbags until their arms and backs ached. They helped evacuate people closest to the flood area. Side by side they worked to save homes, businesses, and possessions. Religion, political views, and ethnicity didn't matter as people strove to stay ahead of the water. "We're all in this together" pulled communities into unity.

We are often at odds with each other about many things, large and small. But Paul reminds us in Romans that we are all sinners. We should not think that others are less important than ourselves. The good news is that *all* sinners—of every stripe and color—can be redeemed by Jesus' sacrifice on the cross. The ground is level at that cross, and justification comes to all who enter the waters of baptism.

The flood of God's mercy pours over each one of us who come to Christ in repentance and faith. Rather than standing apart with criticism, let us join together in thanks and praise. Here on earth, in good times and bad, we, the body of Christ, really are all in this together.

Lord, thank You for giving me the gift of salvation. Remind me that You sacrificed yourself for me and for the rest of the world. In Your name I pray. Amen.

Shine Like a Lighthouse

In the same way, let your light shine before others, that they may see your good deeds and glorify your Father in heaven (Matthew 5:16).

Scripture: Matthew 5:14-16
Song: "Shine"

Lighthouses dot shorelines as landmarks for passing ships. At night, lighthouses shine beacons to guide ships through the darkness. To ensure that ships' crews know exactly where they are, lighthouses have their own unique signals. Each flashes its beacon in a particular pattern known as a "characteristic." When a ship's navigator sees a pattern of flashes, he checks his light list to know which lighthouse he sees.

Jesus probably did not have lighthouses in mind when He told us to shine. However, there are similarities. Like lighthouses, we stand on firm ground. We also shine in individual ways. We each have unique abilities and gifts to offer: cooking, teaching, fishing, doing crafts, making music, or a myriad of other things. We can find ways to use these in our churches, at work, in our neighborhoods, and at home.

We are like lighthouses in another way. They do not shine for their own benefit, but to guide others. Jesus says that our ultimate reason for shining should be to lead others to glorify God. We don't use our gifts to draw attention to ourselves, but to lead others to Jesus.

Jesus, light of the world, thank You that we each have our own special characteristic, shining out to our neighbors. Guide me in discerning my spiritual gifts, and give me the will to use them fruitfully. In Your name I pray. Amen.

The Cure

If your right hand causes you to stumble, cut it off and throw it away. It is better for you to lose one part of your body than for your whole body to go into hell (Matthew 5:30).

Scripture: Matthew 5:27-30
Song: "There Is a Balm in Gilead"

Medical conditions sometimes require amputation to keep disease from spreading to the rest of a patient's body. And sometimes internal organs are fully or partially removed in an effort to contain, control, and cure disease.

Jesus talks about a different kind of ailment in Matthew 5: "sin sickness." He points out how rampant and devious sin is. Overtly sinful acts are easy to identify and maybe avoid, but even a look or thought can be unlawful. So Jesus emphasizes the intent of the law: to move us toward loving God and others.

If we amputated every body part that caused us to sin, there would soon be nothing left of us! Instead, we can use our bodies to glorify God. Rather than chopping off a hand, offer it in aid and friendship. Rather than cutting out a tongue, use it to encourage and build up. Lopping off body parts won't save us from sin; only Jesus can do that.

Medical researchers seek understanding in containing and curing disease. A variety of treatments may be effective, depending on the patient. There is only one cure for sin sickness, though—Jesus, the one whose sacrifice gives us eternal life.

O Great Physician, give skill and wisdom to medical teams. Give Your peace and courage to patients facing surgery. Thank You for Your power to heal body and soul. In Jesus' name, amen.

Does Practice Make Perfect?

Be perfect, therefore, as your heavenly Father is perfect (Matthew 5:48).

Scripture: Matthew 5:43-48
Song: "They Will Know We Are Christians by Our Love"

Late professional basketball player Wilt Chamberlain said, "They say that nobody is perfect. Then they tell you practice makes perfect. I wish they'd make up their minds."

The quest for perfection is a lifelong struggle. So is the balance between perfection and reality. Psychologists write that though striving for perfection can help improve a talent or product, it can be damaging if carried to extremes. Perfectionists place high expectations on themselves and those around them. They can be difficult and driven, with little compassion for others.

In a way, though, practice does make perfect. Jesus calls Christians to practice hospitality by loving and welcoming those ignored by society. He expects us to practice generosity by giving to those who cannot give in return. He challenges us to face the world's meanness by practicing kindness. In those ways, Christians will be known as different from the secular world.

God doesn't leave us alone to reverse our worldly ways, though. Jesus taught us how to pray. Worship and fellowship with other Christians builds us up. The Holy Spirit is with us to guide and encourage us. God is at work, transforming us until the end, when at last, we will be made perfect. Ultimately, then, it's God's work, start to finish.

Lord God, You alone are perfect and worthy of praise! Work in me so that I delight in practicing the Christian way as Jesus describes. In His name, amen.

Traditions to Keep—or Not?

Some Pharisees and teachers of the law came to Jesus from Jerusalem and asked, "Why do your disciples break the tradition of the elders? They don't wash their hands before they eat!" (Matthew 15:1, 2).

Scripture: Matthew 15:1-6
Song: "In Remembrance of Me"

"Tradition, tradition!" sings Tevye in the musical *Fiddler on the Roof*. The song's lyrics explain the role of each member of the Jewish household. These traditions give a sense of order to Tevye and the community. In the story, though, the audience watches Tevye's traditions broken, one after another. At first he balks but eventually comes to accept the new ways because he loves his family. When his youngest daughter marries a Christian, Tevye declares them dead. Yet, he utters the blessing, "God be with you," when they part ways.

Tradition provides security, but clinging to traditions "for tradition's sake" is the problem. In Matthew 15, Jesus defends His disciples by pointing to pharisaical hypocrisy. They kept one tradition that broke another. Being rule-bound doesn't leave room for the Holy Spirit. When a tradition gets in the way of loving God or others, it's time to let it go.

God gave us the Bible to guide us and established the rite of baptism to claim us. Jesus instituted the Lord's Supper in memory of His sacrifice for us. These are traditions to live by and to pass on to others.

Father, thank You for the apostolic traditions that help me remember You. But guide me in knowing which other traditions to consider letting go. In Jesus' name, amen.

Know Him Through Obeying

Know therefore that the LORD your God is God; he is the faithful God, keeping his covenant of love to a thousand generations of those who love him and keep his commandments (Deuteronomy 7:9).

Scripture: Deuteronomy 7:7-16
Song: "Trust and Obey"

The selected Scripture verse for today calls me to "know" something crucially important: God is God (and I am *not* God). How easy to forget!

Even in the most difficult times, we can remember God's faithfulness to us. And though it's sometimes easy to forget Him in times of trouble, He clearly spells out His terms of faithfulness: We simply have to know and remember that He is God—and God alone.

Do we try to do His work for Him? Do we seek to know what's ahead for us, rather than simply doing what is set before us in the moment? I love how Oswald Chambers put it: "All God's revelations are sealed to us until they are opened to us by obedience. . . . Let God's truth work in you by soaking in it, not by worrying into it. Obey God in the thing He is at present showing you, and instantly the next thing is opened up. . . . God will never reveal more truth about Himself till you obey what you know already." Know God, by obeying God!

Lord, I want to know You so much better. So help me today to obey what You have called me to do. In service to You, I will deepen in knowledge of You. In Christ, amen.

May 19–25. **Jimmie Oliver Fleming**, of Chester, Virginia, has written numerous devotions and articles for publication. She enjoys playing piano and recently began taking guitar lessons.

Obey—Because He Loves You

What does the LORD your God ask of you but to fear the LORD your God, to walk in obedience to him, to love him, to serve the LORD your God with all your heart and with all your soul (Deuteronomy 10:12).

Scripture: Deuteronomy 10:12-21
Song: "Jesus Paid It All"

"You don't know how good you have it here at home," a father told his son. "Just wait until you're out on your own and see what happens." It didn't take very long, for being "out on his own" merely entailed walking to the end of the long path that led to the end of the road of their country home. He returned with gratitude and obedience.

Obedience is what God asks of us, and when we obey, this also shows our gratitude to Him. It shows respect too, for when we truly "fear the Lord," we will do it His way.

The important distinction to know is that our obedience flows from our gratitude and not from our desire to earn God's favor. Otherwise, it would be like bribing God!

Sadly, many folks in our society see religion as a means of getting God to like them. They fail to see that He already loves them unconditionally, without limit. If only they might invite Him into their lives and accept that love!

As one theologian once put it, the key calling to every human being, when it comes to God, is simply this: Accept that you're accepted.

Father God, thank You for Your infinite love. Help me to realize the depth of this love when I'm tempted to try to earn Your favor. In Jesus' name, amen.

In the Way?

Love the LORD your God and keep his requirements, his decrees, his laws and his commands always (Deuteronomy 11:1).

Scripture: Deuteronomy 11:1-7
Song: "Open My Eyes That I May See"

"I'm taking guitar lessons," I told my friend, "and it's improving my piano playing."

"Well, good for you," she said. "Because I had enough of that when I was growing up; I was made to take piano lessons. I'm glad I don't even have a piano, since it would just be in the way."

Perhaps the things of God can get in the way as well? It can happen when we lose interest in keeping His "requirements, decrees, laws, and commands" as we're called to do. The great thing is that we can be right back in close fellowship with Him—enthusiastically—with a simple turning of the will.

Christian writer Tim Stafford said: "You can think it will take a lot of time, a month or so of spiritual discipline, to get going again with Him. Then you sit down and discover, in just minutes, that you don't have to do a thing—except take some time. Be alone with Him. In what feels like no time, you are caught up again in your love."

Let us take heart. God will not let us get by with our neglectful behavior forever. Soon we'll open our eyes again to His great mercy and love. And we'll love what He asks us to do.

Heavenly Father, I want to see and remember all of Your majesty. Please help me to open my eyes wide. Unshackle my feet so that I can walk, run, jump, and soar to the heights promised in Your Word. In Jesus' holy name, I pray. Amen.

Keep Them in Your Heart

Do not steal. Do not lie. Do not deceive one another (Leviticus 19:11).

Scripture: Leviticus 19:11-17
Song: "The Way of the Cross Leads Home"

Going from the book of Deuteronomy to the book of Leviticus in writing these devotionals reminds me of two practice tunes in my guitar lesson book, "More" and "Still More." That is, there are still more requirements, decrees, laws, and commands to follow. And any notion of being "home free" has gone out the window.

Jesus made this clear in His Sermon on the Mount. If we appear to be keeping one of the commandments, we might check our hearts: have we actually *desired* to break that commandment? Maybe the circumstances prevented us, for example, from acting on an impulse to steal someone's shiny blue pen. We didn't, but we *would* have if assured of not being caught. It's that impulse Jesus speaks to. He came to give us new impulses, desires that flow from the indwelling Holy Spirit to replace the desires of our old nature.

However, it is true that growth in the Christian life can feel like a real uphill struggle. Hopefully, it is two steps forward and only one step back. With God's help we can become the kind of people, inwardly, who display the character of our beautiful Savior.

Heavenly Father, help me to remember and obey Your Word with the full understanding that I am always accountable to You—while continually relying on Your grace and mercy. I pray through my deliverer, Jesus. Amen.

Praying for Whom?

When the heavens are shut and there is no rain because your people have sinned against you, and when they pray toward this place and give praise to your name and turn from their sin . . . send rain on the land you gave your people for an inheritance (1 Kings 8:35, 36).

Scripture: 1 Kings 8:31-36
Song: "Let It Rain"

It's easy to pray for nice people—but what about the not-so-nice? Solomon prayed to God on behalf of people who had seriously sinned against God.

Why? Because of their need. They needed rain. They needed conviction too, the broken hearts that would lead them to repentance. And so Solomon prayed for them.

Who are you praying for today—and what are you asking? I am hoping to add to my list not only more friends, but some enemies too. I hope to add anyone who has a need, even if they are involved in things terribly self-destructive.

I think of Jesus' words to the man who once asked him, "Who is my neighbor?" After hearing the parable of the good Samaritan, the questioner finally got it. A neighbor is one who shows mercy, pure and simple. When someone is in need, let us reach out with our deeds and in our prayers.

Almighty God and Creator, I am praying for Your rain right now in the lives of those You love. Help me to love them with the compassion that flows from the heart of Jesus my Savior. Give me a renewed sense of Your grace and mercy in my life that I might extend those matchless qualities to everyone in my world. Start today, Lord! In the name of the Father and of the Son, and of the Holy Spirit, I pray. Amen.

Who Are You Following?

LORD, who may dwell in your sacred tent? Who may live on your holy mountain? The one whose walk is blameless, who does what is righteous, who speaks the truth from their heart (Psalm 15:1, 2).

Scripture: Psalm 15
Song: "The Majesty and Glory of Your Name"

The psalmist David led an interesting life. Those who might have tracked him on his Twitter page would have some exciting feats to follow.

We can still "follow" David, despite the lack of cyber data from his day. Many of his amazing deeds are documented in the written Word. And yes, experience does count when it comes to the two questions he asked at the beginning of Psalm 15. Who was better qualified to ask and answer them?

"LORD, who may dwell in your sacred tent? Who may live on your holy mountain?" Can you answer these questions? Is your walk with God blameless? Do you always do what is righteous? If not, fear not. Neither was David's walk without sin — it even included adultery and murder!

God can change for us whatever needs to be changed in our lives. All we need do is ask, with an open heart. Then we too will be following more than the Lord's servant. We'll follow the Lord himself.

O God my Father, help me to follow Your leading as closely as I possibly can. I want to dwell in Your sacred tent and live on Your holy mountain. I want to "fear" You according to Your Word. Please help me, so that I will remain steadfast and not be shaken by any fearful circumstance. In Jesus' name, amen.

Questions and Answers

One of the teachers of the law came and heard them debating. Noticing that Jesus had given them a good answer, he asked him, "Of all the commandments, which is the most important?" (Mark 12:28).

Scripture: Mark 12:28-34
Song: "I Found the Answer"

"Nice that I can ask this doctor questions," said the elderly woman who sat next to me in the waiting area. "My other doctor was always in a hurry. And even when he did answer questions, he didn't explain much." How sad, I thought, for both doctor and patients.

In our Scripture we hear an excellent question coming to Jesus. Will He answer? Will He explain?

Yes! He wanted the questioner to understand much more about the nature of God and His will. That's why I know that I too can always ask Jesus any question I choose. His answers are always good and thoroughly practical. Want to know what's important? "Love the Lord your God with all your heart and with all your soul and with all your mind and with all your strength" (Mark 12:30).

When we begin loving the Lord God like that, He'll bring us to a recognition of the next most important thing: "Love your neighbor as yourself" (Mark 12:31). Full answer, full explanation.

Dear Lord, thank You for Your consistent answers and clear direction in my life. Your Word says it all. Continue to guide me in Your wisdom. I know that when I follow Your leading, I can never go wrong. Do continue to work in me a love for You and a love for those You love. I pray this prayer in Jesus' name. Amen.

Hanging on Jesus' Words

They could think of nothing, because all the people hung on every word he said (Luke 19:48, *New Living Translation*).

Scripture: Luke 19:41-48
Song: "Speak to My Heart"

Our youngest son lives with Sensory Integration Dysfunction Syndrome. He is very intelligent, but he learns differently. For example, he learns best when he is allowed to fidget with something while listening. Although some people may think he isn't paying attention, he is.

I saw this clearly one night as I shared a Scripture verse with my two boys. I noticed my younger son was "focused" on his toy instead of my words. So I asked him to tell me what I had just said, and he basically repeated my words verbatim! I smiled and was reminded: We can't always tell who's truly listening.

We see it in today's Scripture reading. As Jesus approached Jerusalem, He wept because He knew He was going to be rejected. In the temple He found a den of thieves instead of a house of prayer. But as He taught in the temple's outer courts, some of the people hung on His words. It seems the average person paid more attention than the religious elite.

Of course, we Christians desire to "hang on" Jesus' every word. And even though others at times may not think we are listening, Christ surely sees our open hearts.

O Lord, I want my heart to be open to You and Your teachings. May I hear Your word of truth, and may my heart always be soft to Your touch. In Your name, amen.

May 26–May 31. **Pete Charpentier** serves as a senior minister and enjoys camping with his family, reading, writing, and investing in others through personal mentoring relationships.

I'll See You in a Second!

Because of the anger of the LORD this happened in Jerusalem and Judah, till He finally cast them out of His presence. Then Zedekiah rebelled against the king of Babylon (Jeremiah 52:3, *New King James Version*).

Scripture: Jeremiah 52:1-9
Song: "Softly and Tenderly"

A certain man decided to jump from a 10-story building, distraught with his life of running from responsibility—and from God. However, after falling five stories, the man thought better of his choice and cried out to God for forgiveness. As he continued to plummet to the concrete below, he heard these words: "I forgive you, and I'll see you in a second!"

OK, that's meant to be a joke. But as the story shows, God has placed certain physical laws in motion, and one of them is gravity. Such natural laws—and also moral laws—have consistent, predictable consequences when they are broken. God does not suspend them on a whim.

This is illustrated in Jeremiah 52 in a very serious way. Here we see the devastating consequences of Judah's sinful choices over a long period of history: judgment for sin was inevitable; captivity would follow. Yet we also know from Scripture that God eventually made a way for His people to return from captivity. While consequences certainly flow from our choices, God's love for His people truly does endure forever.

Father, thank You for Your great love for me. I praise You for the promise that You will never leave me nor forsake me. I give You thanks for Your mercies that are new and fresh every morning. In Jesus' name, amen.

The Domino Effect

All the army of the Chaldeans, that were with the captain of the guard, brake down all the walls of Jerusalem round about (Jeremiah 52:14, *King James Version*).

Scripture: Jeremiah 52:10-14
Song: "Living for Jesus"

I used to read a bedtime story to my son about a little animal that lived on a farm. It sneezed. And that sneeze sparked a chain-reaction of events that led to complete planetary chaos! This classic tale illustrated the proverbial "domino effect," how one event triggers others in succession.

The story of Zedekiah and the destruction of Jerusalem is a biblical example of a massive domino effect. The carnage is staggering. Not only do we see Zedekiah blinded, chained, and carried off into exile, but we also see his sons slaughtered before his eyes, the princes of Judah executed, and the temple—along with all the houses of Jerusalem—left in charred ruins.

The problems in Jerusalem did not begin with Zedekiah. They began long before him as many of the kings in Judah's turbulent history rebelled against the Lord.

So the "domino effect" is a real phenomenon. One small action can result in major events. But just as negative choices lead to negative results, the opposite is also true: Positive choices lead to positive results. May we daily choose the latter option.

O God, Creator of Heaven and earth, I have many choices before me today. Please enable me by Your grace and strength to set in motion a positive chain reaction of events so that Your name may be praised. I pray this prayer in the name of Jesus, my merciful Savior and Lord. Amen.

God's Guardrails

The people mocked these messengers of God and despised their words. They scoffed at the prophets until the LORD's anger could no longer be restrained and there was no remedy (2 Chronicles 36:16, *New Living Translation*).

Scripture: 2 Chronicles 36:15-21
Song: "Take Time to Be Holy"

I remember the first go-kart my brothers and I had. My dad built it from the metal frame of our bunk-bed set. But its seats had no guardrails. Of course, we didn't notice this oversight until our "maiden voyage" was already underway.

Dad sent out my two older brothers for a test drive, but when my oldest brother took a sharp left turn, my other brother continued straight and out of the go-kart and onto the pavement! At this point, with my brother's scrapes and bruises focusing our minds, we all realized that guardrails would be a great idea.

Isn't this how we often learn in life? Like Israel, we may ignore God's warning signs around us. Having guardrails on a go-kart is a common idea, but when we try to do things from "scratch" instead of learning from others, we tend to learn the hard way.

The old axiom is true: Those who don't learn from history are destined to repeat it. Yet, we can choose to live differently. Instead of ignoring God's warning signs, we can live according to biblical counsel. This is living within God's guardrails.

Lord, thank You for surrounding me with Your guardrails. Please help me to heed the warning signs all around me so that I can walk according to Your wisdom and experience Your protection. In Your name, amen.

We'll Both Sink!

Nebuchadnezzer led King Jehoiachin away as a captive to Babylon, along with his wives and officials, the queen mother, and all Jerusalem's elite. He also took seven thousand of the best troops and one thousand craftsmen and smiths, all of whom were strong and fit for war (2 Kings 24:15, 16, *New Living Translation*).

Scripture: 2 Kings 24:8-17
Song: "Make Me a Channel of Blessing"

There's a rather humorous Jewish proverb about two men stranded at sea. After days without food, their desperate condition began to take its toll on their mental states. One of the men began drilling a hole in the bottom of his side of the boat. When the other man saw what he was doing, he protested, "Stop, or we'll both sink!" But the man drilling the hole shouted back, "I'm only drilling the hole on my side of the boat!"

Scripture constantly emphasizes that sin is a personal choice—but with widespread consequences. In other words, our sin isn't just our business; it impacts others.

Our reading today clearly illustrates this sobering truth. For example, although Jehoiachin was king, his sinful choices led to the captivity of many others. Not only was his family devastated by his unfaithful leadership, thousands of others were also led into bondage along with him.

While we will never live perfect lives, we can leave a legacy of faithfulness that encourages others to do the same. Our good deeds also have an impact on the world. Thanks be to God!

Lord God Almighty, I want my life to be a blessing to others. Please grant me the strength to leave a legacy of faithfulness. I pray in the name of Jesus. Amen.

Restoration

Then rose up the chief of the fathers of Judah and Benjamin, and the priests, and the Levites, with all them whose spirit God had raised, to go up to build the house of the LORD which is in Jerusalem (Ezra 1:5, *King James Version*).

Scripture: Ezra 1:1-8
Song: "Jesus, I Come"

Not long after my wife and I were married, she told me that she wanted a vegetable bin for our little kitchen. So I bought a book of small woodworking projects. It included a pattern for a vegetable bin, and I set out to impress my bride with my carpentry skills. The only problem was that I was in way over my head! While my father-in-law was a master carpenter, I didn't know the first thing about working with wood.

After some time of working hard on my project, I made my vegetable bin perfectly—perfectly crooked. Eventually I swallowed my pride and went to my father-in-law for help. I asked him, "Can you 'heal' this thing?" He sized-up the situation for a moment and said, "No. It doesn't need a healin'; it needs a resurrection!"

Well, whether we need a "resurrection" or a "healing" in life, God is able to give us what we need. The people of Israel made a mess of things, but the Lord still called leaders to pave the way for their restoration. The great news of the Bible is that God restores us.

Thank You, **Lord,** for being faithful when I am faithless. Thank You, Lord, for fulfilling all Your promises and for not letting one of them fail. Thank You, Lord, for restoring my life every time I falter. Through Christ I pray. Amen.

DEVOTIONS®

June

> This is what the LORD Almighty says: "Give careful thought to your ways."
>
> —*Haggai 1:7*

Gary Wilde, Editor | **Margaret Williams,** Project Editor | Photo iStockphoto | Thinkstock®

DEVOTIONS® is published quarterly by Standard Publishing, Cincinnati, Ohio, www.standardpub.com. © 2013 by Standard Publishing. All rights reserved. Topics based on the Home Daily Bible Readings, International Sunday School Lessons. © 2010 by the Committee on the Uniform Series. Printed in the U.S.A. All Scripture quotations, unless otherwise indicated, are taken from the HOLY BIBLE, *NEW INTERNATIONAL VERSION®. NIV®.* Copyright © 1973, 1978, 1984, 2011 by Biblica. Used by permission of Zondervan. All rights reserved. *Holy Bible, New Living Translation (NLT),* © 1996. Tyndale House Publishers. *The Revised Standard Version of the Bible (RSV),* copyrighted 1946, 1952, © 1971, 1973. *New American Standard Bible (NASB),* © The Lockman Foundation, 1960, 1962, 1963.

Provision in Record Time

Now go up into the hills, bring down timber, and rebuild my house. Then I will take pleasure in it and be honored, says the LORD (Haggai 1:8, *New Living Translation*).

Scripture: Haggai 1:1-11
Song: "He Leadeth Me!"

My wife and I stared at the paper. We'd filed our taxes and were looking at how much we had to pay. We owed $1,500, which was our life's savings at that point in our lives. We were in ministry, living from one love offering to another. When I preached, we were paid; when I didn't preach, we weren't paid.

Obviously, we had to pay our taxes. So we went to the bank and borrowed against our savings. Then we went to the post office . . . and found an envelope waiting for us. It contained a letter from a couple who explained that God had led them to send the enclosed gift months before: a check for $1,500.

Now my wife and I stared at the check. The next morning we went back to the bank and paid off our loan in record time. While the Lord has not always provided for us in such sensational ways, He has always met our needs.

Haggai called God's people to trust Him in building the temple. While we all become preoccupied with storing treasures for ourselves, Haggai reminds us to seek God's kingdom first, and He will provide for us.

Lord, You know what I need even before I ask, and nothing is impossible for You. I thank You in advance for Your provision in my life. Amen.

June 1. **Pete Charpentier,** of Hammond, Louisiana, is a senior minister who enjoys camping with his family, reading, writing, and investing in others through mentoring relationships.

Surely, It Was God—It Wasn't Me!

LORD, **You establish peace for us; all that we have accomplished you have done for us** (Isaiah 26:12).

Scripture: Isaiah 26:1-13
Song: "On My Knees"

Bob, our minister, acts out different Bible characters in short, one-act plays during the weeks leading up to Easter, and he's a tough act to follow. He asked me to play Mary for the Saturday before Easter morning. In the 20 minute solo part, Mary speaks her heart to God after her Son's crucifixion.

But I was unable to memorize the part like Bob did his, and I felt fearful and unworthy. As the lights dimmed, I whispered, "Oh God, I can't do this without You!" My heart pounded like crazy. But when I started speaking, I felt peace flow through me. I no longer needed the paper I was holding. For those moments I became Mary. My heart was touched as if watching someone else perform.

When the play ended, there wasn't a dry eye in the sanctuary. I turned to Bob and said, "It wasn't me." He just smiled.

We are promised perfect peace if we live in "righteousness" and "rightness." How do we know and do what's right? God provides the way.

O Lord God! How grateful I am that You keep Your promises, that You never leave me, nor forsake me. Even when it seems as if it is too late, You show up on time. Help me to keep my mind and heart on You and Your ways. I certainly can't do life without You. In the name of Jesus, I pray. Amen.

June 2–8. **SanDee Hardwig,** a retired teacher, and now a freelance writer, lives in Brown Deer, Wisconsin, with her two cats, Odie and Milo.

Let the Words Come Through

I broke the bars of your yoke and enabled you to walk with heads held high (Leviticus 26:13).

Scripture: Leviticus 26:3-13
Song: "There Is a Redeemer"

Keith Green, born in 1953, was a musical child prodigy, playing guitar at 5, piano at 7, writing songs at 8. By the time he was 10 years old, he had a contract with Decca Records. Instead of becoming a rock star, though, Keith is best remembered for his devotion to Jesus Christ.

In 1975, Keith and his wife, Melody, began helping drug addicts, prostitutes, and the homeless. Their Last Days Ministries offered shelter, Christian counseling, and education. In 1976, Keith returned to music, becoming a well-known Gospel singer and songwriter. But on July 28, 1982, Keith Green and two of his young children died in a plane crash, along with missionaries John and Dede Smalley and their six children.

What a tragic loss! But what a wonderful legacy and example this humble man left us.

Keith always urged people not to worship musicians, saying "I repent of having recorded . . . if my life has not provoked you to sell out more completely to Jesus. . . . The Lord will say, 'Well done, good and faithful servant' (Matthew 25:23) to one whose life proves what their lyrics are saying."

So today I am prayerfully considering: Does my own life reflect my words?

My Father God, I repent of any idolatry in my heart. Forgive me for my selfishness, and may the lyrics of my life bring honor to Your name. In Christ, amen.

Fatherly Discipline

If after all this you will not listen to me, I will punish you for your sins (Leviticus 26:18).

Scripture: Leviticus 26:14-26
Song: "I Hear Thy Welcome Voice"

When I was five, Dad married Mom and adopted me. I never considered him my stepdad. He never lifted a hand or a loud voice to me. I loved him so much that whenever he talked, I really listened. When he said no, I didn't challenge him. Except once—I was 12-years-old.

"Come back here, young lady!" Dad yelled. He grabbed an apple tree branch off the ground and chased me across the lawn. That was the fastest I've ever run! He didn't catch me.

What had I done? I don't remember the crime, but it must have been a humdinger.

I thank God often for the gift of my dad. Today's Scripture speaks of fathers, and they are sometimes difficult words to read. Our heavenly Father knows what's best for us. He loves, guides, and provides for us. However, as any good father, he sets boundaries for our good, for our protection—sometimes to keep us from pure self-destruction.

Yes, God must warn and discipline His children if they are truly to be loved. And, conversely, when we have a loving Father, don't we want to listen, please, and obey?

Almighty and most merciful God, I am deeply ashamed when I slip up and sin. Help me avoid disappointing You or grieving Your heart. Thank You for godly mentors You place in my life and for giving me Your indwelling presence to guide me. In the name of the Father and of the Son and of the Holy Spirit, I pray. Amen.

Muffie Moved to the Good Life

Do what is right and good in the LORD's sight, so that it might go well with you and you may go in and take over the good land the LORD promised (Deuteronomy 6:18).

Scripture: Deuteronomy 6:17-25
Song: "From the Inside Out"

The award-winning comic strip "Pickles" features retirees Earl and Opal Pickles. They find the retirement years less than "golden," but make the best of it. They live with their dog, Roscoe, and their cat, Muffie. And I think Earl's a bit jealous of the cat. In one strip Earl asks Opal (sitting with Muffie on her lap) whether the cat really cares for her. "Of course," says Opal.

"I heard about a lady who took great care of her cat for years," says Earl. "She thought the cat loved her. But when a lady down the street put gourmet cat food on her porch, the cat moved without a thought about her owner."

Opal looks down at Muffie, who she's had for years, "You wouldn't do that to me, would you, Precious?" And then a thought bubble appears above Muffie's head: "Well, actually I belong to a neighbor down the block." Looks like Muffie changed her circumstances and moved to the good land.

Ever feel it's too late to change your circumstances? God promises to remove obstacles and lead us into "the good land" for fellowship with Him, moment by moment through our days. We need only keep an open heart, listen for His guidance, and "do what is right" in each decision that comes our way.

Lord God, sometimes I lose hope and patience when things go wrong. Help me to remember that You have my life in Your hands—and You are good! In Christ, amen.

More than Enough

So do not fear, for I am with you . . . I am your God. I will strengthen you and help you (Isaiah 41:10).

Scripture: Isaiah 41:1-10
Song: "Enough"

Last Sunday, our praise and worship team sang, "Enough" by Chris Tomlin. As the song lyrics rang through my mind, I recalled a fable I read somewhere. A king had his servants place a boulder in the middle of a road. Then the king hid to see if anyone would remove the huge rock.

Many of his subjects just walked around it. Some cursed the king for not keeping the roads clear. None attempted to move it, until a peasant carrying a heavy load came along. He laid down his burden, then pushed and strained against the rock until he moved it off the road. When he picked up his bundle, he spotted a purse lying where the boulder had been—a purse full of gold and a note from the king, thanking whoever cleared the road.

The peasant did the right thing and was rewarded. In Isaiah, God called his people into His service, saying: "'You are my servant'; I have chosen you and have not rejected you. . . . do not be dismayed" (Isaiah 41:9, 10). God promises to strengthen us, to help us, and to uphold us in His hand. Since our God does not lie, what better king could we have? What good things can we do to serve Him out of our gratitude today?

Lord Jesus, You are King of kings! Lord of lords! And You're more than enough for me. No words I say can ever praise You enough or thank You enough. I love You, Jesus, who lives and reigns with the Father and the Holy Spirit. Amen.

Priceless Gifts

Wait for the LORD; be strong and take heart and wait for the LORD (Psalm 27:14).

Scripture: Psalm 27:7-14
Song: "Wait, O My Soul, Thy Maker's Will"

Caitlyn Persinger's brother, Chris, was her hero and her mentor. He taught her to tie her shoes, ride a bike, and play sports, which they both loved. Caitlyn (13) was devastated when Chris (17) was killed in an auto accident during his senior year. She threw herself into athletics, making varsity in her freshman year.

Four years after her brother's death, Caitlyn was as good in sports as he had predicted. But she twisted her left knee and severely tore her ACL. When using tissue from Caitlyn was not possible, doctors had to locate tissue from a cadaver. Chris had been a tissue donor when he died.

Knowing it was a long shot, the parents inquired whether any tissue was left. They discovered Chris's gift had helped 63 people in eight states and two continents, and only one piece of tissue from Chris remained. It was exactly what was needed to repair Caitlyn's knee. After surgery and six months of therapy, Caitlyn was back on the basketball court. What a great and good gift from her brother!

The psalmist writes of the goodness of our heavenly Father: "I will see the goodness of the Lord in the land of the living" (v. 13). In His goodness, God has given us His Son and along with Him, every good thing. Let us wait . . . and take heart.

Thank You, **Heavenly Father,** for hearing my voice when I call to You—and for giving Jesus, the greatest gift of all. In Him I pray. Amen.

Restoration Promises

They came and began to work on the house of the LORD Almighty, their God (Haggai 1:14).

Scripture: Haggai 1:12–2:9
Song: "Unless the Lord the House Shall Build"

Kids used to play telephone tricks by calling and asking people things like, "Is your refrigerator running?" or "Do you have Prince Albert in the can?" When someone would answer in the affirmative, they'd giggle and say, "You better catch it before it gets away," or "Better let him out!" Prince Albert was a popular tobacco brand in the early to mid 1900s.

Jen Lang, of Stevens Point, Wisconsin, was rebuilding her kitchen walls when she spotted red, shiny metal cans stacked in the insulation, from the middle of the wall to the floor. Jen says she really did find Prince Albert in a can—88 cans, to be exact. All were unopened and displayed tax stamps from 1918. The previous owner had no idea the cans were there, but said they'd found a lot of empty tobacco cans around the house when they bought it. But do tobacco cans make for good insulation?

Haggai and Zechariah roused God's people to rebuild Solomon's temple. Only the best materials were used, and about 50,000 people worked for years to complete the temple in 516 BC. As God promised, His glory was greater here than in His former house.

O God, when all seems lost, and I can't see a way out, may I cry out to You. You promise to comfort, heal, restore, and renew whatever the enemy attempts to destroy. I praise You, Lord, "God is our refuge and strength, an ever-present help in trouble" (Psalm 46:1). I pray through Christ my Lord. Amen.

A Gorgeous Place

The wilderness and the dry land shall be glad, the desert shall rejoice and blossom (Isaiah 35:1, *Revised Standard Version*).

Scripture: Isaiah 35
Song: "To God Be the Glory"

Winter Mesa, some 40 miles west of our small town in Colorado, is a formation of red Entrada sandstone. Western juniper and pinion trees populate it. Deep canyons of freestanding pinnacles and rock buttresses flank its sides. It's a gorgeous place.

As spring draws near and the mountains remain locked in deep snow, we often go to Winter Mesa to enjoy an afternoon of warmer temperatures and spectacular scenery. Occasionally, we find a few colorful wildflowers in bloom. They've pushed through the dry, desert sand to announce the advent of spring.

The arid, hot summer will soon arrive, and we will not visit Winter Mesa until the next spring. But the desert art gallery of wildflowers will survive the intense summer heat. They will continue to flourish and splash the desert with color.

Isaiah says the desert will blossom abundantly, and God will display His glory. Nothing on our earthly desert will ever be as bright or as welcome as God's glory. And here is one great reason: The wintry season of Satan's control will eventually give way to the incomparable, eternal spring of God's splendor.

Creator God, remind me that this good earth, as beautiful as it is, will some day be no more. Help me prepare my heart for life in Your eternal kingdom! I pray this prayer in the name of my Lord and Savior, Jesus Christ. Amen.

June 9–15. **Vicki Hodges** lives in the mountains of western Colorado with her family. She's a high school Spanish teacher who loves to travel.

The Strength of Obedience

All these blessings shall come upon you and overtake you, if you obey the voice of the LORD your God (Deuteronomy 28:2, *Revised Standard Version*).

Scripture: Deuteronomy 28:1-9
Song: "A Year of Precious Blessings"

While elk hunting, Steve ruptured the distal biceps tendon on his left arm. In the doctor's office, we focused on each word as the surgeon described the extent of my husband's injury. He had a 60% tear from his elbow. If the surgeon didn't repair his arm, Steve would have permanent weakness and lose a lot of his lifting power. But any chance for successful surgery meant operating within the next three days.

Steve was neither thrilled with the prospect of surgery nor with the likelihood of being off work for several months. However, he believed his surgeon's counsel was reliable and wise.

After four weeks of intensive physical therapy, Steve was thankful he'd followed his surgeon's instructions. He obediently did the exercises and stretches prescribed by the therapists, regaining range of motion and strength in his arm.

In today's Scripture, according to God's dependable counsel, He placed conditions on the blessings He promised His people. He wanted them to learn to obey Him in all His commandments. Why? Because He loved them, wanted to save them unnecessary pain, and hoped they'd come back "full strength" in His service.

Father, I see the importance of obedience to Your Word. So remind me today that when my will aligns with Yours, I receive the greatest blessings. Through Christ, amen.

~ Gold Fever! ~

You know that you were ransomed from the futile ways inherited from your fathers, not with perishable things such as silver or gold (1 Peter 1:18, *Revised Standard Version*).

Scripture: 1 Peter 1:13-21
Song: "God Owns the Cattle on a Thousand Hills"

Our family decided to look for gold, but we didn't propose to mine or pan for it. We wanted some of the gold that prospectors had previously squirreled away in hideouts but had never retrieved. Over a century ago, skilled gold miners had chiseled such hideaways in Black Canyon.

Our strategy was simple. Equipped with water and snacks, we hiked our way around slide rock and crevices—avoiding prickly cacti—until we arrived at the lowermost part of the canyon. Afterwards, we relaxed and picnicked, then zigzagged back up the canyon, investigating every pocket we encountered.

Presently, Steve whistled, and we scrambled toward his "strike." We carefully removed stacked rocks in order to access a partially hidden stockpile. We discovered frying pans, shovels, picks, canteens—and the mother lode: a lidded, rusty lard pail!

Steve carefully pried the lid from the pail. He removed a small white sack drawn together at the top, comparable to bags that miners filled with gold dust. We held our breath while he poured the grainy contents into his hand. Then we laughed. *Salt!*

Lord, Your servant Peter reminds me today of the futility of materialism. Through Jesus Christ, we have obtained an inheritance that surpasses earthly treasures; after all, He is more precious than silver or gold. When my heart becomes distracted with the world's trinkets, redirect my focus and help me be content. In Christ, amen.

Connected Through the Word

Having purified your souls by your obedience to the truth for a sincere love of the brethren, love one another earnestly from the heart (1 Peter 1:22, *Revised Standard Version*).

Scripture: 1 Peter 1:22–2:3
Song: "Beloved"

When I was little, my parents bought a set of encyclopedias, and we kids thrilled at the articles and amazing pictures. Two years later, a salesman tried to peddle another set of encyclopedias to us. Dad beamed as he told the fellow we already had a set, but the persistent man said we needed to upgrade. Dad insisted, "Information couldn't have changed that much!"

The Internet now allows us to access vast amounts of information and resources, updated within nanoseconds. We demand and expect faster communication speeds.

In the computing environment, networking is vital. We can easily connect to most of the world through protocol. *Protocol* is a set of actions that paired entities follow when communicating. In computing terms, the TCP/IP model (Transmission Control Protocol/Internet Protocol) describes this framework.

Peter tells us that to have sincere love for each other as brothers and sisters, we must share a "born-again protocol." That is, true believers in Jesus Christ have the same connecting link, the living Word of God, by which they have come to new life. This networking, this bond of unity, allows us to sincerely love one another.

Lord, thanks for the means to love not only believers who are easy to love, but those who are somewhat unlovable. Remind me of our unity! In Jesus' name, amen.

The Flying Frying Pan

You also, like living stones, are being built into a spiritual house to be a holy priesthood, offering spiritual sacrifices acceptable to God through Jesus Christ (1 Peter 2:5).

Scripture: 1 Peter 2:4-10
Song: "Make Me a Servant"

On the campus of the University of Florida, one Christian organization, the Navigators, challenges its students to sacrifice their spring break in order to serve others. In 2010, they caravanned to Nashville to do cleanup where recent tornadoes and flooding had caused much devastation.

When my husband and I learned of their plans, questions flooded our minds. Why would college students exchange a week of sun and surf for sweat and grime? Where would they lodge? What would they eat?

We e-mailed the team leader. He answered, "We expect to sleep on the floor of a local church and devour an enormous amount of pizza." Steve and I felt a simultaneous divine nudge. "Why don't we fly to Nashville and cook for those students?"

For a week, the students painted, installed windows and doors, and shoveled mud, never complaining. The following year, they—and we—traveled to New Orleans. After seven years, Katrina-damaged neighborhoods still needed a helping hand, so the students split into sub-teams and worked at one large church, two schools, and two homes. They became living stones, helping rebuild in the name of our Cornerstone.

Lord, teach me to perceive the world's needs and decide to serve, no matter what the personal cost might be. Cause others to see Christ in me. In His name, amen.

Blessed Cleansing

Since we have these promises . . . let us purify ourselves from everything that contaminates body and spirit, perfecting holiness out of reverence for God (2 Corinthians 7:1).

Scripture: 2 Corinthians 6:14–7:1
Song: "Soul of Jesus, Make Me Whole"

Many people have come to the natural mineral hot springs in Ouray, Colorado, for relaxing soaks and healthy dips. In the 1800s, Ouray, chief of the Ute tribe, spent much of his time in the area. Many of the Utes referred to the springs as the "sacred mineral waters," and Chief Ouray claimed the springs provided him with relief from painful arthritis. He also thought the waters cleansed him of inner impurities as he soaked in them.

In 1992, experts analyzed the water in the natural hot springs. The results showed concentrations of at least 24 minerals. Within these two dozen, I was surprised to see these contents: arsenic is an old-time treatment for arthritis; magnesium helps with muscle relaxation; potassium aids circulation. Additionally, there are three varieties of salts, which help cleanse the body of impurities. These natural minerals, combined with the hot temperatures, offer the sensation of healing and purifying.

Jesus Christ, the living water, is the only one who can purify us spiritually. His sacrificial death perfects and cleanses all who trust in Him. His sanitizing blood brings spotlessness to our contaminated lives. The peace He offers is the best relaxant.

Most Holy God, I come to You in reverent awe, for You are perfectly holy. Yet because of Jesus Christ's pure, atoning blood, I am able to petition You and seek Your mercy. Thank You for humbling yourself to come into my life. In Jesus' name, amen.

Blight Ain't Right

I smote you and all the products of your toil with blight and mildew and hail; yet you did not return to me, says the LORD (Haggai 2:17, *Revised Standard Version*).

Scripture: Haggai 2:10-19
Song: "Holy, Holy, Holy!"

"Did you water the tomatoes last week?" My husband asked as he uncoiled the garden hose.

"Yes, I did. I let the water run extra long, since I forgot to water the week before. Is anything wrong?" I felt guilty, even though I knew I was innocent this time.

"Something isn't right; the leaves are turning brown, and the stems are withering."

After searching the Internet for the probable cause of our tomatoes' sickness, it didn't take us long to discover the culprit: late blight. We learned that late blight is an airborne disease caused by the fungus *Phytophthora infestans* and that it can infect tomatoes and potatoes worldwide. Occasionally, peppers, eggplants, weeds, and a few ornamentals may be mildly contaminated. The spores from diseased plants can travel on the wind for miles before landing on a host plant. In the 1840s late blight caused the devastating potato famine in Ireland.

Haggai knew that sin is highly infectious. Therefore the Lord uses many means to turn people back to himself. Sadly, many choose to remain in the devastating plague of unrighteousness.

Heavenly Father, You are merciful enough to give us boundaries and loving enough to discipline us. Help me to see Your hand at work in the circumstances of life that cause me to correct my course. Through Christ I pray. Amen.

"Why Me?"

Does God listen to their cry when distress comes upon them? (Job 27:9).

Scripture: Job 27:8-12
Song: "We'll Understand It Better By and By"

Injustice. It's far too easy for most of us to recall instances of unjust treatment. Some wrongs are unintentionally inflicted; others were meant to be. No matter the cause, such treatment often raises the question, "Why me?"

"Bad behavior = unpleasant consequences" is an equation most of us learned at a young age. So too is the idea that negative repercussions can be *avoided* by doing what's right. Yet real life invariably proves otherwise. Consider Job. Here was a man who "was blameless and upright; he feared God and shunned evil" (Job 1:1). His reward? He lost everything he had and everyone he loved. And if anyone deserved an explanation it was Job. He never got one. Remarkably, however, Job's hope in God endured (and was eventually rewarded).

Suffering for no apparent reason isn't easy. Yet we need look no further than Job for inspiration. While usually remembered for his patience, Job had something even more admirable—unshakable faith in God's righteousness. His reward wasn't the answer he craved. It was instead a far greater gift: the wisdom to think far less of himself and far more of God.

O God, You bear with me as I foolishly seek answers I will never have until joining You in paradise. In the meantime, Lord, grant me Your wisdom. In Jesus' name, amen.

June 16–22. **Robert Stephens,** a retiree from the metals industry, devotes his time to family, free-lance writing, and speaking. He and his wife, Linda, live in Glen Allen, Virginia.

Look Within

Why, my soul, are you downcast? Why so disturbed within me? Put your hope in God (Psalm 43:5).

Scripture: Psalm 43
Song: "It Is Well with My Soul"

Terrible things happen—often. The story of yet another mugging or shooting constantly appears in the news. Desensitized by the frequency of such things, we quickly move on to the next item. How, though, do we react when personally victimized?

The psalmist is clearly in such pain, though we don't know its source. But his pain is severe, it's recurring, and it evokes a sense of rejection shrouded in spiritual darkness. Surely his suffering results from some catastrophic event, the kind experienced by only an unfortunate few!

Really? Consider the person who first loses job and then home. The marriage disintegrates under ensuing pressures. Newsworthy? Not in today's world. Exaggeration? Sadly, no. Countless people for countless reasons experience such pain in our day.

As the psalmist ultimately realized, however, renewed hope can spring forth amidst painful, troubling times. Though anguished, he wisely chose to look inward, to the soul—and there found comfort.

The solace he experienced remains available to each of us. Look within. For there resides the eternal flame, the hope that prevails in any circumstance: our ever-present, indwelling God.

Precious Holy Spirit, You dwell within me and never depart, no matter how difficult my days. Whenever downcast, may I too place my hope not in temporal remedies but in Your eternal promises. Through the precious name of Jesus. Amen.

How Much Longer?

We wait in hope for the LORD . . . in him our hearts rejoice (Psalm 33:20, 21).

Scripture: Psalm 33:13-22
Song: "Come, Thou Long-Expected Jesus"

I stood so close my breath fogged the glass separating me from the tarmac. It was the 1950s, and those greeting arriving flights were allowed into the gate area. It had been too many months since this exquisite drama last played. I could barely stand another minute's delay. "How much longer, Mom?" I asked.

Vacation time for Dad, an oil-tanker engineer, had begun. Each such homecoming was a blessed event, the return of my hero—master of the oceans, visitor to strange lands. The airport wait, while torturous, enhanced my excitement. And then—

A plane, his plane, propellers slowing, inched into position and finally stopped, followed by an endless stream of nameless faces. "I see him! It's him!" Minutes later I was swept up in his arms, and euphoria reigned. I experienced the very moment the psalmist was hoping for—the arrival of the Father.

Have you known the sweet agony of awaiting a long-anticipated arrival—and the joy it ultimately brings? For we who anticipate the Lord's return, the wait continues. Yet it's a kind of "pregnant pause," filled with hope, for rejoicing and thanksgiving reside just beyond the horizon.

Excited? Me too!

Father, like the psalmist, I trust in You. Guide and direct my waiting. Use me to reflect the light of Christ upon others until all Your children anxiously look forward to Your promised return and the eternal joy to follow. Through Christ I pray. Amen.

Worth the Wait

If we hope for what we do not yet have, we wait for it patiently (Romans 8:25).

Scripture: Romans 8:18-25
Song: "This Is a Day of New Beginnings"

I don't remember counting them, but I did consider each tiny finger and toe among the many wonders of new life. "She's a miracle!" Though years later, the feeling was equally acute when a second daughter arrived. Twice blessed, it was just beginning.

Throughout the years my children have repeatedly enriched my life. I count their transformations into amazing women among my great joys. Yes, reflecting on the past only adds to my anticipation of the future. Yet I know, my dreams aside, the world offers few guarantees. So I place my hope elsewhere.

Paul knew he was saved through his belief in Christ. He knew, infused with the Spirit, he was being continually transformed. He also knew the best was yet to come — that the miracle would only be complete with his "adoption to sonship" (8:23). Placing his hope in God's promise, he was confidently prepared to wait.

Every parent wants their child's future to be filled with happiness, while knowing that some tough times are inevitable. We're comforted by the knowledge that the future our heavenly Father promises exceeds even our wildest hopes. And that's not even the best part. It's guaranteed, and it's worth waiting for.

Thank You, **Lord**, for sending Your Son, Jesus, so that through Him I could be saved. Thank you for the daily guidance of the Holy Spirit. Most of all, Father, thank You for counting me among Your children in the new creation to come. Until then, like Paul, I wait. In Jesus' name, amen.

Divine Contradiction

Even if you should suffer for what is right, you are blessed. "Do not fear their threats; do not be frightened" (1 Peter 3:14).

Scripture: 1 Peter 3:13-17
Song: "O Jesus, My Hope"

According to Webster they are "pointedly foolish." Some, however, are used so often that the inherent contradiction goes unnoticed. I'm speaking of the *oxymoron*—a combination of contradictory words: "It was an open secret that the clearly confused had descended into controlled chaos." *Huh?*

It's hard to imagine the apparent contradictions in Peter's letter slipping past his readers, past or present. He did, after all, write of blessed suffering. To suffer for a righteous cause—or to suffer as the result of doing good—is to be blessed. He went on to suggest that those giving themselves to Christ find not anguish but hope in the midst of suffering. *Wow!*

Imagine the disciples' response upon hearing such things from Jesus. Surely some found it pointedly foolish and contradictory. Christ's teachings, however, clearly produced the intended results. For Peter and others went on to proclaim those same gospel truths. And the cycle endures. For every day the light of Christ shines from those who, though no fault of their own, are suffering. Every day rays of hope, founded in Christian belief, penetrate the bleakest circumstances.

Lord, I struggle to understand much of what You would have me do and be. Yet in Your gentle responses—a Scripture passage revealed, a person placed in my path—I find hope. In the name of Jesus, amen.

Promises, Promises

Let us hold unswervingly to the hope we profess, for he who promised is faithful (Hebrews 10:23).
Scripture: Hebrews 10:19-24
Song: "Go to the Deeps of God's Promise"

"No, really. I *promise.*" We've all heard that one—too many times! It can start early. Your brother promises to keep a secret and then tattles anyway. A dear friend proves not-so-trustworthy after all. Many such breaches have little lasting effect; others can be psychologically damaging, rendering the victim suspicious of all future promises.

Consider those to whom Hebrews was written. These Christians wanted to believe that through Jesus, all had access to God; and that in spite of persistent hardship, their faith would some day be rewarded with an eternity in God's presence. These were lofty promises indeed. No less so today, they continue to come to each of us.

Who knows how the letter's original readers responded? Some probably chose to place their hopes not in Christ but in some other proclaimed savior. Others undoubtedly opted not only to continue in faith but also to "spur one another on toward love and good deeds" (v. 24). The Old Testament, after all, offered numerous examples of those who, having maintained a belief in God's promises, were richly blessed.

One thing is certain. Each of us faces the same choice. God has promised. Dare we believe?

Lord, times have changed greatly since the Scriptures were written. And yet, in Your faithfulness, all of Your promises remain. All praise to You, in Jesus' name! Amen.

Go Ahead, Ask!

What are these two olive branches beside the two gold pipes that pour out golden oil? (Zechariah 4:12).

Scripture: Haggai 2:23; Zechariah 4:1-3, 6-14
Song: "Spirit of Faith, Come Down"

A selection's been made. *It's you!* Feels good being chosen, doesn't it? Gives a lift to the old self-esteem. Then you find out what it is you've been chosen to do. That, unfortunately, could also be when your morale begins to "lose altitude."

Consider Zerubbabel. From among the masses, Zerubbabel got the nod—from none other than the Lord Almighty. Talk about an ego boost! Learning that his task was to oversee the rebuilding of God's temple, angst may have begun to intrude on his excitement. This was no small undertaking. Revelations about "olive branches" and "golden oil," undoubtedly intended to help, led instead to more questions.

Can you relate? Another's explanation of a desired outcome can leave you feeling dropped into a mental labyrinth from which escape seems impossible. And it's a fact: Worldly assignments can end badly.

We needn't worry, however, when doing the Lord's work. Zerubbabel's questions were asked in faith. God responded not in frustration or anger but with an infusion of the Holy Spirit, an inexhaustible supply of "light" to shine on the path until each next step was revealed. A new temple was built. God's purpose was accomplished.

Lord, in spite of my imperfection, I know You're calling me. Yet I'm often uncertain how to respond. Grant me the faith of Zerubbabel today! Through Christ, amen.

Standing Firm

Stand firm in the LORD (Philippians 4:1).

Scripture: Philippians 4:1-7
Song: "Jesus, Stand Among Us"

Making movies was a childhood dream for Kyle Prohaska, a boy from Buffalo growing up in the 1990s. Nothing else captured his imagination like the movies. His first heroes weren't sports stars; they were Steven Spielberg, George Lucas, and other film-making greats.

As a teenager, Kyle and a friend founded Praise Pictures, a Christian production company. By the time he was 21, Kyle was running the company by himself and wrapping up "Standing Firm," his first feature film, for release in August 2010. Within 18 months, the movie was being distributed on the Internet's biggest Christian film sites, available in more than a dozen countries. And Kyle had accumulated 290,000+ Facebook fans.

Kyle and his movie offer two stellar examples of someone standing firm. Kyle himself is one example: he's determined and faithful in pursuing his goal to make Christian films. The second example comes in one of the film's characters, a young man whose steady, committed Christian faith enables him to minister to his own father after a family tragedy.

All of which causes me to wonder: What can you and I do to renew our own commitment to stand firm in our faith?

Lord, please help me resolve to stand firm in my faith this day. And may I have the courage and strength to be faithful every day to come. Through Christ, amen.

June 23–29. **Randall Murphree** is a freelance writer and editor of American Family Association Journal in Tupelo, Mississippi. Missions, reading, and music consume his spare time.

Serving Others

There are different kinds of service, but the same Lord (1 Corinthians 12:5).

Scripture: 1 Corinthians 12:4-11
Song: "The Longer I Serve Him"

Word came to our church office that a local family's mobile home had burned just a few weeks before Christmas. The family had no connection to our church, but that made no difference to Courtney Dean—and no one was surprised when she went into action. Courtney is a stay-at-home mom, so she has plenty of time to do things like that, right?

Well, not exactly. In fact, at the time, she and her husband Neel had three little girls, ages 5, 4 and 2—and Courtney was eight months pregnant. Nonetheless, she secured information about the family and printed up flyers with their specific needs. Then she, Emmy, Macy and Nora, walked through their neighborhood, knocked on doors, and left flyers inviting neighbors to help others in need.

Over the coming days, friends, church members, and neighbors delivered countless boxes and bags to the Deans' garage. Courtney and Neel invited me to join them, and we packed their van and my car full of Christmas for a family who were soon overwhelmed at the gifts from God's people. The Deans' ministry was not only a picture of Christian faith at work, but also a beautiful way for three little girls to learn about serving others.

Lord, help me see the opportunities to serve and minister to others in Your name and in Your strength. Help me remember that each person in the church is drawn to different kinds of serving. May I honor each one. In the name of Jesus I pray. Amen.

Coats of Many Colors

As a prisoner for the Lord, then, I urge you to live a life worthy of the calling you have received (Ephesians 4:1).

Scripture: Ephesians 4:1-6
Song: "My Spirit Longs for Thee"

Any time there's a faltering economy, jobs grow scarce, home repossessions escalate, and more people need financial assistance. Then life becomes a major challenge. But what a great time for the body of Christ to minister! Now the church can feed the hungry, clothe the poor, and visit the prisoner. It's also an important time for believers to listen carefully for God's call.

Robert Wages is one who listens carefully, wholeheartedly investing his gifts in ways that honor the Lord. He has been on his church missions board, traveled on many mission trips himself, sung in the church choir, and served in men's ministries.

But in November 2010, he sensed God's call to do something different, something a little out of his comfort zone. Still, he never considered *not* following.

God called Wages to collect good used or new coats to offer to those who needed one in his hometown of Tupelo, Mississippi. With each coat given away, Wages and a few friends share the gospel message of new life in Christ. Now he's been to six other cities, including Nashville, Tennessee, and Joplin, Missouri. He and his friends have given away 1,700 coats so far—and led some 80 people to the waters of baptism.

Almighty and everlasting God, help me always to be sensitive to Your voice as You call me to new avenues of ministry, even if they're outside my comfort zone. In the name of the Father and of the Son and of the Holy Spirit, I pray. Amen.

Teamwork Gets the Best Results

Just as a body, though one, has many parts, but all its many parts form one body, so it is with Christ (1 Corinthians 12:12).

Scripture: 1 Corinthians 12:12-20
Song: "We Are One in the Spirit"

Paul wrote his Corinthian letters to immature, self-centered believers who weren't using their spiritual gifts well. Instead of working in unity and oneness of spirit, they competed for power and position. So what better metaphor could he have used? He compared the body of Christ to the human body, with its many parts and organs—all of which must work together if there is to be wholeness and health.

I am blessed to work as an editor in a parachurch organization. But beyond that, I am even more blessed to have a staff who truly works together as a team. Sometimes we even approach the unity I think Paul was urging the Corinthians to cultivate. For example, if I'm concerned about the big picture of our work, Rusty's my go-to man. If it's something I don't understand about politics, culture, or the church, I go to Ed. For insights on today's teens and young adults, TJ's the one. And for women's issues—of course, that's Debbie's strong suit.

While we each have our own strengths, they don't divide us. Rather, they make us appreciate that we are a team, one body, with each part functioning in its God-given strengths.

O Lord, help me to be an instrument through which You can bring more unity into all of my circles of influence. And help me to use my gifts to fulfill my role in each group. I pray this prayer in the name of my Savior, Jesus. Amen.

Rejoicing and Weeping

If one part suffers, every part suffers with it; if one part is honored, every part rejoices with it (1 Corinthians 12:26).

Scripture: 1 Corinthians 12:21-26
Song: "He Ain't Heavy, He's My Brother"

The human body is used numerous times in Scripture to illustrate how people who follow Christ should relate to one another —each doing his or her part, but each sharing sorrows and joys together. J.J. Jasper, Christian comedian and on-air personality with American Family Radio network, is heard each weekday morning on dozens of stations scattered across the U.S. After working with J.J. for more than 20 years, I can safely say this: I've never known another Christian who better illustrates the principle of rejoicing (or suffering) with fellow believers.

If a friend wins a contest or gets a raise, J.J. is as happy as if he himself won the prize or received the raise. On the other hand, if someone he knows is grieving, has lost a job, or faces some other challenge in life, J.J. is that person's greatest encourager. He walks with his friends—applauding their victories and encouraging them in their defeats.

Good as J.J. is, no one has ever demonstrated this principle as perfectly as Jesus did. In Hebrews, we're told that, even though He's our high priest, He still sympathizes with our weaknesses and understands our temptations. How can you improve the way you relate to others in your circle of acquaintances?

Lord, help me refocus so I can sincerely rejoice with my friends when they rejoice and sense their deepest hurts when they are suffering. In Jesus' name, amen.

Gifts? Or a More Excellent Way?

Now eagerly desire the greater gifts. And yet I will show you the most excellent way (1 Corinthians 12:31).

Scripture: 1 Corinthians 12:27-31
Song: "I Will Serve Thee Because I Love Thee"

Kirt Kisling and Larry Lapeere began creating humorous but insightful radio spots 30 years ago. They established LifeLine Productions in 1988 with the goal of presenting biblical truth in entertaining ways that not only challenge believers but also plant seeds in the hearts of those who don't yet know Christ.

One LifeLine script features a man approaching a church leader to say, "Hi. I'm looking to serve God."

"Wonderful," the leader replies. "We could use some help in the nursery."

"Naaa—I'm not into diapers."

It goes on like that with other opportunities—greeter, Sunday school teacher, serving soup at the rescue mission, etc. But something's wrong with every option.

The man's final plea is: "Don't you have *something* that would impress my fellow Christians—but wouldn't let my friends know I go to church? And it would be nice if I could do it in front of the TV. Got anything like that?"

Paul says it's OK to desire the greater gifts. But the challenge is to still let God show us "the most excellent way." In other words, we may need to use our gifts and abilities in ways that humble us—even in the nursery or a soup kitchen.

Lord, let me be willing to serve You in any way You lead me to do it. I want to be sensitive to the Holy Spirit as He guides me this day. Through Christ, amen.

Who Are We Following?

I planted the seed, Apollos watered it, but God has been making it grow. So neither the one who plants nor the one who waters is anything, but only God who makes things grow (1 Corinthians 3:6, 7).

Scripture: 1 Corinthians 1:10-17; 3:4-9
Song: "Where He Leads Me"

I was once part of a church that suffered heartbreaking division when a staff member was asked to resign from his position. Many dissenters followed him as he departed, and the bitter poison of division hurt believers on both sides of the issue. That experience helped me grasp this fact: I must always measure my devotion—is it to Christ or is it to human leaders?

Paul must have been disappointed to discover that believers in Corinth were dividing into cliques based on which leader they followed. And it wasn't a matter of doctrine, because these leaders were in agreement on such things. It was simply a matter of personality. Which man did they know best? Whose preaching had led them to faith?

So Paul warns them—and he warns us—of the dangers of following human leaders too closely. God measures our faith not by what Christian leader we follow on earth, but by our hearts' devotion to Christ. Do we humbly mirror the example of Jesus Christ in our lives?

Almighty and Merciful God, please help me to see through the finite appeal of human leaders. May I appreciate them for their gifts, but always recognize that those gifts come from You—and they are to be used to bring You alone the glory. In the precious name of Jesus I pray. Amen.

Don't Grow Old, Grow Up

Speaking the truth in love, we are to grow up in all aspects into Him, who is the head, even Christ (Ephesians 4:15, *New American Standard Bible*).

Scripture: Ephesians 4:7-16
Song: "I Would Be True"

When we were kids at home, we used to sit out on the front porch and watch the cars go by. There weren't many, but we played the game of, "Next car is mine." If it was an expensive car, the "new owner" would cheer and say how rich he was. If it was an old jalopy, we would jeer the one who had claimed it and deride him for being such a ne'er-do-well. So we would judge character by the chance selection of a car! And we loved mocking the other person based on that selection.

Our Scripture points out that I am not to be an immature child, influenced by the trickery and deceitful scheming of the world we live in. Growing up into spiritual maturity is hard, and I may never find my way there. Yet my maturity is to be measured in all aspects by the character of Christ.

He must first be my Head personally, not just theoretically. Thankfully, I can study His character in the Word, asking God in His great grace to make the changes in me that will result in my becoming Christlike. Growing up into Him will cause less of me to be seen and more of Him to be visible, blessing others.

Lord Jesus, my Savior and Head, remold my personality in all its aspects into that which honors You and blesses others. I ask it in Your name, Amen.

June 30–July 6. **Brian Doud** is a retired minister working full-time as the resident violin maker at a well-known violin shop in Cleveland, Ohio. He has also hosted a radio program for about 3 years.

My Prayer Notes

_____
_____
_____
_____
_____
_____
_____
_____
_____
_____
_____
_____
_____
_____
_____
_____
_____
_____
_____
_____
_____
_____
_____

DEVOTIONS®

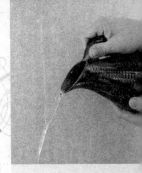

July

"To each one of us grace has been given."

—*Ephesians 4:7*

Gary Wilde, Editor | **Margaret Williams,** Project Editor Photo iStockphoto | Thinkstock®

DEVOTIONS® is published quarterly by Standard Publishing, Cincinnati, Ohio, www.standardpub.com. © 2013 by Standard Publishing. All rights reserved. Topics based on the Home Daily Bible Readings, International Sunday School Lessons. © 2010 by the Committee on the Uniform Series. Printed in the U.S.A. All Scripture quotations, unless otherwise indicated, are taken from the *HOLY BIBLE, NEW INTERNATIONAL VERSION®. NIV®.* Copyright © 1973, 1978, 1984, 2011 by Biblica. Used by permission of Zondervan. All rights reserved. *New American Standard Bible* (*NASB*), © The Lockman Foundation, 1960, 1962, 1963.

How's the Lifestyle?

I am afraid that when I come again my God may humiliate me before you, and I may mourn over many of those who have sinned in the past and not repented of the impurity, immorality and sensuality which they have practiced (2 Corinthians 12:21, *New American Standard Bible*).

Scripture: 2 Corinthians 12:14-21
Song: "Before Thy Throne, O God, We Kneel"

Many of us have family members who have caused us some consternation and grief by their poor choices and careless mistakes. We're sick at heart over the messes they've created, and we feel somewhat responsible because they're our loved ones.

The apostle Paul had ministered in Corinth and led many of the citizens to Christ. Now he'd heard tales of their sinful lifestyles, was planning on visiting them, and was anxious over what he might find to be true of them.

Similarly, our Lord Jesus Christ, having died for us, has gone back to Heaven. He is soon to return — and what would He find if He walked into my church this next Sunday morning? Am I mourning the same things He would mourn?

The sins of the flesh, found in Galatians 5:19-21, are all too evident today in the church. I am not to judge others, but where is my humiliation and mourning? Is my life as pure and holy as it ought to be?

Lord, sinless, pure, and holy, purify all that I am so that I do not cause You grief or cause my brothers and sisters in Christ to be humiliated. In Jesus' name, amen.

July 1–6. **Brian Doud** is a retired minister working full-time as the resident violin maker at a well-known violin shop in Cleveland, Ohio. He has also hosted a radio program for about 3 years.

Christ, for the Other Guy Too

Let us therefore celebrate the feast, not with old leaven, nor with the leaven of malice and wickedness, but with the unleavened bread of sincerity and truth (1 Corinthians 5:8, *New American Standard Bible*).

Scripture: 1 Corinthians 5:1-8
Song: "Wonderful Grace of Jesus"

Sadly, it sometimes happens that in a congregation someone falls into very public sin. Paul is here giving directions for handling the situation with the right attitude. All "church discipline" is to be carried out in a spirit of love, hoping that the one who has fallen will repent and be restored to full fellowship. Yet if the unrepentant offender continues in the group, it may bring about more sin—at least in a judgmental or critical attitude.

In the midst of this difficult subject, God gives Paul clear insight. We are each cleansed from sin by the sacrifice of Christ, our Passover. In any thought or action about a sinning brother/sister, I am not to use the thinking of the unregenerate mind: "malice and wickedness." I am instead to celebrate the sacrifice of Christ by thinking and acting in sincerity and truth.

Wouldn't it help to celebrate, every day, the marvelous truth that Christ died for me—*and for the other person as well?* Then if some difficult situation would arise, I would be in the habit of thinking redemptively, not judgmentally.

Dear Heavenly Father, thank You for providing my Passover sacrifice in your Son. I rejoice today in that wonderful fact. Bless all my brothers and sisters in Christ, and keep them from sin, as You help me walk the narrow road of discipleship. I ask all this in the precious name of Jesus. Amen.

Avoiding Negative Friendships

I am writing to you that you must not associate with anyone who claims to be a brother or sister but is sexually immoral or greedy, an idolater or slanderer, a drunkard or swindler. Do not even eat with such people (1 Corinthians 5:11).

Scripture: 1 Corinthians 5:9-13
Song: "Grace Greater than Our Sin"

My mother stopped talking to me, or even listening to me. I had said something "smart-mouthed," and she was offended. Old enough to have known better, I had definitely crossed the line of bad attitude and unsocial language. Once I recognized what was happening, I hastened to apologize. I had learned what it meant to have fellowship withdrawn, to be put "outside" because of my wrong actions.

The verse for today instructs me to stop having close fellowship with a person who is supposed to be a Christian, but who continues in obvious sin. While all judgment is with the Lord, I can be discerning enough in my friendships to avoid the clearly negative influence.

There is a famous saying, "We bear no neutral influence" — and others bear no neutral influence on me! So, will I have to stop talking to someone I like and love? I'll certainly need to depend on wise discernment here. May God lead me in such situations to be fully aware of my own sin first. Then, with fear and trepidation, may I be ready, in love, to help someone else back onto the path of authentic discipleship.

Lord, grant me the grace and strength to understand this principle and to apply it when necessary. But keep me close to You as I do. In Jesus' name, amen.

You Were, But Are Not Now

Such were some of you; but you were washed, but you were sanctified, but you were justified in the name of the Lord Jesus Christ, and in the Spirit of our God (1 Corinthians 6:11, *New American Standard Bible*).

Scripture: I Corinthians 6:1-11
Song: "Whiter Than Snow"

Most every little boy has "been there": I came in from playing with the other neighborhood boys, and my mother took one look and said, "How in the world did you get so dirty? Company is coming for dinner in 30 minutes, and you are a fright! Run upstairs and clean up!"

And I replied, "I was just doing what the other guys were doing." Then I rapidly went to clean myself up.

Isn't that the point of our verse above? I am no better than any of "the other guys," by myself. I may not now be committing some of the awful acts mentioned in verses 9 and 10, but I may have in the past. I may have thought of doing those things—and might have, could I have been assured of complete anonymity.

So I can't look down on the others, because I too need to be justified (declared not guilty in God's sight) and sanctified (washed, set apart for Him). I can't do that myself. But I can look back to the cross. I can remember that when I trusted Him, He did all these things, and more, for me.

Blessed Lord, I know that cleaning up my act on my own would never be even a start. Thank You for cleansing me from sin. Keep me walking a clean walk for Your sake, because of Your sacrifice, and for the encouragement of others. I pray this prayer in the name of Jesus, my merciful Savior and Lord. Amen.

There for Each Other

The wife does not have authority over her own body, but the husband does; and likewise also the husband does not have authority over his own body, but the wife does (1 Corinthians 7:4, *New American Standard Bible*).

Scripture: 1 Corinthians 7:1-9
Song: "Lord, Who at Cana's Wedding Feast"

My wife and I, married for 52 years, were out for dinner. I had just pushed her wheelchair up to the table, and I bent down to kiss her on the top of her head. I had done that many times before, but this time I overheard a young waitress say to her teammate, "Isn't that sweet?" It felt natural enough to me.

Our verse tells us that a married couple will each honor the other and put him or her first. Primarily, in context, it is about the sexual relationship in marriage, but this principle covers every aspect of life. Husbands, we are to love our wives, just as Christ loved the church and gave himself up for her (see Ephesians 5:25) This isn't merely optional, it is a bedrock principle. It starts before you are married and continues until you both die. So she gets the best chair, the best piece of pie (if she wants one), and the most beautiful "I love you" card in the store. You will be the first to be blessed by her joy.

And wives, you are to honor your husband as your head and leader. Maybe he will "step up" if his leadership is expected and respected when offered.

Lord God, You are the head of my marriage as much as You are the head of the church. Please bring my thoughts and actions into joyful obedience to this verse and to every other command from Your Word. I ask it in Jesus' name. Amen.

I Am Not My Own

Or do you not know that your body is a temple of the Holy Spirit who is in you, whom you have from God, and that you are not your own? (1 Corinthians 6:19, *New American Standard Bible*).

Scripture: I Corinthians 6:12-20
Song: "Oh, Enter, Lord, Thy Temple"

I was one of five boys in our family attending a rural church in Pennsylvania. We were taught early and continually that you wore your best clothes, and were on your best behavior, in church. It was God's house. One very small boy (not in our family) once asked the minister, "Are you God?" It seemed the minister was always there when we got there, seemed to live there. So, logically, if it was his house, wasn't he God?

Actually, since every born-again believer is part of the church, I can't, strictly speaking, "go to church." I *am* the church, at least part of it. My behavior needs to be controlled by the fact that the Holy Spirit is within me everywhere I go. What I think, say, and do should reflect His presence and ownership of my whole life: my ambitions, desires, and plans for the future.

The point is, rebelling against God, or sinning in any other way, would be a sin against the one who indwells me and owns me. Yet, what a contrast to the culture we live in! ("I Did It My Way" is the theme song of the day.)

Blessed Holy Spirit, I once again acknowledge and submit to Your ownership of all that I am. May the desires of my heart please You and spur me to kingdom service today. Fill me with yourself, lead me into and out of everything as it pleases You. I ask it in Jesus' name, amen.

Never Enough

This is an illustration for the present time, indicating that the gifts and sacrifices being offered were not able to clear the conscience of the worshiper (Hebrews 9:9).

Scripture: Hebrews 9:1-10
Song: "Calvary Covers It All"

I was visiting with a lady in Moscow. Through an interpreter she told me, "I always knew that the priest could talk to God in the cathedral. But now that I know Jesus, I have a cathedral in my heart."

She told me that she had been a faithful worshipper, attending services, lighting candles, but did not know the Savior personally. Gifts, sacrifices, religious works can't do what only Jesus can do—and that's what this Russian woman had discovered.

The priests in ancient Jerusalem faithfully brought their sacrifices to atone for their own sins and the sins of the people. They regularly entered the Most Holy Place in the tabernacle. But the one who was sent from the Father paid the final, complete, and total sacrifice for our sins. Now, year after year, we don't need to wonder if any sacrifice that we bring, any religious duty we perform, is adequate to gain God's favor. Thankfully, we don't have to keep wondering if our sins are truly forgiven. A certainty, a clear conscience, is now ours.

I know that I cannot do enough, **O Lord,** to atone for my own sin. I thank You that You provided redemption and forgiveness for me through Christ's sacrificial gift for me. He is the *Agnus Dei,* the perfect lamb of God. In His name I pray. Amen.

July 7–13. **Roger Palms,** former editor of *Decision* Magazine, is a writer, editor, and teacher. Best of all, he is a husband, father, and grandfather.

Worshipping What Is Real

These are a shadow of the things that were to come; the reality, however, is found in Christ (Colossians 2:17).

Scripture: Colossians 2:16-23
Song: "The Light of the World Is Jesus"

"What's your astrological sign?" she asked me. We were at a dinner, and the woman asking me the question is an active member of her church. I told her that I didn't know the answer, which surprised her. So, learning my birth date, she told me my sign.

She has a shadow faith. There is light and there are shadows. Light drives back the shadows. But if the light is dim or doesn't exist, the shadows deepen and become darkness. Scripture tells us that religious activities, even the sacrifices for sins which the priests in Jerusalem conducted for the people, were but shadows. A shadow gives a hint of something; in the shadows we sort of see yet don't really see.

Reality is found in Christ. Whereas others may be content with religious shadows, our job is to live by and point to the light of the world. The light of God, the redeeming Jesus, can push back darkness and cause people to see. We can't argue people into seeing, but we can bring light. God's light is reality.

There is light and there are shadows. Many people have a little bit of both. When we bring people more light, we bring them reality.

I know the shadows, **Father.** I once lived in them. Thank You for sending the light of the world who brought me out of darkness. Help me never to hide that light from others who are still in the shadows. In the name of Jesus, amen.

Just Add

If you possess these qualities in increasing measure, they will keep you from being ineffective and unproductive in your knowledge of our Lord Jesus Christ (2 Peter 1:8).

Scripture: 2 Peter 1:2-11
Song: "Seek Ye First"

We hear it often: "I'm a Christian, but I'm not a very good one." And there is the temptation to reply, "Why not?"

If grace and peace are mine in abundance, and Scripture tells me that they are, and if God's divine power has given me everything I need for a godly life, then why am I not a "good one"?

There's an easy tendency to compare nothing against everything and feel inadequate. But the qualities God is looking for in believers are not complete. They are blossoming, they are building in us "in increasing measure."

Can I add to my faith? Can I add to my goodness and my knowledge and my self-control and my perseverance and my godliness and my mutual affection and my love? The question is not, "Do I have all of these things completely?" The question is, "Can I *add?*"

A 3-year-old child isn't 4 years old. But he is more than 3. A growing Christian may not be as mature today as she will be tomorrow, but she is growing toward that maturity. And here's the thing: No healthy, growing Christian is content to be today where he was yesterday.

Dear Father in Heaven, I don't want to remain a spiritual child. Neither do I want to use my less-than-fully-mature condition as an excuse to stop growing. Help me, through Christ, I pray. Amen.

Invite a Little Bit of Reading

His letters contain some things that are hard to understand, which ignorant and unstable people distort, as they do the other Scriptures, to their own destruction (2 Peter 3:16).

Scripture: 2 Peter 3:14-18
Song: "My Faith Has Found a Resting Place"

Ken was in his mid-80s when I started visiting him. He told me that the Bible was full of errors and contradictions. I replied, "Oh, am I ever glad to be talking with you. I keep hearing that the Bible is full of contradictions and errors, but I've been reading the Bible for years, and I can't find them." Handing Ken my Bible I asked, "Will you show me some?"

Then Ken began to backpedal. He couldn't show me the contradictions and errors because he had never read the Bible. He was only repeating what he'd heard. Two years later, while I was visiting, he surrendered his heart and life to Christ. He ended his confessing prayer with the words, "I want You to take over the rest of my life."

Three months later Ken was in hospice, dying. A friend was in his room when I went to visit him for what would be the last time. I said to the friend, "Ken is a follower of Jesus now." Ken replied, "Yes, and these have been the happiest three months of my life."

Those who distort or disbelieve the Bible don't need me to challenge them. They simply need my encouragement to examine what they say they don't believe.

Thank You, **Lord,** for Your Word, which is truth. And thank You that I don't have to try to defend it. May I simply love every truth seeker. Through Christ I pray, amen.

God Is Judge; I Am Not

Whoever regards one day as special does so to the Lord. Whoever eats meat does so to the Lord, for they give thanks to God; and whoever abstains does so to the Lord and gives thanks to God (Romans 14:6).

Scripture: Romans 14:1-6
Song: "Choose the Living Way"

She likes a more formal worship, with traditional hymns. So, while the praise band in her church is leading the congregation in worship, she stands in the church narthex until the music ends. Her grandchildren, though, stand mute, even sullen, when one of the great hymns of the church is sung. Thus our likes become fixed. What I like is the right way; what the other person likes is clearly wrong.

Paul asked the church at Rome, "Who are you to judge?" (v. 4). Especially, who are we to judge if "God has accepted them" (v. 3)? It all comes down to the heart. Is a person's heart right toward God? Has she thought through *why* she feels that her way is correct instead of relying only on a personal preference?

A tribal group once used drums in their religion's worship. When many came to faith in Christ, they put away their drums because, for them, drums and the gods went together. Two generations later people realized that the problem wasn't the instruments, which could be used for good or evil. What was important was the hearts of the people making the music.

Dear Lord, even though others may be looking on the outside at what I do, You are looking at my heart. Help me to be faithful in my worship and, by a surrendered life, to accept what is acceptable to You. In Jesus' name, amen.

Here or There, I Still Live

If we live, we live for the Lord; and if we die, we die for the Lord. So, whether we live or die, we belong to the Lord (Romans 14:8).

Scripture: Romans 14:7-12
Song: "Face to Face"

I find that living each day under the guidance of God is exciting. But I also look forward to the even greater adventure of being with Him in eternity. Here I live in a limited way, always growing weaker with each passing year. There, I will move into fullness of life with no limitations at all. So, here or there, either way I win.

The believer, who already has new life in Christ, steps from the land of the dying into the land of the living. It is graduation, a commencement; the tuning of the orchestra changes to the beauty of the symphony. We move from discord to delight.

That is, unless I want to live only for myself. Then all I have is my ability, a feeble attempt at trying to live in a world made by God, but without God who created it. I am trying to function as a created one without the guidance of the Creator.

Today is another good day because it is a "God-given day." I can worship Him, follow Him, trust Him, and honor Him— even if, by all appearances, I seem to be having a less-than-stellar time. And if, before the end of this day, I am moved into the day without end, that will be OK too.

Thank You, **Lord,** for the assurance that in Christ it doesn't matter whether I live or die; I belong to You. Help me to show that certainty to the many people I know who have not taken hold of this great promise. In the name of Christ, amen.

Living in Love vs. Living by Rules

Those who think they know something do not yet know as they ought to know (1 Corinthians 8:2).

Scripture: 1 Corinthians 8
Song: "Praise to the Heavenly Wisdom"

I know how everybody else ought to behave—I think.

I know how everybody ought to vote—in my opinion.

I know what is wrong with the country, society, people in leadership, and the church—just ask me. I'll tell you.

But Scripture warns me that what I think I know I do not know—at least I don't know as I ought to know. We are not to be an inflexible, locked-in people. We are fluid before God, allowing His teaching to shape us, mold us, and even recast us as a potter does with clay.

In the early church there were arguments over food that had been offered to idols and then later sold at market. To eat it or not eat it: that was the trying question. The early Christians struggled with it.

Today we have other issues. Can I go there? Can I participate in that? Can I really be a Christian if I watch that? But following rules is much easier than walking with God.

The bottom line for holy living comes in these wise words, "But whoever loves God is known by God" (8:3). Do I love God with all my heart, soul, mind, and strength, or do I love my rules more?

O gracious God, thank You for giving me Your guidance for life. Help me to live today out of love for You, not just out of fear of disobeying the rules. Fill my life so full of gratitude that I will just naturally do what pleases You! In Jesus' name, amen.

Pressure to Solve Problems

When the people saw that Moses was so long in coming down from the mountain, they gathered around Aaron and said, "Come, make us gods who will go before us" (Exodus 32:1)

Scripture: Exodus 32:1-10
Song: "Be Thou My Vision"

At an international conference of ministry leaders in South America, a presenting church leader confided to fellow speaker Anne Graham Lotz that he wasn't sure Jesus was the answer for Brazil. He felt pressure to solve the country's problems and told Anne his ideas for a thoroughly humanistic approach to reform. Mortified by the minister's suggestions, Anne prayed his talk would confuse everyone. Later, his interpreter became so perplexed during his speech that he was unable to continue.

The tendency to seek purely practical answers to problems — without divine guidance — is not new. Aaron faced immense demands from the Israelites as Moses spent over a month on the mountain with God. Eventually, Aaron gave the people a golden calf to celebrate. Sadly, worshipping the manufactured god was an easy but costly choice for everyone.

At times our own faith may be stretched to the point where we seek solace apart from the Lord. But He remains constantly close — as near as the simple turning of our heart back to Him.

Lord, forgive me for pursuing false hopes. You came to give us abundant life. Help me to know this not just as a fact but as my own experience. In Jesus' name, amen.

July 14–20. **Sara Schaffer** happily resides with her husband and two daughters in Colorado. She loves immersing herself in God's Word through study, writing, and speaking.

Violent Holiness

When the LORD Your God has delivered them over to you and you have defeated them, then you must destroy them totally (Deuteronomy 7:2).

Scripture: Deuteronomy 7:1-6
Song: "Victory in My Soul"

The doctor found a tumor, a spot, and finally microscopic amounts of cancer. When all of this had been cut out of my dear friend, she had another surgery which revealed no more malignant cells. Still, doctors ordered chemotherapy and radiation. They wanted to completely eradicate the harmful disease.

We understand such a violent attack on this illness. With a similar passion, Scripture reveals God's instructions to remove false religions. Like the cutting, poisoning, and burning of cancer, He tells the Israelites to break down, smash, cut down, and burn all idols. His goal is the complete eradication of the damaging sickness of sin. He wants His children's spiritual health preserved.

To encourage us to live sin-free, God tells us we will have victory over "enemies" like unhealthy relationships, bad habits, and ugly thoughts. Then we can follow up with replacing old habits with new ways, as we seek to walk in Christ's steps daily. We might need to sever some relational connections, move, change jobs—whatever!—in order to put ourselves in a healthy, holy place.

O Lord God, thank You for giving me spiritual health and victory through the cross of Jesus. Help me seek holiness, and surrender to You completely, in order to have total victory. In the precious name of Jesus I pray. Amen.

Chocolate and Consequences

Then Peter said, "Ananias, how is it that Satan has so filled your heart that you have lied to the Holy Spirit and have kept for yourself some of the money you received for the land?" (Acts 5:3).

Scripture: Acts 5:1-11
Song: "Create in Me a Clean Heart"

"Did you get into the chocolate, Owen?"

"No, Mommy."

My friend looked at her 3-year-old son's sticky, smudged face and asked the question again. Narrowing her eyes, she also warned him he'd receive a consequence for lying. With not-so-innocent conviction, Owen held to his story. His mommy disciplined him, and after several additional reprimands, Owen finally confessed to the truth smeared across his cheeks and chin.

Ananias and Sapphira's guilt was also obvious to Peter. He immediately confronted each one about their greedy lie, but like naïve children they didn't realize they'd been caught. Persisting in the lie brought them to swift judgment.

What would our sins look like smudged across our faces like stolen sweets? God perceives with utter clarity everything we think, say, and do.

Knowing this, let's admit to God that, like Ananias, we want part of the money. Like Sapphira, we want to cover for our spouses. Like Owen, we want some chocolate. When we lie, spiritual life dies in us. But when we confess, God forgives.

Lord, You hold Your children in unconditional love. Forgive me for forgetting this and denying "hidden" sin that breaks our fellowship. In Jesus' name, amen.

Protected from Extinction

The LORD your God is a compassionate God; He will not fail you nor destroy you nor forget the covenant with your fathers which He swore to them (Deuteronomy 4:31, *New American Standard Bible*).

Scripture: Deuteronomy 4:25-31
Song: "Mercy Seat"

In the building of the Hong Kong International Airport, some people feared the Romer's Tree Frog would become extinct. As the world's tiniest frogs, they measure only a couple centimeters in length. However, 200 of the species were rescued from their natural habitat, bred, and released successfully in seven new locations. Surprisingly, a small number of the amphibians even survived near the airport.

Tiny tree frogs don't understand relocation; however, we can trace our present situations to past decisions. Our sin carries us little-by-little from our loving God until we find ourselves in an unfamiliar environment.

Moses gave a difficult but hopeful word to the Israelites. They would be scattered as a consequence of their idolatry, but they would not become extinct.

God cares for His smallest of creatures, and He is crazy about His children. When we find ourselves in foreign lands with life-less gods, we can still seek and find Him. We can break un-healthy habits and change toxic thinking patterns. Then we'll enjoy renewed life in the compassionate embrace of our Father.

Father, forgive my sin that keeps me apart from You. I seek You today with this simple prayer and rely on Your promise to restore me. How I love You, Lord! Amen.

Running Together

**Encourage one another daily, as long as it is called "Today,"
so that none of you may be hardened by sin's deceitfulness**
(Hebrews 3:13).

Scripture: Hebrews 3:7-14
Song: "O My Soul, March On"

At mile eight of the marathon, I grabbed a snack and met
Melanie. We ate power bars, shared stories, and then continued
the event at our own paces.

I sat to stretch several miles later. As I twisted my aching
back, I heard Melanie say, "How are you?"

"How do I look?" I said pathetically.

"You must be OK; you're still smiling!" she replied, reaching
out her hand. I snickered at myself as she pulled me up and
walked with me briefly. Feeling refreshed, I ran on.

With only five miles left, I made another acquaintance. As we
talked, her pained expression became a smile. Before long, she
moved on, quickening her steps, motivated now to finish.

In daily life we benefit by exchanging encouragement with
fellow believers. Each day we can walk beside somebody, buy
someone coffee, pray for another's need, write a letter—find a
way to hold one another firmly to our confidence in Christ.

After the marathon I never felt so sore or so elated! Exercis-
ing encouragement is also a workout, but the Scripture warns
that the alternative is a hardening of the heart. Let's cheer one
another on and remain spiritually fit and strong.

Lord, You are the greatest encouragement of all, for You promise to be with me always. So may I be a joy and encouragement to others today. In Christ, amen.

Knowing the Fact

I do not want you to be ignorant of the fact, brothers and sisters (1 Corinthians 10:1).

Scripture: I Corinthians 10:1-5
Song: "Turn Your Eyes upon Jesus"

Growing up I was close to my friends in Sunday school and youth group. Year after year we learned more about God and each other. By high school we'd experienced numerous classes, church traditions, road trips, and summer camps together.

In my senior year, however, only a handful of us remained to celebrate graduation—and even fewer still claimed to be Christians! Despite sitting under the same weekly instruction and receiving similar blessings from our parents and ministers, few of us came through the desert of adolescence as serious believers.

In many circles, even at church, acting the part can convince others we belong. God won't be fooled, though; His vision is sharp, and His standards are high. Do we belong to the group, or do we belong to Him?

Specifically, God wants us to have more than a corporate religious resume. He desires a personal relationship that stands firmly and only on Him—not church background or loved ones. Let's know this: only a life pleasing to the Lord matters.

How do we please Him? Seek Him and His will first. Love Him authentically and invite Him into each thought, word, and action today. He is easy to please, but hard to satisfy.

Lord, let any purely religious busyness fall away from my life. You alone are my God; guide me into service in Your kingdom. Through Christ I pray. Amen.

The Example

These things occurred as examples to keep us from setting our hearts on evil things as they did (1 Corinthians 10:6).

Scripture: 1 Corinthians 10:6-22
Song: "And Can It Be?"

After years of excessive smoking, drinking, and distance from family, my Uncle Bud was diagnosed with terminal cancer. He returned home to loved ones for his final months of life and lived with us while receiving treatment.

One evening he listened as I practiced piano. Between songs we started talking. At one point he looked at me with grave sincerity and said, "Sara, don't mess up your life like I did."

Looking into his remorseful, repentant eyes I had no reply. He had rebelled against family and God, but in the end he turned back to both.

I was 14 when Uncle Bud's body slowly eroded and his spirit gently opened to us and the Lord. Years after his death, he remains to me an example of how not to "mess up my life" and how to grow closer to Jesus Christ. It's really never too late while the breath of life remains.

What type of examples are we? Would God point to our lives as examples of what to do or what *not* to do? I remind myself today: It's best to live a sensible life of integrity as a model for others — and to the glory of our God.

Almighty and most merciful God, I don't know who's watching me, but I pray they see Your amazing love and grace working in my life. Keep my heart open to Your working and, as I come to You in repentance, wash me clean. In the name of the Father and of the Son and of the Holy Spirit, I pray. Amen.

Me First!

I wrote to the church, but Diotrephes, who loves to be first, will not welcome us (3 John 9).

Scripture: 3 John 2-12
Song: "Empty Me"

I have two young sons, and as any parent of multiple children will tell you, any situation can easily deteriorate into an argument between the two of them. Many such spats have to do with who is going to be first. They each want to be the first to get dessert, go down the slide, and play the video game. They even argue about who will receive the first haircut when we take them to the barber! They both love to be first.

While it is unacceptable, it's at least *understandable* among young children. But when this type of me-first attitude comes through among mature believers in Christ, we rise to an entirely new level of impropriety.

There is no place for a me-first mentality in the body of Christ, especially when it comes to nonessential issues like the style of music, dress codes, etc. Even if I don't like something stylistically, I should be able to see how much it is blessing somebody else. It can then reside within my "latitude of acceptance."

Let us remember that the Bible commands us to value others above ourselves (see Philippians 2:3, 4). That's why, in the church, the me-first mentality gets kicked to the curb.

Lord, help me see others as You see them and serve others as You serve them. For You have told us: the first shall be last, and the last first. In Your name, amen.

July 21–27. **Mike Edmisten** is minister of the Amelia Church of Christ in Amelia, Ohio. He and his beautiful wife, Nicki, have two sons. He loves God, his family, his church, and the Cincinnati Reds.

Lord Willing; the Crick Don't Rise!

Instead, you ought to say, "If it is the Lord's will, we will live and do this or that" (James 4:15).

Scripture: James 4:13-17
Song: "Sweet Will of God"

I knew an older lady who always used the phrase, "Lord willing and the crick don't rise." (For those who are unfamiliar with southern Ohio farmer lingo, the word *crick* actually means "creek.") For example, if you were to say, "Ruth, will you be at church tomorrow?" she would respond, "Lord willing and the crick don't rise."

Ruth would never commit to anything without saying this phrase. It was her homespun way of saying, "I intend to do such-and-such, but the final outcome is out of my hands. If God allows me to do it, then I'll do it. But in the end, it's all up to Him."

That is a very godly, biblical approach to life. In fact, that is James's exact point in today's Scripture. We don't actually know what is going to happen tomorrow, after all. We make our plans, but if our plans aren't also God's plans, then our plans are all in vain.

It's a lesson in seeing everything through the lens of God's sovereignty, a reminder of how little we actually can control. It is an affirmation that our lives, our plans, and our futures are all in the hands of our heavenly Father.

O God, help me to see all of my plans in light of Your ultimate plan. And when my plans do not line up with Your plans, help me accept that my plans will be altered, changed, or abandoned. Through Christ I pray. Amen.

Honoring Our Leaders

Have confidence in your leaders and submit to their authority, because they keep watch over you as those who must give an account. Do this so that their work will be a joy, not a burden, for that would be of no benefit to you (Hebrews 13:17).

Scripture: Hebrews 13:16-21
Song: "Jesus Shall Reign"

The man was red-faced with anger, the veins in his forehead popping. He was yelling at me—in the church parking lot—at the top of his lungs about something I didn't even do.

I wish I could say this was an isolated incident, but it's not. I've been a minister for 18 years now. In that time, I have received more love, encouragement, and affirmation from people than I could ever detail in writing. But I have also been the recipient of the nastiest, most hateful vitriol you could ever imagine. Sadly, it goes with the territory.

No doubt more ministers have been run out of the ministry by church members than by Satan himself! They've loved God, loved people, and possessed a God-given gift for ministry. But they left their calling because of the constant pressure, criticism, and downright disdain they received from their people.

Today's text should be a wake-up call for all of us in the church. Godly, humble, biblical leaders deserve our love, our encouragement, and our honor. Before another moment passes, why not pick up the phone or send an e-mail?

Lord, thank You for godly leaders. Protect them. Guard their families. Bless their ministries. And use me as an encourager in their lives. In Jesus' name, amen.

A Lesson from the Ball Games

Warn a divisive person once, and then warn them a second time. After that, have nothing to do with them (Titus 3:10).

Scripture: Titus 3:8-14
Song: "The Church's One Foundation"

When I was a boy, one of my favorite pastimes was playing baseball with some of the other kids in my neighborhood. We'd pretend we were big leaguers. We would be our own umpires and even called our own play-by-play. Pretty impressive, when you consider there were usually only three or four of us!

These ball games were my favorite part of summer—until Kenny decided to start playing with us. (Kenny wasn't his real name, but that's what we'll call him.) Kenny was older than us. He was convinced he knew more than us. And he ruined every game he was a part of. So we all wised up and decided to play our games elsewhere.

Simply put, Kenny was a divisive force among us. Whenever he was around, arguments and fights were inevitable, because divisiveness is contagious.

That's why the Bible specifically instructs us to give only limited warnings to a divisive person. We warn them. We warn them one more time. And then we "have nothing to do with them." Healthy churches do not allow divisive people to get a foothold. The possibility of contagion is just too great.

My Lord Jesus Christ, You prayed for unity among all Your followers. Use me as a unifying force, and give me the courage to take a stand against those who seek to divide your church. Let me be an instrument of peace, as You lead me. In the name of the Father and of the Son and of the Holy Spirit, I pray. Amen.

A God of Order

God is not a God of disorder but of peace—as in all the congregations of the Lord's people (1 Corinthians 14:33).

Scripture: 1 Corinthians 14:27-33
Song: "You're Worthy of My Praise"

I'm not a very organized person. My desk is usually cluttered, to put it mildly. I found a newspaper article a few years ago that said people with messy desks are often the most creative and innovative people around. I'm not sure if that is actually true, but I pretend that it is.

It's just not in my nature to be organized and orderly. Truthfully, I like to think of God in much the same way. The Bible portrays God as being wild and untamed, which He most certainly is. But in His perfect nature, He is also orderly. He is wild, but He is not chaotic. Our worship should reflect that.

This principle takes different forms, depending on the nature of a particular church. Some churches hold services that are absolute chaos. No one is sure what is happening other than, "The Spirit is moving." In other churches, the service may resemble a come-as-you-are party, largely because everything has been thrown together at the last minute. There has been no prayer or preparation. The songs are haphazard. The sermon is a "Saturday night special." And the people come expecting nothing exceptional to happen, because nothing ever does. The same principle applies to both churches: God is not a God of disorder, whether it is planned or just tolerated.

Lord, You are wild and yet orderly. May I worship You in a way that reflects the depths and the riches of who You are. Through Christ I pray. Amen.

Agreeing on the Rules

If anyone thinks they are a prophet or otherwise gifted by the Spirit, let them acknowledge that what I am writing to you is the Lord's command (1 Corinthians 14:37).

Scripture: 1 Corinthians 14:37-40
Song: "Word of God Speak"

If we can't all agree on the basic rules, then nothing else matters. I was reminded of this when I was playing a game with one of my sons. It's a game that he made up, so apparently he also believed that he could change the rules whenever he felt like it. He employed this tactic whenever I was winning. I finally explained to him that if we don't have an agreed-upon set of unchanging rules, the game is meaningless.

That is the apostle Paul's key point in today's Scripture. He said, in essence, "If anyone is going to follow the Lord or do anything for Him, it begins by acknowledging that what I'm saying is the Lord's command. It begins with an absolute respect for Scripture as the Word of God."

Anyone who preaches or prophesies on anything apart from the Word of God is speaking meaningless things. They have rejected the authority of God's Word, which means there is no need to go any further. If two people have different foundational authorities, there is going to be never-ending conflict. Everything we do, say, preach, or pray must rest on this unchanging principle: what we read in the Bible really is the Word of God.

Heavenly Father, your Word is truth. If there is anything in my life that conflicts with Your Word, I pray You would cut it out of my life. I look to You to lead me today in all things. In the precious name of Jesus, amen.

Want Them to Understand?

In the church I would rather speak five intelligible words to instruct others than ten thousand words in a tongue (1 Corinthians 14:19).

Scripture: 1 Corinthians 14:13-26
Song: "Jesus Saves"

When my dad was in Japan for his job, he had to give a speech before several hundred people. Most of those in the crowd spoke English, but Dad wanted to make a good impression on them, so he opened the speech with a line in Japanese.

Much to his surprise, the place immediately erupted in laughter. Obviously, something had gotten "lost in translation." So Dad asked the man who introduced him, "What did I just say?"

The man, who was laughing hysterically, said, "You just asked me if my mother washes herself properly!" That's not exactly what my father was trying to say, but that is indeed what everybody heard.

In today's text, the apostle Paul makes one point incredibly clear. When speaking in the church, five intelligible words are worth more than ten thousand words that are misinterpreted.

The church has often been guilty of talking in a "code" that insiders understand but seekers don't. So, before we choose to use religious verbiage and Christian clichés, let's ask ourselves a simple question: Wouldn't we like those who still need Christ to at least understand what we're saying?

Lord, I thank You for the people in my life who shared the gospel with me. I thank You that they presented Your message to me with clarity and conviction. Now, use me to do the same for others in my world. Through Christ I pray. Amen.

I'm Not Afraid

God is our refuge and strength, an ever-present help in trouble (Psalm 46:1).

Scripture: Psalm 46
Song: "O God, Our Help in Ages Past"

Kathy's sense of humor brought lighthearted fun to our writers' meetings. One time, however, tears flowed down her cheeks when she requested prayer. "I don't know what's wrong with me. I just know my legs hurt—they hurt so much I can't think."

She called me a few weeks later. "Did you get the results from your bone scan?" I asked.

A long pause followed. "Sue, they found cancer in every bone in my body," she said. "The doctor says I have a couple weeks, maybe a couple months."

I couldn't speak. Tears welled up in my eyes.

"I'll be Home soon," she said. I closed my eyes, imagined her sweet smile and heard her say, "I'm not afraid."

It was just like Kathy to encourage a friend when she endured incredible pain. She suffered through kidney disease, breast cancer, and then metastasized bone cancer. Yet, when I think of her, I remember her beautiful smile, her faith in God, and how she relied on Him for help and strength. Kathy is in the presence of our Lord today and forever, but she left a legacy of wonderful stories of faith that will continue to bless others.

Father God, thank You for friends like Kathy who faithfully show me how to live in Your strength. In the name of Jesus, amen.

July 28–31. **Sue Tornai** lives with her husband, John, and dog Maggie in Carmichael, California. She's taught Sunday school for 23 years and enjoys camping and fishing with her family.

Around the Block

There is no one like the God of Jeshurun, who rides across the heavens to help you and on the clouds in his majesty (Deuteronomy 33:26).

Scripture: Deuteronomy 33:24-29
Song: "Days of Elijah"

I tripped over a cable at work, which flipped me to the ground and sent the mail I carried flying in all directions. The fall broke my hip, and surgeons installed a titanium plate in my upper right leg. Then began a time of recovery, physical therapy, and learning to walk again. During that time, my husband, John, drove me everywhere I needed to go, and I grew to depend on him. Four weeks later, when it was time for me to return to work, I begged him to drive me, but he wouldn't. All my insistence fell on deaf ears.

Standing by the passenger side of the car, tears filled my eyes. John looked at me and said, "Drive around the block, and if you still want me to drive, come back and get me."

I moved into the driver's seat, put the key into the ignition—and prayed. It was as if the God of Heaven waited for me to turn to Him for help. Peace and confidence overwhelmed me. I backed out of the driveway, drove around the block and on to work. That day I was sure that God indeed rode on the heavens to help me and on the clouds in His majesty. How could I be afraid?

Lord, it is wonderful to know You ride on the heavens in Your majesty, and I take great comfort in knowing that You are as close as a prayer. There is no one like You, and I praise You! In Jesus' name, amen.

To Whom Can I Turn?

LORD, there is no one like you to help the powerless against the mighty (2 Chronicles 14:11).

Scripture: 2 Chronicles 14:1-12
Song: "No One Like You"

My grandson, Luke, was born seven weeks early with a serious deformity. Lying motionless in his tiny bassinet, under monitors, tubes, and an oscillating ventilator, he had no power, no strength, and only a 30 percent chance of survival. I cried and I prayed. *Lord Jesus, who else can we turn to? You are the resurrection and the life. You are the master healer. Please heal our baby, Luke.* As a grandmother, prayer was the only (and best) thing I could do.

King Asa also cried out to God when his circumstances grew dark. He found his people in a defenseless position, as they faced the vast Cushite army ready to destroy them. Against all odds, he prayed, *Lord, there is no one like you to help the powerless against the mighty.* The Lord struck down the Cushites before Asa and Judah. Although the Cushites fled, Asa pursued and defeated them.

Sometimes God has a different plan, one we don't expect. But I am glad He brought victory to Judah under King Asa—and especially glad He healed our little Luke. My 9-year-old grandson reminds me how God answered our prayers, bringing him through his critical birth and surgeries.

Lord God of Heaven and Earth, thank You that I can turn to You in times of great despair and trust that You are in control. Whatever happens, draw me close to You and keep me in the shadow of Your omnipotent wings. In the holy name of Jesus, my Lord and Savior, I pray. Amen.

Blessed to Bless

It is more blessed to give than to receive (Acts 20:35).

Scripture: Acts 20:28-35
Song: "Bless the Lord"

In our troubling economy, it made me happy to be able to help a few people who had experienced significant loss. Then my supervisor shocked me when she announced the company had eliminated my position. Questions flooded my soul. Where would I go if not to work? How would I pay my bills? The question that bothered me most was: How can I help others now that I myself need help?

Like Paul, I've found great pleasure in giving and, like him, I've worked hard to make that happen. But without a job, I didn't know how I could give.

I didn't have the answers, but kept working at one thing or another, mostly volunteer jobs. My applications for work brought few interviews, and they didn't bring any full-time job offers. I continued to pray, though, that God would make me a good steward of the blessings He gave me.

Thankfully, the severance and unused vacation pay allowed me to become debt free. Now that I'm not working, God is showing me new ways to contribute to the needs of others by sharing my time, talents, and service in addition to limited financial giving. It amazes me that as I give—whatever the gift—God blesses me so I can keep giving.

Father God, I find so much joy in giving to others as You have given to me. Thank You that as I give in faith, even in troubling times, You bless me so I can keep giving. In the name of Jesus, amen.

DEVOTIONS®

August

"Be still, and know that I am God; I will be exalted
among the nations, I will be exalted in the earth."

—*Psalm 46:10*

Gary Wilde, Editor | **Margaret Williams,** Project Editor | Photo iStockphoto | Thinkstock®

DEVOTIONS® is published quarterly by Standard Publishing, Cincinnati, Ohio, www.standardpub.com.
© 2013 by Standard Publishing. All rights reserved. Topics based on the Home Daily Bible Readings,
International Sunday School Lessons. © 2010 by the Committee on the Uniform Series. Printed in
the U.S.A. All Scripture quotations, unless otherwise indicated, are taken from the *HOLY BIBLE,
NEW INTERNATIONAL VERSION*®. *NIV*®. Copyright © 1973, 1978, 1984, 2011 by Biblica. Used
by permission of Zondervan. All rights reserved. *King James Version (KJV),* public domain. *New
American Standard Bible (NASB),* © The Lockman Foundation, 1960, 1962, 1963, 1968, 1971,
1972, 1973, 1975, 1977, 1995.

He Is My Strength

Pray continually (1 Thessalonians 5:17).

Scripture: 1 Thessalonians 5:12-22
Song: "The Joy of the Lord"

My supervisor called me to the conference room where she waited with one of my coworkers who had a complaint against me. Reluctantly, I walked down the long hallway, wishing I didn't have to go. After I closed the door, my peer blasted me with one false accusation after another—raising her voice and shaking her finger at me. Silently I prayed, "I need your help, Lord Jesus."

My natural tendency would be to retaliate and humiliate her, to make her feel as small as she made me feel. All I could say was, "That's not true." Finally, the woman took a breath and I looked at my manager, who seemed to share my surprise at the woman's outburst. I asked, "May I leave now?" Speechless, she nodded. As she stayed calm and neutral, I felt God's peace in answer to my prayer.

The high-stress nature of working in financial services often sent our emotions reeling out of control. Knowing God was always with me, I relied on the power of prayer to deal with some of the difficult people around me. I even found opportunities to encourage others with the same comfort I had received.

Thank You, **Lord,** for making me strong when I feel weak and for showing me how to stay calm in stressful situations. Thank You for being with me, especially when I feel alone and discouraged. In Christ's name, amen.

August 1–3. **Sue Tornai** lives with her husband, John, and dog Maggie in Carmichael, California. She's taught Sunday school for 23 years and enjoys camping and fishing with her family.

Faithful Friend

Your love has given me great joy and encouragement, because you, brother, have refreshed the hearts of the saints (Philemon 7).

Scripture: Philemon 3-7
Song: "How Great Our Joy"

I dreaded going to the Christmas tea, and as the time approached for me to speak, anxiety mounted within me. I think of public speaking in the same category as going to the dentist. I'd rather be someplace else. After giving my testimony, I felt relieved but still a little shaky.

Then a woman came forward to thank me. I welcomed her gentle smile and encouraging comments. It was as if God sent her to calm my fears about how my words had affected others.

A few days later I met this woman, Carole, again at a mutual friend's birthday party. We talked as if we had known each other for years. Before we parted, she asked if I would like to pray with her on a regular basis. That was 13 years ago, and we are still friends and prayer partners.

Carole is my Philemon. She is committed to missions and frequently opens her home to students and missionaries. Regardless of her difficulties or personal challenges, she makes room for guests with joyful hospitality. The joy she shares in providing a home-cooked meal for God's laborers, her willingness to pray for and support them, refreshes and inspires many — especially me.

Thank You, **Father,** for friends like Carole, who inspire me in new ways to serve You. Show me how to use all the spiritual gifts You've given me. In Jesus' name, amen.

Everyone Needs Compassion

Praise be to the God and Father of our Lord Jesus Christ, the Father of compassion and the God of all comfort, who comforts us in all our troubles, so we can comfort those in any trouble with the same comfort we ourselves receive from God (2 Corinthians 1:3, 4).

Scripture: 2 Corinthians 1:3-11
Song: "Mighty to Save"

My kids are grown and have kids of their own, but I still enjoy remembering when they were little. As a toddler, my son used to hold his stuffed bear over his shoulder, close his eyes, and gently pat the bear on its back. When I heard him murmur, "O-o-o," it occurred to me that he showed love to his bear the way I showed love to him.

God calls us to love others as He loves us, but some of the things people do are not lovable. It's not easy for me to love the guy who cuts in front of me in traffic or the woman who pushes her way to the front of the checkout line. What makes people so impatient and angry? As the question enters my mind, I see a picture of myself a few years earlier. I'm thankful that in my despair I remembered from childhood to cry out to God for help. He heard me and lavished His love on me.

My heart aches for people who don't know they can turn to God. Maybe the only God they will ever see is the Holy Spirit living in me. So today I'll make an effort to exchange a smile for a frown or a prayer for rude behavior.

Lord, I pray for those who have lived their lives without knowing You. As far as it depends on me, help me to love them today. In Jesus' name, amen.

Impossible Perfection

Through Him everyone who believes is freed from all things, from which you could not be freed through the Law of Moses (Acts 13:39, *New American Standard Bible*).

Scripture: Acts 13:36-41
Song: "Only the Blood of Jesus"

My son, Brian, works as a manufacturing engineer for a maker of high-end binoculars and scopes. Several months ago, the company enrolled Brian's group in a program to improve product quality. The goal: reduce the number of defects, as a percentage, from parts-per-thousand to parts-per-million.

For example, one computer-controlled machine cuts the metal rings that hold the scope onto a gun. The tooling wears as it works, and at some point no longer cuts accurately. But no one knew when it began to produce unusable parts. When the operator finally discovered defects, he would shut down the machine, replace the worn-out tooling and sort the rings, tossing many bad ones. The process was costly, in time and materials.

Under the new program, an engineer statistically studied the process and discovered that the tooling wears enough after cutting only 10 to 20 rings to compromise quality. With the new information, he has set the machine to automatically compensate.

My point is this: even measuring every fifth ring does not produce perfection, any more than the Law produces it in our lives.

Thank You, **Jesus**, for freeing me from pursuing righteousness through keeping rules. Only Your sacrifice on the cross can provide salvation. Through Christ, amen.

August 4–10. **Patty Duncan** teaches fifth grade at Eugene Christian School in Eugene, Oregon. She loves to teach art to kids and train teachers for sharing art literacy lessons with their students.

The Cardboard Parade

If we confess our sins, He is faithful and righteous to forgive us our sins and to cleanse us from all unrighteousness (1 John 1:9, *New American Standard Bible*).

Scripture: 1 John 1:5-10
Song: "The Wonderful Cross"

"Yesterday we had a cardboard parade at church," said Pam, my teaching colleague, as we met to pray before school.

"People in our church had cut cardboard from big boxes and used markers to write words that described their lives before Jesus saved them. One man walked across the platform holding a sign that said 'Addict' then flipped the cardboard and it read 'Free.' A woman raised a sign announcing 'Depressed' and turned it over to show the word 'Joyful.'"

"Oh, yes," I said, "Our church had a parade like that once, and it was powerful."

"I talked about it with a friend after church," Pam continued, "and she said to me, 'I knew you and Luther before you came to the Lord, and your lives were a mess.'"

"I had forgotten," Pam told me, "but she was right. Our lives were a mess."

Her eyes sparkled. "Isn't Jesus wonderful?"

God didn't wait for Pam and her husband to clean up and act right before rescuing them. He did what the Law couldn't do by His unconditional love and His pure grace.

Dear Heavenly Father, I would need an armful of cardboard signs to list the ways You have changed my life and rescued me. I'm so grateful to You! I pray through my deliverer, Jesus. Amen.

Practice the 5 A's

If your brother or sister sins against you, rebuke them; and if they repent, forgive them (Luke 17:3).

Scripture: Luke 17:1-6
Song: "You Are My King"

The students at the Christian school where I teach love buddy chapel, when young students sit by their older buddies. After chapel recently, I noticed another teacher talking sternly to one of my students and a younger child.

Moving closer, I heard the teacher admonish, "Socking each other is not right. Now what exactly happened?"

Jessica offered, "I patted him on the shoulder to say hi, and he turned around and hit me."

David retorted, "Then she hit *me!*" The teacher continued working with the two until they both admitted they had done wrong—and had asked and received forgiveness.

Children sometimes have trouble getting along, so we teachers mediate disputes using the 5 A's of conflict resolution, based on Scripture. We teach the children what to do if they hurt another child's feelings. The 5-A steps include: *Admitting* I have done wrong; *Apologizing*; *Accepting* consequences; *Asking* for forgiveness; and *Altering* my choices in the future.

I'm glad Jesus didn't teach doormat psychology, that we should let people walk over us emotionally. He included healthy confrontation in dealing with someone who sins against us. He required repentance before extending forgiveness.

Lord, when I consider what You went through on the cross to forgive me of my many sins against You, I'm so much more able to forgive others! In Your name. Amen.

Generous to the Max

In Him we have redemption through His blood, the for-giveness of our trespasses, according to the riches of His grace which He lavished on us (Ephesians 1:7, 8, *New American Standard Bible*).

Scripture: Ephesians 1:3-10
Song: "God of Wonders"

God isn't stingy in His creation. My organic-gardening friend tells me millions of microscopic creatures in one teaspoon of soil benefit plant growth. Instead of tilling her garden, she digs a hole for each plant and leaves the rest of the ground undisturbed. God has provided abundantly to nourish the seedlings.

Underfoot, insects scurry between blades of grass, more in number than all other animals put together. And the next time you're enjoying a summer walk at night, look up at the sky. Each pinprick of light represents a star that might host circling planets like our own solar system. In fact, astronomers have not found an end to the galaxies and stars.

Consider your own body. Here we find an intricate defense system rivaling the strategy of the strongest army in history. In a world replete with germs, few succeed in making us sick, thanks to our intricately designed immune systems.

The abundance of His provisions gives us valid reasons to trust Him for our salvation. After all He has lavishly, abundantly given of himself. Now all the riches of His grace are ours. God isn't stingy with His children.

Jesus, You told me to consider the sparrow and ponder the lilies of the field. When I go outdoors, I see so many reasons to trust Your lavish grace. In Christ, amen.

Survive to Five

If by the transgression of the one, death reigned through the one, much more those who receive the abundance of grace and of the gift of righteousness will reign in life through the One, Jesus Christ (Romans 5:17, *New American Standard Bible*).

Scripture: Romans 5:15-21
Song: "Lord, Reign in Me"

The struggle between death and life is no more obvious than among the children of the world's poorest people groups. A letter from World Vision recounted the story of Moses, a boy born in Kenya. His mother died birthing him, and the baby barely survived. He struggles against incredible odds to stay alive in an area where life-threatening diseases claim so many very young children. Lacking adequate nutrition and medical care, Moses may not live to see his fifth birthday.

World Vision has launched a fund-raising campaign, "Survive to Five," targeted at cheating death for millions of children like Moses. Funds will go to fight severe malnutrition, pneumonia, diarrhea, malaria, neonatal infections, cholera, and tetanus.

Death has reigned on earth since Adam sinned, but life comes through Jesus Christ. Spiritual rebirth and forgiveness of sins bring life to us, and He also reaches out through us in very practical ways to fight for physical life among us. I pray that offerings given to "Survive to Five" will bring many children to their fifth birthdays—and well beyond—that they may know and love their Savior forever.

Lord, have mercy on the poorest of the poor in the world, and especially on the children. Spur me to help and give! In Your life-giving name. Amen.

Jesus Pizza

We are a fragrance of Christ to God among those who are being saved and among those who are perishing; to the one an aroma from death to death, to the other an aroma from life to life (2 Corinthians 2:15, 16, *New American Standard Bible*).

Scripture: 2 Corinthians 2:12-17
Song: "Let the Lower Lights Be Burning"

Two years ago, Brian, a senior at Southridge High School in Beaverton, Oregon, wanted every student in his school to know who Jesus is. He and his minister researched ways to hold an evangelistic event at the school, knowing he'd meet resistance.

And he did. Because the idea was student-generated, Brian gained permission to hold the session in the school cafeteria, over objections from teachers, students, and the principal.

He and his friends put up a banner advertising the meeting, and a few minutes later it was torn down. They hung it up again and again the sign came down. But at the meeting, the minister spoke about Jesus, and kids came in faith to Him.

Afterward, the new group of believers wanted to continue talking about Jesus, so they met at lunch on Friday, eating pizza provided by the adults. The first week, 40 kids came, and they decided to meet the next week. Sixty kids showed up. By the fourth week, 120 students attended. The "Jesus Pizza" Friday lunches continue, two years after Brian shouldered a burden for his school and took action.

Lord, thank You for this young man's holy boldness and his compassion for the kids closest to him. Let his story inspire me to share You with my neighbors, by word, deed, or just by the "aroma" of a life that gives forth Your character. In Christ, amen.

Kept by the Power of God

So that no advantage would be taken of us by Satan, for we are not ignorant of his schemes (2 Corinthians 2:11, *New American Standard Bible*).

Scripture: 2 Corinthians 1:23–2:11
Song: "Our God Is Greater"

In 1923 the U.S. government took Jeff Yellow Owl's grandmother from her parents and put her into a boarding school to immerse her in the white man's culture. She remembered bumping along in a wagon, watching her home and family disappear in the rolling hills of the Blackfeet Indian Reservation in Montana near Glacier Park. She was 5 years old.

Forbidden to speak her native language, she never saw her parents again. Released as a teenager, hungry for love, she married young. Her husband became an alcoholic.

Instead of growing bitter, Jeff's grandma drew close to God and became a gospel preacher. She'd hold house meetings in her living room, teaching from her well-marked Bible. She'd call the grandkids in from outside, fervently pray for them, and say: "It's not what man has done to you but what God will do for you."

Later, as a young man working away from home, Jeff would call his grandmother from a pay phone. "Grandma, I'm messed up on drugs and alcohol," he'd say. "What should I do?"

"My boy," she'd say, "you need Jesus." Because she refused to succumb to Satan's scheme of bitterness, her life poured faith and hope into her grandson.

Father, You've held me close through difficult trials. I pray that Your faithfulness to me provides a heritage of faith for my children and grandchildren. In Jesus' name, amen.

A New Generation

Even when I am old and gray, do not forsake me, my God, till I declare your power to the next generation, your mighty acts to all who are to come (Psalm 71:18).

Scripture: Psalm 71:17-24
Song: "Lord, Through All the Generations"

"I may be gray headed, but I'm bursting with purpose," I said, as I felt God's nudge to teach a first-grade Sunday school class. After a month, I learned that teaching children whose parents are nonbelievers is quite a mission. *Am I having an effect on these kids?* I wondered. I wanted to be seen as the kind grandmother, with a passion to introduce children to Jesus. But I did not foresee the misery that filled their lives. I prayed hard for each child.

One Sunday during class, 7-year-old Robbie became frantic. I'd passed out smiley faces and said, "When you are troubled, hold up the smiley face and remember God loves you!" Robbie ran screaming to the corner. While attempting to maintain peace, I knelt in front of him.

"I love you," I said, "but you need to calm down. Know that God loves you too!"

But he would not respond to me. With a heavy heart, I shut my eyes briefly and silently prayed, "Oh God, touch that little boy." When I turned around, one of my students held up her smiley face and said, "God loves us all, Teacher!"

Lord, help me remember that teaching a Sunday school class isn't about how well I speak. It's about Your love. Reach the children through me, in Christ's name. Amen.

August 11–17. **Shirley Reynolds** is a freelance writer living in the mountains of Idaho. Riding her ATV through the backwoods, hiking, taking pictures, and writing are her favorite things to do.

God's Everlasting Love

The LORD hath appeared of old unto me, saying, Yea, I have loved thee with an everlasting love: therefore with lovingkindness have I drawn thee (Jeremiah 31:3, *King James Version*).

Scripture: Jeremiah 31:1-6
Song: "Have Faith in God"

As I've matured, I still don't fully comprehend God's love for me, but when He comes near, I am drawn to Him. He has reminded me of His love for me when I was a child, sitting on a dark landing and singing "Jesus Loves Me." Yet I stuffed years of anger over childhood abuse into an imaginary backpack and carried it throughout most of my adult life. When my deep-seated anger began to overflow and influence my life, I knew I could not journey on without giving everything to God. I've felt as if He said, "It's time for you to deal with your past!"

I drove to the mausoleum where my parents were buried. As I laid my hands against the cold concrete wall, I prayed for God to turn my anger into love. He was there with me. Tears fell. I let go of my burden and walked from that place, sure that I was hundreds of pounds lighter.

Throughout my life, I have felt God's tap on my shoulder. Now, like the Israelites of long ago, I've discovered how much God loved me, even from birth. Amidst the world's chaos, I've sometimes forgotten. And then He's drawn me near once again.

Father, keep me from becoming so caught up with life's problems and heartaches. When faced with a crisis situation, You are near me, loving me. Thank You for drawing me close and helping me love and forgive as You do. In the name of Jesus, amen.

God Gives the Strength

If ye be reproached for the name of Christ, happy are ye; for the spirit of glory and of God resteth upon you: on their part he is evil spoken of, but on your part he is glorified (1 Peter 4:14, *King James Version*).

Scripture: 1 Peter 4:12-19
Song: "Faith Is the Victory"

I read a book titled, *Tramp for the Lord,* by Holocaust survivor Corrie ten Boom. She told about a message she delivered to a congregation of concentration camp survivors. After her talk ended, she saw a man walking toward her. Her first response was—"Oh great, I'm exhausted. I would like to go back to my room and sleep!" Then the man stood in front of Corrie, held out his hand, and said, "Please forgive me."

What? Who is this man? she thought. But then the years melted away, and she remembered him as a guard from Ravensbrück Camp, where she had been imprisoned for so long.

She silently argued with God. She did not want to forgive him, since he was the cruelest of the guards. But God spoke to Corrie ten Boom, and she placed her hand in the hand of the man, and said, "Yes, I forgive you."

The Spirit of God came upon Corrie ten Boom with awesome glory. When I read her words, I prayed for God to give me that same power and strength to forgive those who have wronged me.

O Lord, when anger looms up or mistrust enters my mind, help me see that what I face is nothing in comparison to the pain You endured in giving up the glories of Heaven to endure the cross. Thank You for taking care of me! In Jesus' name, amen.

Satan's Turf, God's Avenue

Be sober, be vigilant; because your adversary the devil, as a roaring lion, walketh about seeking whom he may devour (1 Peter 5:8, *King James Version*).

Scripture: 1 Peter 5:8-14
Song: "Onward, Christian Soldiers"

"When you're working with street youth, you'll walk where they walk—on Satan's turf! You must be prayed-up," the Safe House Director said. Here I was, Ms. Susie Suburbia, fresh from the comfort of my church upbringing. But I listened.

Weeks later, during a late night outreach, I walked up a side street with my staff partner. A cluster of hardened street youth ambled out of an entryway of an abandoned building. They blocked our path, while cursing and threatening harm.

"Why're ya talkin' bout God all the time," they heckled. A trickle of fear ran down my spine. I was a newbie and not prepared for their taunting. My streetwise partner began to pray. Following his lead, I sat down on a curb and prayed. My director's words came to my mind—"This is Satan's turf."

Being alert to Satan's attacks was my first step toward being equipped. Calling on the name of the Lord was a sure way to defeat the enemy. When I opened my eyes, the terrifying group had wandered down the street.

My partner casually said, "One thing you need to remember: If you're not being attacked by the devil while working here, then something is wrong! Always be ready!"

Father, as I walk with You, don't let complacency enter my life. Make me aware of Your presence always, and help me recognize the opposition! Through Christ, amen.

Slipping Away

Whosoever transgresseth, and abideth not in the doctrine of Christ, hath not God. He that abideth in the doctrine of Christ, he hath both the Father and the Son (2 John 9, *King James Version*).

Scripture: 2 John 1-9
Song: "Jesus, with Thy Church Abide"

I have struggled with allowing God to have all of my life, not fully understanding the word *all!* One morning, I'd awakened in a grouchy mood. While trying to grasp the idea that we might be losing our home, I'd discovered I had built a chasm between God and me, and I didn't want that feeling.

Leaning over our railing, I tried listening to God instead of filling my thoughts with my own problems. A ray of sunshine landed on a pile of rocks that my grandson called his landscaping. A shiny object gleamed from the top of a flat rock. *What is that?* I wondered, as I ran down the hill. It was a silver pocket cross I'd given to Michael. *How did it land here? Did Mikie drop it while playing?*

Later, after a phone conversation, he said, "Grandma, I put the cross on top of the rock so you would know that God takes care of your home too!"

Wiping away my tears, I was aware that I had taken life's problems in my own hands—once again. It took God, a little boy, and his silver cross, to bring God's truth to my mind.

Father, help me to remember, at all times, that "letting go" and abiding in You includes my thoughts. Remind me, that when I try to solve my own problems, I create a huge gap in our relationship. Today I give all of me to You. Through Christ, amen.

Always More to Learn

But ye, beloved, building up yourselves on our most holy faith, praying in the Holy Ghost (Jude 1:20, *King James Version*).

Scripture: Jude 17-25
Song: "Build on the Rock"

When my husband turned 70 years old, his family held a party at our church. More than 50 family members attended. When I looked around, I was stricken with the thought—"How many of these have I shared Christ with throughout the years?"

Later, I could hardly wait to go to my quiet place to pray. I was weary, but it seemed as if God wanted me to listen to Him, instead of spouting. I'd been praying for months for God to light a fire inside of me, so that I could be a mirror of His grace to friends, family, and acquaintances. Through my prayers, it seemed as if God were saying: "Think about each day. Think about what you can do to further my message to your immediate family." I sat in the quiet, smiled, and said, "Thank You, Lord."

I needed to stop dwelling on what might have been and act on the future possibilities. I thought about my relatives and about the people in my church, and then I knew. I'd allowed God's Spirit to go before me! There was no end to the outpouring of His nature.

Sitting in His presence that night, I didn't want to leave. Words like *encourage*, *hug*, and *love* came to mind. It almost seemed too simple.

Lord, help me to learn to pray in Your power and strength. Teach me to be a mirror to the world, showing only Your reflection. Through Christ, amen.

A China Teacup

We are hard pressed on every side, but not crushed; perplexed, but not in despair (2 Corinthians 4:8).

Scripture: 2 Corinthians 4:1-15
Song: "Before the Throne of God Above"

My grandson, Mikie, was about to serve what he called "a cup of vanilla tea!" When he's come to stay with us, we've observed this tradition before bedtime. He would be the waiter and serve from a gold-striped teapot. We drank from small china cups, and we'd talk about our day.

One evening, as he poured tea into my cup, he accidentally bumped his teacup, and it fell to the floor and broke. He burst into tears and said, "I'm so sorry, Grandma!"

Stooping down, I picked up the broken pieces. It had not shattered, so I placed the pieces on the table. Checking our supply cupboard, I found the glue, and the two of us promptly began to put the broken pieces back together. Yet he continued to say, "I'm sorry," while tears dampened his face.

I assured him that we could fix the cup. "I forgave you a long time ago," I said.

When the glue dried, he was thrilled. "You can't even see the crack!"

"You're right Mikie," I said. "It's just like Jesus. He comes along, picks up our broken pieces, and tells us to get going. The memory is there, but He is the glue!"

Lord, help me to remember that when bad things crash into my life, that I need never be in despair; You promise to be with me through it all. Though I may be "dumbfounded" for a time, my life is in Your good hands. In Jesus' name, amen.

Christian Re-Offending

Are you thinking of killing me as you killed the Egyptian yesterday? (Acts 7:28).

Scripture: Acts 7:23-28
Song: "I Want a Principle Within"

When Fred started out in his painting business, he decided to save money by diluting his paint. Since his first customer was a small church, he reasoned that if they discovered his deception they would have to forgive him. So after Fred finished and the minister inspected the job, he found the newly painted walls were splotched and streaked. "I know you used diluted paint," the minister told Fred. "What you need to do is repaint and thin no more!"

That's silly of course but whether it's Fred's duplicity or Moses' murder of the Egyptian, the minister's pun-ridden advice is entirely correct—to change and not repeat the offense. However, that's not so easy, especially when, like the Israelite in our passage, others doubt our ability to start anew and continually remind us of it. It also makes it likely we will fail again.

So what to do? We can't control what our friends say, but we can certainly manage how we regard our pardoned offenses. That's because once God forgives—and then as He forgets the offense—He invites us to continued service for Him. And with that reassurance, who really cares what others say or think?

Father, when I fail, help me tune out the opinions and reactions of others and concentrate only on You and Your loving guidance. Through Christ I pray. Amen.

August 18–24. **Anne Adams** is a writer and teacher living in Houston, Texas. She has published two books and also writes for various Christian and secular publications.

Illogical Love

You see, at just the right time, when we were still power-less, Christ died for the ungodly (Romans 5:6).

Scripture: Romans 5:6-11
Song: "What Wondrous Love Is This?"

A king invaded a neighboring nation, captured its monarch and his family, then interviewed his captives. He asked the monarch: "What will you give me if I set your children free?"

"Everything I possess," he replied.

"And what will you give me if I release your wife?" The prisoner turned to his wife and grasped her hand. "I will give myself." The conqueror was sympathetic, so he ordered the release of the man and his family. As they left, the former prisoner turned to his wife. "Isn't he a noble man?" The wife replied. "I only see you—the one who was willing to give himself for me."

We might understand how a husband can love his wife enough to sacrifice himself for her. But it's incomprehensible that a perfect Son of God could be willing to love and sacrifice himself for an ignorant, antagonistic, and apathetic world. It's just illogical!

Yet God doesn't operate on human logic; His love flows from His character alone, not on something worthy in us. Illogical though it seems, salvation is available only to sinners. It comes complete, with nothing we could add. As someone has said, "Christ picked up the tab at the cross, and even left the tip."

O Lord, may I confront the skepticism of my world with the unconditional grace of Your salvation. May others embrace Your humanly illogical love as I display it in my own life. I pray in Jesus' name, amen.

Enemies No Longer

Once you were alienated from God and were enemies in your minds because of your evil behavior. But now he has reconciled you by Christ's physical body through death to present you holy in his sight (Colossians 1:21, 22).

Scripture: Colossians 1:15-23
Song: "I've Found a Friend"

Union and Confederate forces met at the Battle of Gettysburg in July 1863, a great tragedy of Americans fighting Americans. The issues involved meant hatred and alienation that often continued even after the war ended in 1865. Yet 50 years later, in the summer of 1913, more than 50,000 veterans gathered at the Gettysburg battle site to commemorate the event. It was a peaceful reunion between the former enemies.

President Woodrow Wilson addressed the group, saying: "We have found one another again as brothers and comrades in arms, enemies no longer . . ." On the same battlefield where they once struggled, former opponents stood together as friends.

We find reuniting enemies inspiring, but with God it's standard procedure. As Paul put it, He treats as friends we who were once His enemies. Yet with God there's a difference. In our world, when combatants reunite they may still retain antagonism. But with God that's not an issue. Why? Because when we believe in Christ, it's as if we were never His enemies at all, but always His friends. He forgives and forgets.

Father, I'm thankful to know what it means to be Your friend. When I fail You, I need never feel estranged as Your enemy. Help me comprehend that Your friendship is never based on my conduct, but on Your unchanging grace. Through Christ, amen.

It's All New!

If anyone is in Christ, the new creation has come: The old has gone, the new is here! (2 Corinthians 5:17)

Scripture: 2 Corinthians 5:16-21
Song: "How Can I Keep from Singing?"

In the Houston area we have a community that illustrates a common problem in real estate development. When it was established years ago, the municipality was largely composed of small bungalows placed along tree-lined streets. In the last few years as young affluent families sought homes near to the city center, developers turned to this community.

However, they realized that the bungalows were just too small for contemporary buyers. But since the community was entirely surrounded by the bigger city, there was no room to expand. So, to accommodate the young families, developers purchased the small homes, remodeled what they could, but usually just cleared the lot and rebuilt from the ground up.

It's the same in our lives when God assumes control and seeks to remodel us to suit His purposes. As He does, it means that we must forget and discard our ideas when they are not compatible with His planned renovations. After all, when we consider all that God wants to accomplish with us, then our own efforts become insignificant in comparison.

Truly, as we believe in Christ, our old life is over and all things are new. All God seeks is an empty lot and a willingness for the reconstruction to proceed.

Lord, Your plans are always superior to mine. You've made me a new creature, and I welcome all You have planned for me. Through Christ, amen.

Playing Second Fiddle

Who is wise and understanding among you? Let them show it by their good life, by deeds done in the humility that comes from wisdom (James 3:13).

Scripture: James 3:13-18
Song: "Take Up Thy Cross"

"What is the hardest instrument in the orchestra to play?" someone once asked the great conductor Leonard Bernstein. "Second violin," he responded. "There are many who want to play first violin, but there are very few who want to play 'second fiddle' with enthusiasm. But without the 'second fiddle' there is no harmony."

When James spoke of working for God, he advised that we not boast about such service—and this continues to be good advice. Do you know someone who brags about their accomplishments? How does that make you feel when you do your best and yet don't get much attention? Like a second-rate Christian? It's almost as if playing "second fiddle" is a waste of time.

Of course, we may forget that we are serving God, not ourselves. Just as an orchestra produces beautiful music when all the instruments play together harmoniously, so do we as Christians glorify God best when we work at our assigned tasks, no matter if we are actually "backstage" and obscure.

What pleases Him is what's important. So continue your service—and remember that neither you nor your service is ever obscure to God.

Father, help me remember that unless You promote me, then I am not promoted. Let me be content to let others get the credit. In the name of Jesus, amen.

Anger into Action

You have heard that it was said to the people long ago, "You shall not murder, and anyone who murders will be subject to judgment." But I tell you that anyone who is angry with a brother or sister will be subject to judgment (Matthew 5:21, 22).

Scripture: Matthew 5:21-26
Song: "His Words Are True"

Jerry's basketball team in the college playoffs faced an opposing team that was skilled but tricky, particularly their star player, Butch. In one complicated play, Butch deliberately rammed an elbow in Jerry's face. But the referee didn't see it and, in fact, called a foul on Jerry.

There was a time-out, and as Jerry nursed his painful nose, his teammates urged him to get back at Butch. He declined. Then as they returned to play, displaying no visible emotion, Jerry repeatedly seized the ball and dashed down the court to score, over and over. Because he focused his anger into action, Jerry's team came from behind and won the game.

People react differently to anger—some with violent retaliation. Others, like Jerry, focus their rage on a solution to the situation. However, it's interesting to note that, as Jesus indicated, while the Mosaic law forbade angry acts, He stressed the importance of controlling the emotion of anger. After all, the overt act is merely a reaction to the thought.

Almighty and most merciful God, help me learn to subdue my anger into focus and concentration on Your purposes in frustrating situations. Then, O Lord, enable me to resolve ill-placed emotion to follow Your will. In the name of the Father and of the Son and of the Holy Spirit, I pray. Amen.

What a Difference a Day Makes!

Behold, now is the accepted time; behold, now is the day of salvation (2 Corinthians 6:2, *King James Version*).

Scripture: 2 Corinthians 6:1-13; 7:1-4
Song: "O Happy Day, That Fixed My Choice"

July 4 is important to Americans, for on that day in 1776 the Declaration of Independence was signed. However, other important events in American history have occurred on the same date. For example, in 1802 the U.S. Military Academy opened at West Point, New York; in 1817 construction began on the Erie Canal; in 1848 the cornerstone of the Washington Monument was laid; in 1881 the Tuskegee Institute opened in Alabama; and in 1934, at Mount Rushmore, George Washington's face was dedicated.

What is your special date? If it's a day of joy, then it might be your birthday or your child's birthday or your wedding anniversary? Or if it's a day of sadness, then it might be the day that a loved one died.

We all have our own ideas about what is the most important day. But as Christians we certainly agree that the day of our baptism shines bright on the calendar! Though the actual dates may vary—and you may not even remember the specific day—it's what actually occurred that matters. Paul called it the "day of salvation," and that made all the difference—an eternal difference.

Father, it is perhaps hard to believe that one day's decision for salvation can have so much meaning, but I see the action from Your viewpoint today. What seemed like a decision had its basis in the suffering and death of Your Son. In His name, amen.

Go and Sell!

"One thing you lack," he said. "Go, sell everything you have and give to the poor, and you will have treasure in heaven. Then come, follow me" (Mark 10:21).

Scripture: Mark 10:17-27
Song: "All to Jesus, I Surrender"

"Congratulations, You have been appointed to Samoa" the telegram read. Living in Samoa from 1977 to 1997, an adventure of different languages, people groups—and definitely different interpretations of the Bible—became our way of life.

At our garage sale we told people we were going 5,000 miles away and could only take a container 6' x 8' x 4'. We sold, we gave to the poor, and we left.

Whatever Jesus asks us to do, always remember that He looks at us and loves us. He loves us for who we are, not for what we do. But if we love Him, we need to do what He wants.

Sell all! We want to hang onto a little bit instead of giving all. In our Scripture, the young man couldn't turn loose of what he loved, thus gaining only what he could not keep. He did not trust God to provide. He held too tightly to the things of the world.

That was the young man, but what about you? "Go, sell": Are you willing? What, exactly, would that mean for you in the days and months ahead?

Lord, help me this day to be willing to let go of what I am counting on for my security, my self-image, and my identity. Today I look to You for all my needs. In Christ, amen.

August 25–31. **Francine Duckworth** of Brush, Colorado, has written for several devotional publications over the years.

Be Kind to Him?

He is kind to the ungrateful and wicked. Be merciful, just as your Father is merciful (Luke 6:35, 36).

Scripture: Luke 6:34-38
Song: "Be Ye Kind to One Another"

"Give, and it will be given to you" was the verse I wanted to use for this devotional piece. So often I had given, and the Lord had given back. That's easy to write about! But be "kind to the ungrateful and wicked"? That's a little harder to handle.

A young mother of three asked us to watch her boys over night. I said, "No," because I knew what she wanted to do with that night. But God seemed to say, "Yes." Did He want me to be kind to the ungrateful and wicked?

I was kind, though I wanted to give her a less-than-kind lecture. *Lord, You know I want people like her to get their just reward. They have milked the system, gotten more than they should have from churches. They have used my car, my gas, and my house.*

The Lord seemed to ask: *Whose things are these?*

Oh, You are right, Lord, they are Yours. You have given them to me so that I might be kind to the ungrateful and wicked.

The very next verse in our Scripture passage calls us to be merciful. *Strong's Exhaustive Concordance of the Bible* says, "Mercy is an essential quality of God." If it is an essential quality of God, then it needs to be an essential quality of mine.

Dear Father, would You please replace this frustration and disgust with people who are wicked and ungrateful with Your loving kindness? Help me to be kind the next time I work with folks who aren't particularly lovable. Show me my own sin, my own unworthiness of Your salvation, for which I am eternally grateful. Through Christ, amen.

Review Them?

If I give all I possess to the poor and give over my body to hardship that I may boast, but do not have love, I gain nothing (1 Corinthians 13:3).

Scripture: 1 Corinthians 13:1-7
Song: "Love Divine, All Loves Excelling"

"Review 1 Corinthians 13:4-8" the contract said. I didn't need to review those verses; I lived them! *I'm the leader of this Bible study,* I said to myself. I'm a missionary, a real one, in the South Pacific. We distribute clothes and food to families, help in the church and community. A real missionary . . . or was I?

Lord, are You trying to tell me something? Do I need to review those verses like the contract said?

I read somewhere to put your name in the place of "love." Do I live by these verses? Can I put my name in the place of love? Let's try it!

Francine is patient . . . Lord help me.

Francine is kind . . . though not all the time.

Francine does not envy, does not boast, is not proud. . . . but . . . Francine is not rude, is not self-seeking, is not easily angered, keeps no record of wrongs . . . however . . .

I didn't have to go on. I knew these statements weren't true. On my knees, going over those verses one by one, I asked the Lord to make His love flow through me, that the character of His Son might blossom, more and more. Love, then give. Love, then teach. Love, then help. Love, then be a missionary.

Jesus, You are the example of pure love and compassion. Let Your love flow through me this day. Through Christ, amen.

Show These Men!

Show these men the proof of your love and the reason for our pride in you, so that the churches can see it (2 Corinthians 8:24).

Scripture: 2 Corinthians 8:16-24
Song: "They'll Know We Are Christians by Our Love"

Paul wanted the Corinthians to prove their love for him! Forty-one years in ministry, 48 years of marriage, 68 years old—and my husband and I were feeling God calling us somewhere else. The Lord had worked in many ways over the year. We'd seen His love poured out to others in marvelous ways. But after almost 15 years as ministers of this church, it was time to leave.

Lord, show the new minister and his family, the community—anyone who comes and visits—the proof of Your love! For 15 years we tried to point people to Jesus and not to us. We wanted them to fix their eyes on Him and His love.

Through the years we had started projects, gotten excited about legitimate things. But our prayer was that people would accept Jesus, look to Him, and live by God's Word.

A friend mentioned that they had been going to church all their life. But they had never gone this long to a church without some big problem. You know what can happen. A church can split; brothers and sisters can argue, get upset with someone, and leave. So, I invite us all today: Let's look inside our hearts and inside our churches. Do we need to fix our eyes on Jesus so others will see the proof of our love?

Lord, You are with us. Help us to fix our eyes on You and let Your love flow through us to others. In Jesus' precious name, amen.

Finish the Arrangements

I thought it necessary to urge the brothers to visit you in advance and finish the arrangements for the generous gift you had promised. Then it will be ready as a generous gift, not as one grudgingly given (2 Corinthians 9:5).

Scripture: 2 Corinthians 9:1-6
Song: "Give of Your Best to the Master"

Pledges, promises, and commitments need to be kept. Yet reverses come, jobs are lost, children get sick. Nevertheless, as much as it is within us, we need to keep our word.

It seems that Paul wondered whether the Corinthians would keep theirs. Is that why he sent "the brothers" ahead of him? Yes, he sent them so the Corinthians would be ready.

It makes me consider today: Am I ready to follow through with all that I've promised or pledged?

Paul was talking about a gift. But I've been in charge of a program or project and not finished it. In a moment of emotion I have said, "I can do that." Then, later I have said, "I can't."

We want God to bless people we're planning to minister to . . . then other good things come along, pulling our focus to something else. A commitment unkept!

Someone needs to go to the doctor or a single mom needs you to help with her children. Let's keep our word whether it involves a monetary gift, an act of kindness, or a project. Let's finish the arrangements and just do it.

Almighty and everlasting God, I want to give my best to You. Remind me that all I say and do is a direct reflection upon You. So please help me to give what I said I will give and do what I said I will do. In Jesus' name, amen.

Two Sides of Goodness

Do what is just and right. . . . Do no wrong or violence to the foreigner, the fatherless or the widow, and do not shed innocent blood in this place (Jeremiah 22:3).

Scripture: Jeremiah 22:1-9
Song: "I'll Tell the World That I'm a Christian"

As a young mother, I was discouraged, thinking I'd never do "big things" for God—never be a missionary, give large sums of money, or lead a national ministry. Then I began to understand God's two basic instructions for pleasing Him. One, we should actively seek to benefit others; two, avoid creating pain.

These ideas were small, but within my ability. And when I looked for ways to apply them in my world of children and chores, the change became very "big" indeed. I'd been raised in an abusive home, and I'd continued rather vehement disciplinary practices. But now I could remind myself to "do no violence" as a way to please God. I found creative ways to order my home without the slaps and yells that had become so common.

On the other side, looking for ways to actively help encourage my children became an enjoyable challenge. You see, preparing a warm drink for a sick five-year-old is an act of worship that makes God smile. I might not be changing the world for Jesus, but I am changing my part of His world, one kind word and one good deed at a time.

Lord, as I move through the coming day, open my eyes to see the good I can do for others. I pray in the name of Jesus. Amen.

September 1–7. **Elizabeth Baker** is a retired counselor drawing on 35 years of experience helping individuals apply biblical principles to real-life situations. She currently lives in Pittsburg, Texas.

DEVOTIONS®

September

"So you will be my people, and I will be your God."

— Jeremiah 30:22

Gary Wilde, Editor   **Margaret Williams,** Project Editor   Photo iStockphoto | Thinkstock®

DEVOTIONS® is published quarterly by Standard Publishing, Cincinnati, Ohio, www.standardpub.com.
© 2013 by Standard Publishing. All rights reserved. Topics based on the Home Daily Bible Readings,
International Sunday School Lessons. © 2011 by the Committee on the Uniform Series. Printed in
the U.S.A. All Scripture quotations, unless otherwise indicated, are taken from the *HOLY BIBLE,
NEW INTERNATIONAL VERSION®. NIV®.* Copyright © 1973, 1978, 1984, 2011 by Biblica. Used by
permission of Zondervan. All rights reserved. *The New King James Version.* Copyright © 1982
by Thomas Nelson, Inc. *King James Version* (KJV), public domain. *Contemporary English Version* (CEV), © 1991, 1992, 1995 American Bible Society. *The Revised Standard Version of the
Bible* (RSV), copyrighted 1946, 1952, © 1971, 1973. *The New Revised Standard Version* (NRSV)
(Anglicized Edition), copyright 1989, 1995 by the Division of Christian Education of the National
Council of the Churches of Christ in the United States of America. Used by permission. All rights
reserved.   Volume 57 No. 4.

Nothing the Boss Wouldn't Do

The LORD said to me, "Proclaim all these words in the towns of Judah and in the streets of Jerusalem: 'Listen to the terms of this covenant and follow them. From the time I brought your ancestors up from Egypt until today, I warned them again and again, saying, "Obey me"'" (Jeremiah 11:6, 7).

Scripture: Jeremiah 11:1-10
Song: "Lead On, O King Eternal"

When I saw that the man parking cars was also my boss, I couldn't help but stare. Why was Dr. Gene Getz spending his Saturday at a women's retreat doing hot, dirty work for which few others would volunteer? When I first became part of his large staff, I was surprised to find that budget concerns, scheduling conflicts, and personnel issues arose in ministry work, just as in business. But as I watched our senior minister take orders and sweat in the sun as 500 women arrived—all needing parking space and luggage help—I realized a wonderful difference between business and this ministry: an emphasis on people. Thus, my boss led by example. He certainly didn't ask others to do what he himself was unwilling to do.

When God gave Jeremiah the discouraging task of calling a stubborn, rebellious people to repentance, it wasn't a work He, himself, refused to do. The Almighty had been calling the people for generations. And in love, He called them still.

Father of all glory, how wonderful it is to know that You humbled yourself, through the incarnation, to walk where I walk, feel what I feel, and do work very similar to my own. May I see the nobility in all work You give me to do each day. I pray in the name of Jesus, Son of God. Amen.

Everything in Its Proper Place

The lofty looks of man shall be humbled, The haughtiness of men shall be bowed down, And the LORD alone shall be exalted in that day (Isaiah 2:11, *New King James Version*).

Scripture: Isaiah 2:10-19
Song: "O Praise Ye the Lord"

The abundant, healthy blooms in the hanging basket were ample payment for all my careful tending. Pruning and watering had brought them life, but the nitrogen and phosphorus snuggled firmly at their roots made the real difference. What a glorious display of purple and white!

These same elements provide bounty for supper tables all across the world. Yet, when such fertilizers—both chemical and organic—leave the land and enter the ocean, death can result instead of life. The nutrients feed algae which, in turn, may grow beyond their natural boundaries. Eventually, the overabundant green sucks oxygen away, creating "dead zones" in the water.

God created all things—but with order and limits. Why? Because order gives life. There's a place for everything, each filling a spot perfectly, according to His design for the whole.

The Lord also reserves a proper place for himself. If we're to enjoy life to the fullest, let us exercise our freedom within the boundaries He has set and honor the proper place of everything. This includes honoring the holy place of exaltation that is reserved for the one who created everything.

Holy Creator, cause us to know the proper place You have given to all things and people. Teach us to honor each other and respect Your earth as we stand in awe of Your holiness. I am so thankful for Your wise creativity! In Jesus' name, amen.

The Place of Communion

Go down to the potter's house, and there I will give you my message (Jeremiah 18:2).

Scripture: Jeremiah 18:1-10
Song: "Open My Eyes, That I May See"

Richard Foster's words in *Celebration of Discipline* played over and over in my mind: "In contemporary society our adversary majors in three things: noise, hurry, and crowds." How often had I resolved to be alone with the Lord daily, only to have my commitment quickly fade? Worries, anxieties, and responsibilities were the reasons I needed time with Jesus. Yet these very things kept me away. Was there no way to solve the dilemma?

Finally, I admitted there would never be a consistent *time* slot for me. Life moved too quickly. Schedules constantly shifted. However, I could prepare a consistent *place*, and I was pleasantly surprised to find that, when the place was ready and waiting, shifting moments of time became easier to utilize.

When both the children and our house were very small, the only private space was the family bathroom! And it had a lock. I could store Bibles and devotional material in a basket. A prayer list and notepad hid in the medicine cabinet. Years later, my "place" was a corner of the bedroom, complete with lamp and scented candle. Now, it is often my garden.

But where is your place? Like God agreeing to meet Jeremiah at the potter's house, Jesus is always waiting there for you.

Father, how wonderful to know that the God who's dwelling place is unapproachable light has seen fit to condescend and meet me in a place of prayer! Help me to hear Your voice that I may be guided by Your Spirit this day. In the name of Jesus, amen.

He Wants to Be Found

Then you will call on me and come and pray to me, and I will listen to you. You will seek me and find me when you seek me with all your heart (Jeremiah 29:12, 13).

Scripture: Jeremiah 29:10-14
Song: "Room at the Cross for You"

As a professional counselor, I was amazed at how often married couples argued because each wanted the other to accept them and understand them. Yet, so often, neither was willing to risk exposing their true needs and desires. "If you really love me," you'll automatically choose the right present, say the right things, and understand my deepest unspoken needs. Teaching couples to risk disappointment by clearly stating their needs was a constant challenge. Few were ready to change.

Thankfully, God doesn't "love" in such a secretive way! The almighty Creator is more than willing to be known. In fact, sometimes the openness of God is frightening as He reveals His holiness and desire for heartfelt worship. God never compromises right or overlooks evil.

But these aren't the only motivations that cause Him to act. When God opens His heart to Jeremiah, He reveals His compassion, tenderness, and a longing to provide good things for those He loves. Best of all, He conveys a grand promise: If we are willing to seek, He is more than willing to be found.

Immanuel, You are the God who is with us and desires to be found by every seeker. Teach me to honor everything You have revealed about yourself. And stir in my heart a desire to know You better each day. In the name of Jesus, amen.

They Kept Praying

But after I uproot them, I will again have compassion and will bring each of them back to their own inheritance and their own country (Jeremiah 12:15).

Scripture: Jeremiah 12:14-17
Song: "Revive Us, O Lord"

I grinned as Facebook pictures filled the screen. Nathan stood with a gun over one shoulder and the end of a long pole balanced on the other. A couple of well-armed friends balanced the other end, and between them hung some small game animals. The message read, "Tacos for dinner tonight!"

I shook my head. My nephew's journey had been a long one. Although raised in church, Nathan had drifted into drugs and theft in high school. His family prayed, but Nathan continued to drift. The drugs became harder, the crimes more serious. But amidst the car wrecks, lost jobs, failed rehabs, and brushes with the law, his family kept praying.

Then a change began to take root. While on parole, he decided to attempt five years of staying clean while jumping through every hoop and paying every fine the government demanded. His family kept praying as Nathan's drift changed to an upstream battle for a new life.

Freedom day came. The judge expunged his record, and Nathan walked out of the courthouse sober, clean, and free to join a mission team struggling in Sudan, Africa. And yes . . . his family kept on praying.

Lord, teach me to wait patiently, even in discouraging situations. No situation is beyond Your redemption, and no person beyond Your reach! In Jesus' name, amen.

Letters of Hope

Write in a book all the words I have spoken to you (Jeremiah 30:2).

Scripture: Jeremiah 30:1-3, 18-22
Song: "Spirit Divine, Attend Our Prayer"

I was going through a particularly wearisome time of spiritual dryness. I wasn't even sure I wanted ever to write again. It was too much hard work, too little reward. God had many excellent writers in His fold; He didn't need me.

Then I pulled an old prayer journal from the shelf and began thumbing through it. What I found changed my world. As I read my prayers, I was amazed at how many victories slipped quietly into the past without my notice. Problems had been solved. Growth had taken place. Moods had changed.

Yet, I had taken so little notice. Where had I been when *that* prayer was answered? Why didn't I notice when my cloudy mood was lifted?

I pulled down another journal. Forgotten memories surfaced like neglected friends. Over and over they testified that the choices I made and prayers I prayed had made a difference. The clouds of discouragement began to lift. Why had I thought new dreams, new prayers, and new horizons weren't worth pursuing? It was like coming up from under water and taking a gulp of fresh air. Memories of answered prayers pointed the way to a new future.

Lord, remind me of where I have been, lest the marvelous things You have done slip by without notice. Today may I hold on to those victories from the past—and be encouraged by them—that I might gain courage for tomorrow. In Jesus' name, amen.

There's a Better Way

But in fact the ministry Jesus has received is as superior to theirs as the covenant of which he is mediator is superior to the old one, since the new covenant is established on better promises (Hebrews 8:6).

Scripture: Hebrews 8:1-7, 13
Song: "Jesus, My Strength, My Hope"

"There's got to be a better way!" How many times have I uttered that desperate cry when trying to fix a leaking pipe under the sink . . . or looking over the clumsy first draft of an assigned devotional piece? (Sometimes that's a much bigger challenge.)

I once served as a delegate to a group with both lay and full-time ministry representatives. We were stuck on an issue, vote after vote. Finally, a "better way" was shown to us by a surprising source. "Let's get on our knees and pray to the Lord for the answer," said a wealthy CEO. The next vote carried decisively.

But such challenges are small compared to the better way of Hebrews. The writer hoped to persuade recent converts to stay the course of the new covenant. Some were wavering. He used the word *better* often to make his case—twice in the sentence of Scripture quoted above and 13 times in the whole book. Of course, the point of all these "betters"—better hope, better angels, better promises—is that now God has spoken to the people through His own Son rather than mere prophets.

Almighty Father, help me guard against complacency in the good life You have granted me. Urge me to keep searching for better ways. In Jesus' name, amen.

September 8–14. **Phillips Huston** is a retired editor and writer living in Naples, Florida. He does write novels in his spare time, though, and enjoys singing in the summer choir.

My Anonymous Hero

He did not enter by means of the blood of goats and calves; but he entered the Most Holy Place once for all by his own blood, thus obtaining eternal redemption (Hebrews 9:12).

Scripture: Hebrews 9:11-15
Song: "Jesus Calls Us"

In our newspaper occasionally there's a letter thanking an anonymous person for a favor: Someone stopped and changed a tire for a distressed elderly couple and then drove away; another found a wallet, looked up the owner, and delivered it with money and cards intact—and declined a reward. These are everyday acts of Christian kindness done by unsung heroes.

I have an anonymous hero: the unknown writer of the book of Hebrews. He wrote such beautiful and persuasive words to wavering early Christians. It's a sustained argument about the superiority of the new covenant to the Judaism they had been raised on. The writer intended to keep backsliders within the Christian fold, and the message still sustains us, 2,000 years later, with words like these: So "that those who are called may receive the promised eternal inheritance" (v. 15).

Was my anonymous hero successful with the earliest Christians? He must have been. Christianity continued to flourish in those first decades after Jesus (probably before AD 70). To me, the author of the book of Hebrews belongs in the pantheon of greatness, maybe just a notch or two below Peter and Paul and the gospel writers.

Heavenly Father, make me aware of opportunities where I can effectively lend a hand, not for acclaim but for simply doing Your will. In Jesus' name, amen.

No Comparison!

Our competence comes from God. He has made us competent as ministers of a new covenant—not of the letter but of the Spirit; for the letter kills, but the Spirit gives life (2 Corinthians 3:5, 6).

Scripture: 2 Corinthians 3:4-11
Song: "Fight the Good Fight with All Thy Might"

Ever needed to accept the "uncertain new" for the "comfortable old"? It's difficult! In making a move to a new city, for instance, it can be challenging to learn to relate to the unfamiliar minister in our new congregation. "He's OK, I guess, but he's certainly no brother Ted," we may say (and elaborate, too). In dealing with changes, Christians sometimes forget their strongest resource for help and discernment is prayer, not gossip; encouragement, not a critical spirit.

But the adjustments we undergo are nothing compared to what those first-century, Jewish Christians were asked to believe. In effect, they were told, "You no longer need to make animal sacrifices: Jesus' sacrifice is sufficient for all your sins. Instead of shunning the Gentiles, you will treat believing Gentiles as family. You will no longer please God by keeping the letter of the law, but by being guided by His indwelling Spirit."

Can you imagine the adjustment? It was such a radical departure, it's no wonder Paul resorted to a sledgehammer approach: "For the letter kills, but the Spirit gives life." Praise be that Paul was tough! Praise be that his listeners believed!

Heavenly Father, give me a listening ear to help me understand and accept change the way the early Christians did. Thank You for their example! In Jesus' name, amen.

Homecoming!

Behold, I will bring them from the north country, and gather them from the coasts of the earth, . . . a great company shall return thither (Jeremiah 31:8, *King James Version*).

Scripture: Jeremiah 31:7-11
Song: "Going Home"

Homecoming! What a warm and wonderful word. Going back to your 25th high school reunion . . . enjoying periodic gatherings of family . . . welcoming back prodigal sons, biblical and modern. I especially enjoy seeing men and women, some battered, coming back from serving in the military in remote lands. And in today's Scripture reading, God himself, through Jeremiah, promises a glorious homecoming for the remnant of Israel.

There's one potential homecoming I'd like to facilitate but have not been very successful at doing. That's bringing home into the Lord's welcoming tent former church members who have strayed away. These are people of my own generation and especially those of the following two generations. Their parents did their jobs, but in our increasingly secular world, the parental guidance hasn't stuck.

Of course, I need to realize that every one who has left isn't *ready* to return. And I must learn to identify those who may be ready but may not realize it. Then I can share in a very special homecoming—the return of good people, one or two at a time, to an active, reciprocal love in God's tent.

O Lord God of Heaven and earth, give me a discerning mind and a facile tongue so that I can help return strays to the fold. Remind me that You haven't given up on them or me! Through Christ I pray. Amen.

A Garden: Nearer God's Heart

They will be like a well-watered garden, and they will sorrow no more (Jeremiah 31:12).

Scripture: Jeremiah 31:12-17
Song: "The Garden of My Heart"

At the Bok Singing Tower in Florida, an inscription by Dorothy Blomfield reads, "One is nearer God's heart in a garden than anywhere else on earth." How true! I'm retired, but in the workaday world there was no time I felt closer to the Lord than when messing about in our garden when I got home. Oh, I could search Him out in other places, but out in the garden I was always aware of His presence—from the miracle of the planted seed to the harvest.

Our garden had a lot going for it: space, full sun, fairly good soil (for Connecticut)—but also rabbits, woodchucks, and deer. So when we produced a decent little crop, the beans, tomatoes, and carrots somehow tasted better than those we bought at roadside stands of "real" farmers. Our own impatiens, iris, and tulips seemed more beautiful. And today my granddaughter, cooped up in a tiny apartment in a metropolis, similarly exults in triumphs with herbs in her window boxes.

The Bible begins in a garden and continues with agricultural metaphors for good things throughout. In today's Scripture Jeremiah rejoices over God's love in terms of the grain, wine, and young sheep. And, for him, a watered garden stands for the ultimate in the good life.

Heavenly Father, thank You for harvests that nourish our bodies. Lead me to ways to share Your bounty with those less fortunate. In Jesus' name, amen.

Saying You're Sorry

After I had turned away I repented (Jeremiah 31:19, *New Revised Standard Version*).

Scripture: Jeremiah 31:18-25
Song: "Redeemed, Restored, Forgiven"

Charles "Chuck" Colson was one of the major figures in the Watergate scandals that brought down the Nixon White House. He was convicted of his crimes and served time in a federal prison. As Colson faced arrest, a friend gave him a copy of *Mere Christianity* by C. S. Lewis. Colson read it, and that lead him to become an evangelical Christian.

In prison he became increasingly aware of injustices done to prisoners and was overwhelmed with the need to do something. After his release Colson founded Prison Fellowship to promote prison reform and prisoner rehabilitation. Over the years he wrote more than 30 books, had a radio program, and won a million-dollar prize for progress in religion. All prizes, fees, and royalties were turned over to Prison Fellowship.

Chuck Colson wonderfully personifies repentance, a foundational tenet of the Christian faith. Even three-year-olds learn that saying "I'm sorry, Mommy," will get them back in Mommy's good graces. When adults find themselves in situations where they too must say they're sorry, it isn't as easy as it is for toddlers. We know, so much better than they do, that appropriate actions must follow, proving the sincerity of our words.

Dear Lord, I know that when I sin against my neighbor I sin against You. Accept my repentance and my desire to serve You. Then give me the courage and strength to carry through on my intentions to live in a new way. In Your name, amen.

The Original Futurist

Behold, the days are coming, says the LORD, when I will make a new covenant with the house of Israel and the house of Judah (Jeremiah 31:31, *Revised Standard Version*).

Scripture: Jeremiah 31:31-37
Song: "There Is a Green Hill Far Away"

Writers of the nineteenth and early twentieth centuries such as Orwell, Verne, and Wells based their novels on predictions of life in the future. But consider how their fantasies have been eclipsed by the realities of the computer, space travel, and heart transplants.

However, the revolutionary prophesies of one writer, about 26 centuries earlier, have held up perfectly. Through Jeremiah, God forgives Israel for the broken Sinai Covenant, looks ahead to a homecoming for the remnant, and foresees a new covenant based on forgiveness and love. Thankfully, the New Testament, foreseen in the book of Jeremiah, became a reality under God's forgiving hand and His Son's sacrifice.

When I visited the Sistine Chapel, I saw Jeremiah staring down at me from the ceiling, along with other major biblical figures (and God himself). The great prophet looks exhausted and sad. Perhaps Michelangelo was depicting Jeremiah as the author of Lamentations rather than the exciting prophet of the new covenant in Jeremiah chapter 31.

Who am I to criticize the greatest painter/sculptor the world has known? But I do wish he'd painted his Jeremiah a little more upbeat. He proclaimed a bright future for God's people.

Lord, whose example of forgiveness to Your people stands as a model for us, help me through "forgive and forget" situations with an admired friend. In Christ, amen.

He'll Lead You Out

You brought your people Israel out of Egypt with signs and wonders, by a mighty hand and an outstretched arm and with great terror (Jeremiah 32:21).

Scripture: Jeremiah 32:16-23
Song: "His Love Endures Forever"

Which of the following sounds like a big challenge to you: moving to a different city? leading a small group? changing your negative thought patterns? deciding what to do in retirement? Advancing into new territory can be scary, even when we know it will be change for the better. In the movie *The Shawshank Redemption*, the character "Red" (played by Morgan Freeman) powerfully portrays such a challenge.

Having been in prison for decades, Red has certainly spent a lot of time dreaming of freedom. And yet, when finally released to live as a free man, he becomes lonely, helpless, and discouraged. Red depicts the part of verse 21 above about beginning his new life "with great terror."

Thankfully, Red had some help. His friend and former prison mate invited him to join him in a new venture in a beautiful, faraway place. Red willingly accepted.

While new territory can be frightening in its uncertainty and instability, remember that the Lord is able to lead you out with "signs and wonders." You don't have to be afraid.

Father, just as You led the Israelites out of Egypt, so You are able to lead me into new territory with Your mighty hand. Praise to You, through Christ. Amen.

September 15–21. **Karis Pratt** has a song for everything, speaks three languages, and lives in Seattle, Washington, land of great outdoor activities and beautiful sunsets.

Turn Towards God

They turned their backs to me and not their faces; though I taught them again and again, they would not listen or respond to discipline (Jeremiah 32:33).

Scripture: Jeremiah 32:26-35
Song: "Hosanna (Praise Is Rising)"

My mother told me about when I was a toddler and wanted to touch a hot stove. In order to teach me that it was dangerous, she lightly slapped my hand when I reached for it. But I seemed to think it was a game and reached again. Another slap—this time a little harder. This continued until I was nearly in tears from the painful slaps, but I still thought I was just playing a game. Don't we do this sometimes with God? We are drawn to things that aren't good for us and even put our hope in them, rather than in the Lord. He may try to show us a better way, to draw us back to Him. But we naively ignore the warnings and continue in our unhealthy patterns. We turn our backs to Him, and though He teaches us "again and again," we do not listen.

Take a moment to think about an area of your life where you are running into obstacles. Is it possible that God is using those difficulties to get your attention? Consider whether He may be trying to call you back on course. As an old English proverb says: "A smooth sea never made a skillful mariner."

Almighty God, show me an area of my life where You want to get my attention and draw me back to You. Open my eyes to anything that I have mistakenly put my hope in. Help me to be open to Your teaching and correction, that I might repent and walk in righteousness, keeping my face turned towards You. In the name of Jesus, amen.

I Want to Be One of Those!

In that day the remnant of Israel, the survivors of Jacob, will no longer rely on him who struck them down but will truly rely on the LORD, the Holy One of Israel (Isaiah 10:20).

Scripture: Isaiah 10:20-25
Song: "Faithful Men"

Does the word *remnant* sound more like cookie crumbs or leftovers than something great you want to be a part of? A couple of movie examples may help us understand who the *remnant* really are. In the movie *The Matrix,* most of humanity has been deceived by machines about what is real. But a few people remain who know the truth, and they launch a risky mission to restore a true existence on earth. In *Invasion of the Body Snatchers,* aliens begin taking over the humans until it seems there will be no one left who has their own free will or knows the truth.

Even though we aren't (apparently) in danger of being taken over by machines or aliens, surely there are forces at work trying to distract us from the truth. Media and advertising can lead us to believe that a new product, activity, or relationship will bring us the ultimate fulfillment. Even something that is good can distract us from what is significantly better.

I plan to commit today to being one of the remnant. It's a moment by moment decision, I realize. But I want to be one of those who will not stray from God's truth ever. I want to continue walking in obedience and service to Him.

Lord, every day I face questionable interpretations of reality. I confess that sometimes they draw me in. But I praise You for revealing truth through Your Word! Help me use it to confront falsehood that I may be one of the *remnant*. In Christ, amen.

Actions Reveal the Heart

They will be my people, and I will be their God. I will give them singleness of heart and action, so that they will always fear me and that all will then go well for them and for their children after them (Jeremiah 32:38, 39).

Scripture: Jeremiah 32:36-44
Song: "Step by Step"

Have you noticed how much better things seem to work out when your heart and your actions are on the same page? I see this when I have an event to go to.

In my heart I want to arrive exactly on time . . . I think. But I get distracted while getting ready—I will check my e-mails, wash up some dishes, or make one more cup of tea. Suddenly it's time to leave, but I'm still not dressed, and my hair is a mess! I end up being stressed out all the way to the event where, of course, I arrive late.

In today's key verse, God gives His people the gift of "singleness of heart and action," which will lead to a healthy fear of their Lord. And besides that, "all will go well for them."

Today, let us consider whether we could exercise more singleness of heart and action in our relationship with the Lord. James 1:8 calls double-minded people "unstable in all they do." So I ask myself: In what areas of life does my heart want to do God's will . . . but my actions say something different?

Lord God Almighty, sometimes my actions don't line up with what my heart truly wants. Please help me to recognize when I do this. Help me to align my actions with my deepest desire to serve and please You. And thank You for Your grace and great patience! In the name of Jesus my Lord, amen.

Unity of the Spirit

In that day the Root of Jesse will stand as a banner for the peoples; the nations will rally to him, and his resting place will be glorious (Isaiah 11:10).

Scripture: Isaiah 11:1-12
Song: "He Reigns"

There is something quite moving about the opening ceremonies of the Olympics. For a few weeks, athletes from each country, regardless of their politics or religious beliefs, join forces under their respective national flags, united. Their mission? To perform their absolute best in a physical contest for their homeland. The Olympic symbol unites athletes from every nation under the ideals of sportsmanship and the pursuit of excellence.

In our Scripture passage, Isaiah refers to the coming Christ as a banner for the peoples: "The nations will rally to him." On that day, the thrill of the Olympics won't compare to the great drama of people from every nation uniting under Jesus.

Let us not forget that this is God's great desire and that one day it will come to pass. Today, meditate on what this means to you—to know that you will one day join hands with countless believers very different from you. Whether it's your neighbor who cheers for rival sports teams or someone from the opposite corner of the globe, you will be united. The current invisible unity of our fellowship in the Holy Spirit will one day become fully evident to the whole universe.

Lord, it's awesome to imagine the visible unity that all believers will share one day. Help me to keep this grand perspective in all my relationships, especially with those who seem very different from me. I pray in the name of Jesus. Amen.

A Reason to Sing to the Lord

For he has done glorious things; let this be known to all the world (Isaiah 12:5).

Scripture: Isaiah 12
Song: "Praise the Lord!"

I have a song for everything. Almost any word, phrase, or action can inspire me to burst into song. What makes you sing?

I heard about a mission team ministering in Mongolia. While traveling through an especially desolate area, they sensed that the Holy Spirit was leading them to stop, set up their musical equipment, and sing worship songs. Even though it seemed odd for them to perform with no audience to hear them, they obeyed the prompting. When they sang, they were certainly singing for a good reason—to proclaim the glorious things God has done, simply because He is worthy of praise.

But not far from the team's location were some nomadic people who were hidden from their view. When the music began, they came and heard about the Lord.

Consider some of the "glorious things" God has done for you. Some of these things might be aspects of His loving providence, in which He keeps the world going, causing the sun to rise each morning and the rains to fall. Others might be specific: a new job, a healed relationship, or some kind of breakthrough that came to You through His indwelling presence. Determine to sing to the Lord, thanking Him for these things. And look for a way to tell someone about what God has done for you.

Father, You have done glorious things, both in my life and all throughout history. Thank You for the many blessings that I now name before You. Through Christ, amen.

Help Me Wait!

Take these documents, both the sealed and unsealed copies of the deed of purchase, and put them in a clay jar so they will last a long time. For this is what the LORD Almighty, the God of Israel, says: Houses, fields and vineyards will again be bought in this land (Jeremiah 32:15).

Scripture: Jeremiah 32:1-9, 14, 15
Song: "Standing on the Promises"

Have you ever had to wait a long time for some good thing? What kept you hopeful? I remember how hard it was for me, as a child, to wait for a big event. If my parents told us we would be taking a trip some two or three months in the future, I seemed to suffer for years before that time would come!

Christmas, of course, always felt as if it would never come. But something kept our hope alive—the promise from someone we trusted. Even if we grew weary in the waiting, we believed our parents' promises and could continue to hope for their fulfillment.

In our passage today, God's promise that the Israelites would one day return to their land is symbolized by a deed in a jar. We may not always have a tangible symbol of God's promise, but we do have God's Word as our hope. If you are tired of waiting for something in your life, look to God and His promises. He is trustworthy, and His word is true. So why not ask the Lord to give you a Scripture to hold on to this day?

Dear Lord, thank You for Your Word. You are trustworthy, and You keep Your promises. It is hard for me to continue to wait for the things I need, but I now commit to standing on Your promises and renewing my hope in You. Through Christ, amen.

Nothing to Do With It

In repentance and rest is your salvation, . . . but you would have none of it (Isaiah 30:15).

Scripture: Isaiah 30:9-17
Song: "Trust and Obey"

My son Joshua loves animals and enjoys watching documentaries about them. He asked to watch a television show about crocodiles that was advertised for a Friday night. I told him it came on after his bedtime and that he would need a nap when he came home from school. He agreed.

That Friday was a beautiful day, and when Joshua wanted to play outside and ride his bike, I reminded him about the show and his need for a nap. "Oh, I can make it. I'm so excited I won't go to sleep," he said. Encouraging the nap a couple of more times, I decided to let him choose.

Later, we brushed our teeth, put on pajamas, and sat down, awaiting the anticipated documentary. Five minutes prior to the show, though, Joshua fell asleep. My husband asked, "Wouldn't take a nap?"

"He would have nothing to do with it," I said. I knew he wouldn't have the energy to stay up; I had watched him too many times.

Our Lord watches us and knows our ways. As He did with His chosen people, He does with us today. He calls, pleads, and gives instruction. He doesn't want us to miss any good thing.

Father, You know me better than I know myself. You know my needs before I do. Help me to repent, rest, and trust in You when You lead me to do so. In Christ, amen.

September 22–28. **Carol Bradfield** lives in LaGrange, Georgia, with her husband, Jim, and their two sons, Joshua and Jacob. She's a mother, a Sunday school teacher, and worship team member.

Remember Him

Does a young woman forget her jewelry, a bride her wedding ornaments? Yet my people have forgotten me, days without number (Jeremiah 2:32).

Scripture: Jeremiah 2:26-32
Song: "Take Time to Be Holy"

At a family gathering, several relatives noticed my 15-year-old niece looking at a bridal magazine. Granddaddy asked her if she were getting married soon. She said, "No, just *planning* my wedding." I smiled. I had started planning my wedding around her age. Most young girls dream of their wedding and study dresses, shoes, hair styles, and jewelry far in advance.

Young ladies in biblical times planned also. Once the betrothal was announced, the groom added more room to his family's house. The bride planned what she'd take with her when he came to take her home and considered what she'd wear on the wedding day.

Her friends would loan her jewelry, for she'd be adorned gloriously. A bride, in those days, would not forget her wedding ornaments, just as a bride today wouldn't forget to wear her wedding dress.

I'll never forget my own wedding day. But I have to admit that I rarely think about it. And it makes me realize: Our days can become so busy that we walk through them without a thought for the Lord, as well. When have we remembered Him last? When have we spoken with Him last?

Lord, forgive me when I forget You. You have led me, protected me, and provided for me. You love me. You deserve my appreciation and attention. In Christ, amen.

Calling Us Home

You are unfaithful children, but you belong to me. Come home! (Jeremiah 3:14, *Contemporary English Version*).

Scripture: Jeremiah 3:11-15
Song: "Jesus Is Calling"

Cathy was 16 when she ran away from home with her boyfriend. The couple went to Hollywood to become movie stars and to live a romantic life. Her parents were heartbroken. They had worried about her relationship with the young man and had even forbidden it. Now their worst fears had come true.

They tried to stay in touch with her, though. They sent her letters and money, praying she'd use it wisely. They continued this for a couple of years, despite rarely hearing from her. Then one day they received a letter. Her boyfriend had left for another relationship, but she didn't want to come home.

Her parents continued to correspond, send money, and invite her home. After some time, they received a letter of apology and a request to return to them. They bought her ticket and met her when she arrived.

There are many reasons we could walk away from the Lord, for years or for mere moments—anger, unbelief, disappointment. For whatever reason we may have walked away, if we'll listen closely we'll hear a heavenly call to come home. A merciful Father looks for us, awaiting our return and actively hoping to lead us once again. The Scripture gives us His attitude: I am not willing that any should perish (see 2 Peter 3:9).

Father, forgive my wayward heart. Your heart is to lead me with wisdom and knowledge. Increase my faith and help me be faithful. Through Christ the Lord, amen.

What's in the High Place?

Surely the idolatrous commotion on the hills and mountains is a deception: surely in the LORD our God is the salvation of Israel (Jeremiah 3:23).

Scripture: Jeremiah 3:19-23
Song: "I Worship You, Almighty God"

After I graduated from college and obtained a good job, I worked hard to create a substantial savings account. Although I benefited from some scholarships while in college, I still had to work part-time to pay for gas, school supplies, and my share of the phone bill. I counted pennies.

So when I graduated, I wanted to know there was money in the bank that could "bail me out" of some unforeseeable event. It made me feel secure.

I thought about it and talked about it often. It became an obsession, virtually an idol. Wasn't God enough for me?

I used to think the Israelites were crazy to make an idol and then worship it. The hills and mountains, the high places, resounded with their sounds of worship. Then I realized how I had done something so similar in spirit.

Having a savings account is fine and prudent, of course. Putting my security there and giving it a higher place than God was not. Today I try to remember: What, really, am I trying to build? Am I giving anything a higher place than God in my life?

Lord God, help me keep You as Lord of all in my heart. Help me keep my focus and reliance upon You. Help me worship You alone. Show me where my heart is, and keep it focused on bringing glory to Your name in my words and deeds. Nothing else and no one else can save me. I pray in the name of Jesus, amen.

Lift Me Out

Heal me, LORD, and I will be healed; save me and I will be saved, for you are the one I praise (Jeremiah 17:14).

Scripture: Jeremiah 17:12-17
Song: "Healing Waters"

My 5-year-old son loves to help me wash my car. He flits back and forth from the car to the bucket of suds. One day while I was rinsing the car, he ran just as I pulled the hose. It pulled his feet out from under him and his bottom landed in the bucket.

"Mama, help!" he cried. I turned to see him seated up to his knees in the bucket, kicking his feet. He was trying to lift himself out without any success. He then looked at me with outstretched arms. I, of course, lifted him out and set him back on his feet.

Stuck in anything today? a situation at work, an illness, or physical challenges? an addiction, a financial situation, or a family problem? We are helpless to heal the hurts or to save ourselves.

Thank Heaven we have a God who longs to heal and promises to save. The Lord helps those who can't help themselves. That's the whole message of the cross, isn't it? Born trapped in sin and death, we need salvation. We have a benevolent Savior who bends down to help and lift us up. He can heal and He can save. And He is worthy of our praise.

O God, Creator of Heaven and earth, I cry out to You in my need. Thank You for the salvation You have already provided and for the grace to help me with my current situation. May my life and lips praise You! I pray this prayer in the name of Jesus, my Savior and Lord. Amen.

It's Who You Know

Let the one who boasts boast about this: that they have the understanding to know me, that I am the LORD, who exercises kindness, justice and righteousness on earth, for in these I delight (Jeremiah 9:24).

Scripture: Jeremiah 9:17-24
Song: "Knowing You"

A couple stopped their car at an apple orchard, and a worker in faded overalls greeted them. The couple told him how the kind orchard owner said they could have some apples. The worker asked them how many they'd like. "Oh, two baskets full will be fine," they replied.

As they picked, the worker asked how they knew the owner. He listened as they told of being old family friends; in fact, they'd just spoken with him in the local hardware store. The man helped them to the car, smiled, and said, "I'm that kind orchard owner, and you may have these apples as a gift from me today. But do not come here boasting about knowing me again."

The red-faced couple quickly left. The owner had a reputation for being kind, and he was kinder than expected.

We can brag about many things and tell about who we know. God wants us to be unashamed about knowing Him—and to boast that we do. Before we can, though, we must truly know Him—His kindness, justice, and righteousness. Best of all, we should understand how much He delights in us as we are growing to be like His Son, Jesus.

O God, I'm proud to know You and to be known as Yours. You are kind and just. Teach me to know You more and to share You more. In Jesus' name, amen.

Clean and Beautiful

I will cleanse them from all the sin they have committed against me and will forgive all their sins of rebellion against me (Jeremiah 33:8).

Scripture: Jeremiah 33:1-11
Song: "You Make Beautiful Things"

I loved painting with Joshua when he was a toddler. It didn't matter whether we used brushes, sponges, or our fingers. I loved watching him mix colors, make bright snakes, and create lopsided crocodiles.

One day while painting, he thought it was fun and funny to paint his hands, face, and clothes. "That's enough!" I said. "Paint on paper or we'll put the paints away."

He looked at me. His eyes narrowed. His lips curved slightly. The monster lifted his arms and pounced. Before the battle ended, I had paint in my hair and on my hands, arms, and shirt. Small globs splattered on the floor, table, and chairs. He smeared it on the wall and bathroom door as I monster-handled him in there. I washed him, changed his clothes, and made him sit down. I cleaned walls, floors, table, chairs, and clothes. I can attest that a little rebellion goes a long way!

Despite it all, the paints came back out again later. More great works were created and displayed for all to see. Similarly, despite our acts of rebellion, God cleanses and forgives. He longs to make beautiful things with us, in us, and through us for all to see.

Gracious Father, help me see what You see today. Help me see the beautiful things You want to paint in and through my life. In Jesus' name, amen.

Surprising Grace

Look at the nations and watch—and be utterly amazed. For I am going to do something in your days that you would not believe, even if you were told (Habakkuk 1:5).

Scripture: Habakkuk 1:1-5
Song: "Guide My Feet"

Do you ever struggle with a negative inner voice? That inner critic, the can't-be-pleased-no-matter-what perfectionist, always finds fault and constantly puts us down. When we think "enemy," we most often picture the barbaric flesh-and-blood types. But what of our inner enemy?

Continually fighting that inner critic is draining. Habakkuk must have felt frustrated in the face of his enemy too, yet God promised to do something that he would never believe possible.

As an obese child, I learned early to criticize myself. But two years ago, when I returned to running after the birth of our son, I heard God encouraging me to challenge myself further, to become an endurance athlete. "Me?" I wanted to laugh. My name and the word *athlete* hardly go together. But over two years, God has shown me, again and again, that depending on Him for mental, emotional—and yes, physical strength—helps me grow.

I take one step, then the next, certain that He never leaves me. Even when the critical voice becomes loud, I keep looking forward, ready to be "utterly amazed."

Father, help me to hear Your voice, even in the middle of my doubts and fears. Remind me that You created me to trust You. In Jesus' name, amen.

September 29, 30. **Joy Choquette** enjoys exploring her faith in relation to fitness and food, and she blogs about her adventures. She and her family live and play in Swanton, Vermont.

Habakkuk's Second Complaint

You have made people like the fish in the sea, like the sea creatures that have no ruler (Habakkuk 1:14).

Scripture: Habakkuk 1:12-17
Song: "The Love of God"

I remember a particularly sunny afternoon in the lake as a child. I was wearing my first pair of swim goggles. Gently, I'd slip beneath the water's surface, not wanting to disturb the sandy bottom. Imagine my surprise when, in the shallow waters where I played, something moved out of the corner of my eye — a fish!

I watched the area closely and saw not one, but two, then three, and then a whole school of silvery fish. They darted in toward the shore, then back out again toward deeper water. I followed them, swimming close to the surface so I could draw in breaths.

What are some attributes of fish? That they're helpless, silent, defenseless? All true. As Habakkuk points out in verse 14, God made us "like the fish in the sea." Not a very flattering comparison, is it?

But whatever our surroundings, however disturbed, afraid, worried, or confused we are, let us remember that God is in control. He's in control when life is going smoothly and we're healthy and happy, and even when, like a school of fish, we move in a panic, driven more by fear than faith.

Father, there is so much to fear in today's world. Remind us, please, that You hold us in Your loving grasp. No matter our circumstances, You are everlasting and will never leave us. Thank You, in the name of Christ. Amen.

My Prayer Notes

DEVOTIONS®

October

I am under vows to you, my God;
I will present my thank offerings to you.

—Psalm 56:12

Gary Wilde, Editor   **Margaret Williams,** Project Editor   Photo iStockphoto | Thinkstock®

DEVOTIONS® is published quarterly by Standard Publishing, Cincinnati, Ohio, www.standardpub.com.
© 2013 by Standard Publishing. All rights reserved. Topics based on the Home Daily Bible Readings,
International Sunday School Lessons. © 2011 by the Committee on the Uniform Series. Printed in
the U.S.A. All Scripture: quotations, unless otherwise indicated, are taken from the *HOLY BIBLE,
NEW INTERNATIONAL VERSION*®. *NIV*®. Copyright © 1973, 1978, 1984, 2011 by Biblica. Used by
permission of Zondervan. All rights reserved worldwide. *New American Standard Bible* (NASB),
© The Lockman Foundation, 1960, 1962, 1963, 1968, 1971, 1972, 1973, 1975, 1977, 1995. Holy
Bible, *New Living Translation* (NLT), © 1996, 2004, 2007 by Tyndale House Foundation. Used by
permission of Tyndale House Publishers Inc.   Volume 57 No. 4.

Is God Down on Me?

Why call me Naomi? The LORD has afflicted me; the Almighty has brought misfortune upon me (Ruth 1:21).

Scripture: Ruth 1:12-21
Song: "His Eye Is on the Sparrow"

The young woman seated near me at the writer's conference was thin, stylishly dressed, and to top it off, completely kind and friendly. Instantly my inner judge points out all these attributes. It was hard not to feel inferior.

But as we exchanged bits of personal information between bites of salad, she said, "I'm hoping to publish a book about the experience of my daughter's death." I sit, fork midway to mouth, stunned. Her infant daughter had died in her arms, she explained, as I mumbled how sorry I was.

"God brought me through it," she replied, "and I feel called to write this book, to give another mother strength."

Have you ever felt that God has turned His hand against you? I've never experienced anything as painful as what this woman went through. But I've certainly felt abandoned by God at times and questioned His motives.

Naomi, whose name means "pleasant," thought God was afflicting her. But she became the ancestor of a king. More importantly, she experienced God's love and comfort through her daughter-in-law Ruth and ultimately from her Father himself.

Father, so often I don't understand the "why" of things. Be with me in these moments and help me feel Your presence and peace. In Jesus' name, amen.

October 1–5. **Joy Choquette** enjoys exploring her faith in relation to fitness and food, and she blogs about her adventures. She and her family live and play in Swanton, Vermont.

Would I Keep Trusting?

"Your sons and daughters were feasting . . . when suddenly a mighty wind swept in from the desert and struck the four corners of the house. It collapsed on them and they are dead, and I am the only one who has escaped" (Job 1:18, 19).

Scripture: Job 1:13-21
Song: "'Tis So Sweet to Trust in Jesus"

I have a confession to make: I avoid the book of Job because it makes me feel like such an insufficient Christian. My faith is fairly strong. But if I found out my family had been killed and oh, by the way—my bank accounts and retirement, funds had been liquidated—kneeling down to worship God probably wouldn't be my first reaction. *Would I still be able to believe?* I wonder.

We wrestle with this question, wonder if we'd be up to the task, then pray we never have to find out. There are other hurts that cause us to question God too: the promotion at work we should have gotten, given to someone else; the checkbook balance screaming zero when there is still a stack of bills to pay; the medical diagnosis that we can't believe is real.

When experiencing a hurt, a tragedy, or a scare, we face a serious decision: do we trust God or turn away? Trusting doesn't mean that we slap a smile on our face to cover what we're thinking and feeling. No, it simply means being completely open with God. We keep the relationship going, looking for Him to show the way through.

Father, thank You for Your love that continues, no matter what. I can trust in You, knowing that You'll never leave or forsake me. Help me to stay open and truthful with You, no matter what my circumstances. Through Christ I pray. Amen.

Help for the Anger

Because of their wickedness do not let them escape; in your anger, God, bring the nations down (Psalm 56:7).

Scripture: Psalm 56:1-7
Song: "There Is a Balm in Gilead"

We all have days when it feels like our enemies are in hot pursuit, don't we? Whether it's a conflict with a child's teacher, an unjustified reaming out at work, or simply an irate driver in the car behind us, we often pray, "Lord, make that person act differently!"

What's easily forgotten is that in every conflict, we play a role: it could be large or very small, depending on the situation. David says, "When I am afraid, I put my trust in you" (v. 3). That seems like an odd feeling to experience: fear in the midst of the anger he surely harbored toward his persecutors. That seems true until we look deeper. Anger is often a mask for fear—fear that we might not get our way, that others might be judging us unfairly, or that our pride will be hurt.

When we feel the heat of anger, it grows like wildfire. But let's remember the rest of David's comment, "I put my trust in you." No matter how justified our anger is in the day-to-day, our responsibility as Christians is to turn that emotion over to God. It's often quite hard to do, but asking for His help in the middle of our fiery rage can make all the difference.

Father, You have more reason than any of us to be angry, disturbed by all that's wrong in the world. But still You love me and offer me a chance in each and every moment to begin again. Help me to remember Your healing power and offer up my anger to You that I may direct it to righteous ends. In the name of Christ, amen.

Prescription for Joy

I am under vows to you, my God; I will present my thank offerings to you (Psalm 56:12).

Scripture: Psalm 56:8-13
Song: "Great Is Thy Faithfulness"

Imagine a groom standing at the altar who tells his bride, "I'll probably stick with you . . . most of the time." Or if, standing before one's military squadron, a soldier pledges allegiance to his/her country and his/her new band of sisters and brothers, "When it's not too inconvenient."

Granted, it's tough to keep our vows, yet we expect those who utter them to take them seriously. But suppose one has come "under vows" to God, as the psalmist states? Is it a hopeless endeavor?

I like to think that I'm under vows to my Lord in this way: I'm pledged to be thankful every day for the chance of a new life through Christ. I hope to remain obedient to His Word and to continually keep my focus on Him and His desires.

I don't always succeed, of course. Yet committing to our heavenly vows requires the same traits as committing to our earthly vows: faith, loyalty, love, and patience.

In spite of our failures to be perfectly consistent in our desires to please God, we can hold onto this: because of our commitment, we will have a better life. We have given ourselves to a transcendent cause. That is always a prescription for deep joy.

Father, thank You so much for the opportunity You've given me to become one with You through Jesus. Strengthen my commitment to love, honor, and serve You this day and every day. In Jesus' name, amen.

Lead Me . . . This Way!

Though the fig tree does not bud and there are no grapes on the vines, though the olive crop fails and the fields produce no food, though there are no sheep in the pen and no cattle in the stalls, yet I will rejoice in the LORD, I will be joyful in God my Savior (Habakkuk 3:17, 18).

Scripture: Habakkuk 2:1-5; 3:17-19
Song: "They That Wait Upon the Lord"

God calls us, then often asks us to wait. Have you noticed that? My writing career has often known that pattern. I worked full-time that first year and made a somewhat decent living. *It's all going to be up from here,* I thought.

It wasn't. The next year the economy collapsed, and we had a baby. Still, I hoped that once that second challenging year was out of the way, my career would take off.

It didn't. But despite the twists and turns, the red eyes, and the slim margins in our checkbook register, I can pinpoint when things changed: when I gave my writing hopes over to God, asking Him to lead. This differs from the prayers I'd prayed countless times before: "Father, please lead me . . . but here's the direction I'd like to go."

Henry Blackaby says that God can make things happen in days or weeks that we'd struggle with for years on our own. But sometimes His answer is "wait." Our responsibility during those times of waiting isn't to sit and do nothing, but to draw closer to Him and follow His lead.

Father, I'm so impatient to make things happen! Help me remember that Your plan is much more perfect than anything I could dream up. Through Christ, amen.

Just Us

Have pity on me, my friends, have pity, for the hand of God has struck me (Job 19:21).

Scripture: Job 19:13-21
Song: "In the Garden"

I stood in the doorway and watched the white Chevy S10 disappear through the trees. I was alone. As a widow, I found it devastating to lose my last child to college.

The forest echoed my sobs. My daughter had been my main companion. My brother never called, I didn't fit in with the "widow groups," and my friends had their own families to attend. I was an outsider, and God seemed uncaring.

I sank into self-pity like a comfortable bed and pulled the covers of despair over my head. I tried to understand, but human reasoning couldn't solve my problem. It wasn't until I entered the presence of God that I knew: He wanted to restore me in the quiet woods of my home. It was a time to heal and be alone with Him before moving into new areas of service.

I entered the sanctuary of God in my heart. There mysteries are solved, plans revealed, and love given. I marvel that here God meets me and gives me His undivided attention. In this place, it is just He and I. Knowing that the Creator of the universe loves me so intimately erases doubt and self-pity. I'm filled with unspeakable joy.

Lord, Your presence waits for me in my inner sanctuary. This intimacy with You calms my spirit and comforts me beyond all things. Thank You, in Jesus' name. Amen.

October 6–12. **Barbara Durnil** is a retired medical worker and a freelance writer in Southern Idaho. Listening to God and writing His voice is her joy and passion.

Look and Wait

Why do You stand afar off, O Lord? Why do You hide Yourself in times of trouble? (Psalm 10:1, *New American Standard Bible*).

Scripture: Psalm 10:1-11
Song: "The Rock That Is Higher Than I"

The water foamed against the banks of what had been a quiet ripple of a river. I'd crossed earlier on a large stone that parted the water circling a dry platform. Now, however, that rock hid beneath whitewater and debris. I gulped as I realized I could no longer see the stone; it was gone. *How will I return?*

Reason replaced fear, though, for I knew the rock was still there, just concealed from my eyes. I needed only to wait and trust that the water would recede.

Another person on that same path might say, "There is no stone on which to step, so I will swim across. I am a strong swimmer and can conquer the current." He would miss the danger of the granite that he could not see. Though others warned him, he might scoff and dive to his death in the torrent.

I trust that God is there, even when the water runs high and I cannot see Him. He gives me faith to wait on Him in times of trouble. The water recedes, and He then leads me across to the other side.

Have you lost your "rock" momentarily? God is not gone . . . look closer and wait on Him.

Father God, may I never doubt Your presence. Make me always aware that You are near. No matter what I think I need to do in my own strength, remind me that waiting for You is better than going it alone. In Christ's name I pray. Amen.

The Right Choice

Is there any God besides me? No, there is no other Rock; I know not one (Isaiah 44:8).

Scripture: Isaiah 44:1-8
Song: "The Shadow of the Rock"

I opened the closet door, and the contents seemed to mock me. There stood the bottles of cleaners, each one with a promise of immaculate perfection. The instant food choppers, magic lint removers, and the phenomenal marble-sucking vacuum cleaner all claimed space.

Abandoned in the corner were the rubber bands, twirling discs, bouncing balls, squeezy springs, collapsible platforms, and mountains of videos, all guaranteeing a slimmer, tighter me in 30 days. Obviously, I fell for every "as seen on TV" promise, and now the worthless items consumed my closet.

The advertising was mostly false; the items were of little value. I needed some truth in my life, and I knew where the real truth could be found. I closed the door and went to the genuine article, the only one that I trusted. I placed my full confidence in God, knowing He would not fail me.

There is nothing false about God. I can stand on His promises, assured they do not fail. The rest can be discarded as worthless trash . . . all those idols that promise satisfaction, joy, and wealth in my future. God is a living, true Lord. He is my rock. Over all else, He is the right choice.

O Father, my God and my Rock, there is no other God that is the first and the last. There is no other God that is trustworthy and true. I trust all Your promises; help me never be distracted by false claims and worthless ads. Through Christ, amen.

Wings of Protection

Have mercy on me, O God, have mercy! I look to You for protection. I will hide beneath the shadow of your wings until the danger passes by (Psalm 57:1, *New Living Translation*).

Scripture: Psalm 57:1-6
Song: "Under His Wings"

"I don't know what I did!" I sat at my desk confused and hurt. This morning's board meeting was brutal. Why the attack? After relocating to the city, I accepted the position offered to me on the board of a women's organization. It wasn't a difficult decision, for I'd held the same position before, and this board needed to fill the slot.

I felt growing animosity from the president, however, and this morning the "spear hit the wall." She seemed threatened by my presence.

Following God doesn't guarantee peaceful coexistence, even in the church. Every Christian eventually meets his or her "Saul," who is determined to do battle. The reason may be unclear, but the conflict can be cruel and relentless.

I knew it wasn't time to grab my sword and fight. Instead, I looked to God for protection and hid in Him until He resolved the matter. To wait for God's help from Heaven is better than going to war with little defense, only to return bloody for the effort. Under the shadow of His wings is a good place to be . . . until the storm passes.

Lord, how thankful I am that You protect me! I watch the wild duck gather her babies under her against storms and danger. They disappear from view and are warm and secure. This is how I feel under Your protection. Thank You, in Jesus' name. Amen.

My Decision

My heart, O God, is steadfast, my heart is steadfast; I will sing and make music. Awake, my soul! Awake, harp and lyre! I will awaken the dawn (Psalm 57:7, 8).

Scripture: Psalm 57:7-11
Song: "I Will Sing of the Mercies of the Lord"

The police officer stood in front of the classroom, and six-year-olds stayed riveted to their seats as the man in full uniform repeated his words. "Now, what are you going to do if a stranger grabs you?"

Hands shot up around the room. They knew the answer; they'd been practicing all morning. Their plan was set. My son, as an adult, once told me, "Mom, if I play the scene in my mind and rehearse the actions, I don't falter when the need comes, I know what to do." The "stranger/child" teaching had followed him into adulthood.

Some decisions need to be set-in-stone beforehand. These include making up our minds about what we believe and what action that decision dictates. My own life is adjusted by that commitment. When events contradict that predetermined choice and threaten to tumble me, I don't have to reconsider my options.

God is who He says He is. He does not go away when storms come. To set my heart and determine to stand will anchor me. I will sing and make music. I will awaken the dawn with praise. I will stay true to my God.

Thank You, **God,** that You are my anchor. Accept my song and music as a joyful sacrifice to You. Help me awake with You in my heart, lighting the day with a flood of devotion for who You are and all that You mean to me. In Christ I pray. Amen.

The Correct Gift

Ascribe to the LORD the glory due His name; Bring an offering, and come before Him; Worship the LORD in holy array (1 Chronicles 16:29, *New American Standard Bible*).

Scripture: 1 Chronicles 16:28-34
Song: "With Gladness We Worship"

I hung up the phone and glanced at the clock. I didn't need to, though, for I had been watching the minutes throughout the conversation. It wasn't that I didn't want to talk with Dad, but I was busy. His birthday was next week; I could get him something then. I remembered the fly rod advertisement. It was hi-tech and very expensive. I could drop the rod off before work.

A week later, I fumed with anger. No recognition of the gift came to me. The problem, however, wasn't Dad, but my gift. It was unacceptable. To give him the honor due him, the rod needed to be exchanged. What he wanted and deserved was devotion. Only the offering of time, conversation, love, obedience, and honor was good enough.

My Lord God is my heavenly Father, arrayed in majesty far above what I can comprehend. To recognize His strength and glory is the first step to understanding the magnitude of the offering due Him.

Everything belongs to God, except my choices. The acceptable offering, then, is not money or things. It is my choice to honor Him with a personal relationship.

O God, how can I truly understand Your glory? To see a particle of dust and to imagine the end of the universe and everything that lies between only begins to reveal Your majesty. I choose to worship You with the offering of myself! In Christ, amen.

Define the Battle

"How long will you torment me and crush me with words? . . . As for me, I know that my Redeemer lives, and at the last He will take His stand on the earth" (Job 19:2, 25, *New American Standard Bible*).

Scripture: Job 19:1-7, 23-29
Song: "The Battle Belongs to the Lord"

"I think you should resign your position; you are unfit for the job. You don't have the intelligence for it." What? *Where did that come from?*

She continued her assessment of my abilities and character as I stood there, blindsided and helpless. How could she say that? People were being helped. We had the day care and mothering classes. We were tutoring students and providing counseling. How dare she talk to me that way! I was ready to attack. But wait, *Where did that come from?*

Maybe the source went deeper than the woman standing before me. Who stood to lose most by people becoming better students and mothers? Who would be most angry with improved lives . . . individuals leaving darkness and walking in the light?

It was not this ambitious socialite. The source of this assault was spiritual, and I needed to change the target of the counter-attack. I needed to turn to my Redeemer and let Him go before me into battle.

Praise to You, **O Lord God of all!** The outcome of the battle is already settled. I need not be afraid, for I know You are in control. I gladly place myself in the chorus to blow the trumpet and sing the praise. The victory is Yours, through Christ my Savior and Lord. Amen.

Go Out and Eat Worms?

"At least there is hope for a tree: If it is cut down, it will sprout again, and its new shoots will not fail. . . . and its stump die in the soil, yet at the scent of water it will bud and put forth shoots like a plant" (Job 14:7-9).

Scripture: Job 14:7-13
Song: "I Know That My Redeemer Liveth"

The short story *The Lady or the Tiger?* and Shel Silverstein's *The Giving Tree* reign as classics of children's literature. The first has no closure, although I recall having to write a short paper on what or who came from behind the door. Being a little girl, I chose the Lady, and the happy duo "lived happily ever after." (That's not the ending the little boy who sat next to me wrote.)

I liked *The Giving Tree* no better; with its sad ending. I didn't yet know the truth about trees that Job relates in this passage. "It will sprout again" and "at the scent of water it will bud." When times of suffering come, I begin to think like Job. I either mentally put on sackcloth and ashes or wonder if I should go out and eat worms. In other words, I have myself a pity party.

How foolish! Centuries lay between Job's complaint and the death and resurrection of Jesus Christ. Here I sit, centuries on the other side of that triumphant fact. For Job, his redeemer was only anticipated. No need for me to go out and eat worms.

Lord, remind me of all that lies ahead in Your plan for the world. Keep my heart and mind focused on Your promises of no more pain, sorrow, or sighing. Thank You that You keep Your promises! In the precious name of Jesus I pray. Amen.

October 13–19. **Katherine Douglas** and her husband, Mark, live in rural Fulton County, Ohio. She enjoys drinking sweetened, iced coffee while writing.

This Holds Onto Me

If someone dies, will they live again? All the days of my hard service I will wait for my renewal to come (Job 14:14).

Scripture: Job 14:14-22
Song: "I Know Who Holds Tomorrow"

My dear friend, Debbie, experienced a crisis of faith two years ago. She said later that, had anyone asked her if she still believed God had all things in His control and that He could be trusted, she would have answered, "I'll have to get back to you on that." Her despair was a dark hole from which the prayers of those who love her—and God's boundless grace—ultimately restored her faith.

After Job lost everything, he too almost reached that point of hopeless despair. The amazing thing is that he never quite did. Throughout the book that bears his name, hope—however slight and transient it seems in the narrative—always sneaks in.

Even in today's passage, centuries before Christ defeated sin and death by His atoning sacrifice and resurrection, Job still affirmed, "I will wait for my renewal to come . . . you will cover over my sin" (vv. 14, 17).

I have not been where Debbie has been. Nor have I suffered to the extent of the patriarch Job. But like Job, I know where my help comes from. "My help comes from the Lord" (Psalm 121:2). That's what I hold onto today and what—more importantly—holds onto me.

O God, when I'm at my lowest point, hear my cry to You. When I feel I can't hold on any longer, please hold me, gracious God. I know You alone understand my pain, and I throw myself on Your mercy. In Jesus' name, amen.

No Matter the Cost

LORD, you understand; remember me and care for me. Avenge me on my persecutors. . . . think of how I suffer reproach for your sake (Jeremiah 15:15).

Scripture: Jeremiah 15:10-18
Song: "Find Us Faithful"

An angry mob besieged the home of a minister and his family about 30 miles from the city of Bangalore, India. Laxmi Gowda, an independent Christian minister, suffered painful injuries. The 2007 attack consisted of beating the man in front of his wife and two children, then throwing kerosene on him and attempting to set him afire. Eventually, a mob of a thousand paraded him through the streets, naked.

Why this horrible abuse? The local police claimed the attackers didn't want Christian prayers and meetings to take place in Gowda's house. "We have asked the Christians to give us a complaint in writing, but they don't want to press charges against the attackers," he said.

Being Christ followers can become costly and torturous for any of us at any time. God's people have always known persecution. Jeremiah, for instance, died in exile among his people, who were driven from their land. As I survey world news today, I don't have to look far to see suffering Christians who daily encourage me in my own walk with the Lord. I want to delight in the Word of God all my life too—no matter the cost.

Father, I pray for fellow believers who suffer for the name of Christ. Protect them from evil. Shield them by the power of Your name. Give them a glimpse of Your glory—and help me too, O God, to persevere through difficulty. In Jesus' name, amen.

Bring on the Rain

Do any of the worthless idols of the nations bring rain? Do the skies themselves send down showers? No, it is you, Lord our God (Jeremiah 14:22).

Scripture: Jeremiah 14:14-22
Song: "There Shall Be Showers of Blessing"

Raised in the suburbs, I never knew about digging or having a well. When my husband and I built our first house in the country, my education about wells and well water began. "You'll have to hire someone to witch a well," my sister-in-law said. A dull lightbulb went on in my head. Did she mean hiring someone to use a "divining rod"?

I thought she was kidding, but she wasn't. I didn't know such practices continued today, even in the western world. It's done routinely, I learned.

She and my brother had done just that when they had to dig a new well on their property. My husband, however, was adamant about not using a "witcher."

"That comes from witchcraft," he told me. "I won't do it. I'm going to pray and ask God to show me where we should dig."

Long story, short: we ended up with the best water and water pressure in our part of the county. When I take a nice, cool drink, I remember: Whether it comes from an underground spring, a lake, or the sky, God alone supplies the thirst-quenching water of life.

God, I know that You alone control all things. When times of drought or flood or other natural disasters come, help me to be a person of prayer and not complain or panic. Thank You that when I'm helpless, You remain all powerful! In Jesus' name, amen.

A Safe Place?

I would flee far away and stay in the desert; I would hurry to my place of shelter, far from the tempest and storm (Psalm 55:7, 8).

Scripture: Psalm 55:1-8
Song: "Where Could I Go?"

Michelle and her family were on their way home from vacation when the sky took on a sinister look. They'd just arrived at a fast-food restaurant. When they got out of the car, the swirling clouds and a heaviness in the air alerted them to danger.

Inside, the restaurant manager was calm but insistent. "There's a tornado warning, and danger is imminent," he said. "Everybody get into our walk-in freezer. It's our safest place." Michelle, her family, and a half dozen other people did as the manager suggested. Then they waited.

The devastating twister struck only a short distance from where the strangers huddled and prayed in their chilly refuge. Devastation surrounded the restaurant, but none of them had been harmed. One couple's car was damaged, but drivable. Michelle and her family were able to continue on their way.

David wanted to seek shelter in the desert wilderness, away from the "violence and strife in the city" (55:9). He knew the desert, not usually a friendly place, would be a safe place now. But a fast-food restaurant's freezer? Thankfully, God provides for us as He sees fit.

Lord, You know that my world is a frightening place sometimes. I ask for Your calm assurance and peace. Please protect me and my loved ones from violence and strife. Help me remember that You hear when I call out to You. In Jesus' name, amen.

Betrayed!

If a foe were rising against me, I could hide. But it is you, a man like myself, my companion, my close friend (Psalm 55:12, 13).

Scripture: Psalm 55:12-23
Song: "No, Not One!"

An American couple we know of lived in the Middle East for several years. Because the government in the country where they live and work is hostile to Christianity, they were discreet in sharing the gospel. They finally reached a point, however, where they could host a small house church with Bible study and prayer.

One of their early converts served alongside them. He was one of the first with whom they had shared the message of new life in Christ. His eagerness about the gospel and his partnership with them encouraged them in their ministry.

But then, he went to the local media with his story. He had faked his Christianity all along! He was neither their friend, nor a Christian. The other nationals in their group had been put in grave danger, and soon the couple's attempts to bring light to a dark place ended. For the safety of the new believers, they disbanded their study group.

Some of us have been shocked and hurt by those we considered trusted friends. Jesus knows what such betrayal is like. He can sustain us when we've been deceived.

Dear Lord, I want to be a faithful friend to all who depend on me. I pray that I never betray a confidence. Thank You that You are trustworthy, and You understand like no other when I'm hurt by friends who prove to be false. In Jesus' name, amen.

Where's the Justice?

God drags away the mighty by his power; . . . He may let them rest in a feeling of security, but his eyes are on their ways (Job 24:22, 23).

Scripture: Job 24:1, 9-12, 19-25
Song: "Tell It to Jesus"

In his book *Your God Is Too Safe,* Mark Buchanan tells of a godly friend for whom nothing in life seems to go right. This self-employed tradesman works hard, does good work, and treats his customers well. He does the task he's hired to do and never lacks for projects. What he does lack for is . . . payment!

His customers end up paying him less than agreed upon, or not at all. It doesn't stop there. Disasters seem to plague him. The car breaks down. The water heater needs replacing. His children only add fuel to the fire by doing things that wound him. He loves God and God's Word, and he lives it out. Yet he still finds himself a victim, time after time after time.

Job begins this chapter today asking, "Why does the Almighty not set times for judgment?"(v. 1). When the good suffer and the evil don't, we cry out for justice.

Yet justice doesn't always come speedily. Sometimes it doesn't come at all in this life. What happens all too frequently to the hardworking tradesman will likely continue to happen until God's justice comes. Yet the Word of God promises us: someday it will cascade down. We can count on our just God.

God, I thank You that You are king and judge of all the earth. When I fall victim to injustice, help me remember that You know and see all. Strengthen me, O God, to wait on You. In the powerful name of Jesus I pray. Amen.

By His Wounds We Are Healed

My friends and companions avoid me because of my wounds; my neighbors stay far away (Psalm 38:11).

Scripture: Psalm 38:9-15
Song: "O Sacred Head Now Wounded"

Our minister recently told a story about a missions trip he participated in when he was a teenager. During this visit to Africa, he met a little boy who was said to have leprosy. No one hugged, kissed, or even shook hands with the child. He was an exile, even among his own family members. Our minister's cousin eventually broke down and hugged the child but didn't catch any kind of disease. It turned out that, through a translation error, the child's *epilepsy* was misinterpreted as leprosy.

Although He bore no illness or sin, Jesus was deserted by His friends at a crucial time. In fact, the great apostle Peter claimed he didn't even know Jesus (see Luke 22). Of course, when no angry crowds were present, Peter trusted Jesus, even to the point of walking on water for a time. Yet once Jesus was vulnerable, the disciple deserted his Lord.

The wounds Jesus' endured enable Him to identify with our suffering. Jesus is God in the flesh, yet His hands and feet bear scars. When we are wounded in body, mind, or spirit, let us remember that Jesus is the friend who will not desert us. He has the scars to prove it.

Lord, thank You for the scars on Your hands and feet. They are tangible proof of how much You love me. Thank You for suffering for my sins. In Your name I pray. Amen.

October 20–26. **Lisa Earl** teaches online writing courses from her home in western Pennsylvania. She enjoys ice skating and spending time with her husband and young sons.

Sovereign King

All the nations you have made will come and worship before you, Lord; they will bring glory to your name (Psalm 86:9).

Scripture: Psalm 86:1-10
Song: "O Worship the King"

In 2012, political ads for the U.S. presidential election dominated the news media. Politically charged commercials derided both the sitting president and his opponent, often exaggerating their weaknesses. By contrast, proponents of both candidates testified that their man would solve all of the country's problems.

It's easy to look for hope in earthly leaders, but we must be careful. When the Israelites cried out for a king, God spoke through Samuel to warn them about the demands such a ruler would impose on them (see 1 Samuel 8). An earthly leader would become a drain on family, fields, and flocks.

Jesus is a different kind of king—one who gives rather than takes, even to the point of giving His very life for us. And today's passage predicts that all nations will one day acknowledge such heavenly leadership. Every knee will bow and every tongue will confess that Jesus is Lord (see Philippians 2:10, 11).

In our church, the prayer time includes responsive readings. One part of the liturgy asks that Christ would be acknowledged as "sovereign king over all the people." While we look for hope in earthly leaders, our true king—Jesus—is already sovereign.

Lord, help me acknowledge Your sovereignty in my life, family, career, community, country, and throughout the world. In Jesus' name I pray. Amen.

An Undivided Heart

Teach me your way, LORD, that I may rely on your faithfulness; give me an undivided heart, that I may fear your name (Psalm 86:11).

Scripture: Psalm 86:11-17
Song: "God Sees the Little Sparrow Fall"

I recently made an unpopular decision. I stopped posting pictures of my 1-year-old son on social media sites. Once he started walking and stopped napping, I had less "down time" to devote to sharing pictures of him with relatives. (I found myself looking at pictures of him online instead of *looking at my actual baby!*)

I chose to leave the virtual world in order to enjoy the real one. Likewise, today's passage warns against dividing our hearts between God and the world. Just as ignoring my son hurts my relationship with him, neglecting God detracts from the reverence He deserves.

Perhaps God needs us to "unplug" from whatever is keeping us from prayer these days or from spending time in His Word. Thankfully, we have a perfect example to emulate. Our heavenly Father gives His full attention to His creation. Jesus said that not even one sparrow "will fall to the ground outside your Father's care" (Matthew 10:29).

Let us rest assured that our Father is giving us His undivided attention. We can only hope to reciprocate one small portion of that devotion.

Lord, today I hope to turn away from distractions so I can focus on You. Give me a calm heart and a peaceful mind, that I may remember Your abiding presence throughout the day. In the name of Jesus, amen.

Marked from Birth

When you believed, you were marked in him with a seal, the promised Holy Spirit, who is a deposit guaranteeing our inheritance until the redemption of those who are God's possession (Ephesians 1:13, 14).

Scripture: Ephesians 1:11-19
Song: "Gracious Spirit, Dwell with Me"

When my son was born, the first thing the doctor said was, "He has a dimpled chin!" I laughed because I knew exactly where he had gotten this feature — from my husband. The distinctive dimple marked our precious infant as his father's son.

Friends and strangers alike continue to comment about how much little Levi looks like his daddy. Likewise, when we're baptized into Christ, we are set apart with a seal — the Holy Spirit. The world will know that we are sons and daughters of the most high God because of the characteristics the Spirit imparts: "Love, joy, peace, forbearance, kindness, goodness, faithfulness, gentleness and self-control" (Galatians 5:22, 23).

When we doubt God's love for us, let us be reminded of these spiritual "birthmarks" that seal our identity in Christ. Our identity lies in who we are in Christ, not what we do. Even when we sin, we are still God's children.

My husband and I love our son unconditionally (but our human nature limits our patience at times). But God's fatherly love is perfect, and He will never leave us or forsake us. Let us live in light of that promise today.

Heavenly Father, thank You for sealing me with Your indwelling Holy Spirit. Help me to live in such a way that others can see I'm Your child. In Jesus' name. Amen.

Because of His Strength

Truly he is my rock and my salvation; he is my fortress, I will not be shaken (Psalm 62:6).

Scripture: Psalm 62:1-8
Song: "A Mighty Fortress Is Our God"

Martin Luther is often quoted as saying, "Here I stand, I can do no other" when asked to recant his position regarding salvation by faith. Such a powerful statement seemingly came from a man of unwavering strength.

In reality, Luther struggled against depression. He was only able to stand up to the church leaders of the day because his conscience was "held captive to the Word of God." By relying on the strength of God and His Word, this sometimes melancholy man led the Protestant Reformation, transforming not only the church of the day but arguably the entire history of western civilization.

Today's passage reminds us that God alone is our fortress, and our strength comes from Him. We don't need to have it all together or even have the power to face each day on our own. Because of Him, we will not be shaken—not because of ourselves.

Just think what we can accomplish, individually and as a church, when we acknowledge Christ as the source of our strength. The Bible promises that through Christ we can do all things (see Philippians 4:13). What is God calling us to do through Him today?

God, You are my rock, my strength, and my fortress. Guide me in doing Your work today. Through Jesus Christ, who gives me strength, amen.

Tsunami of Sin

When we were overwhelmed by sins, you forgave our transgressions (Psalm 65:3).

Scripture: Psalm 65:1-5
Song: "Love Lifted Me"

In 2011, Japan experienced one of the most powerful earthquakes in recorded history. A tsunami with waves reaching over 100 feet followed, sparking a series of nuclear accidents near shore. The disaster claimed thousands of lives and injured countless others. Cleanup continued for years.

Likewise, sin often overwhelms us, shaking us to our core. Our transgressions cause waves of destruction that overtake us, permeating all aspects of our lives, causing a "heart meltdown." While we might scramble to overcome the consequences of our trespasses, we are powerless to overcome sin and its effects by willpower alone

God offers the way forward: forgiveness—a fresh start. Rather than condemning us for our sins, He forgives us through Jesus Christ. Our heavenly Father sent His son not to condemn the world, but to save it (see John 3:17).

While recovery from natural disasters can take years and cost billions of dollars, forgiveness is immediate and free. The process of sanctification continues throughout our lives, but we can rest assured that God is leading the cleanup effort. We need only surrender to the work of His Spirit within us.

Father in Heaven, create in me a pure heart. Clean up the effects of my sin and restore me to the person You want me to be. I pray this prayer in the name of Jesus, my merciful Savior and Lord. Amen.

Love Your "Frenemies"

After Job had prayed for his friends, the LORD restored his fortunes and gave him twice as much as he had before (Job 42:10).

Scripture: Job 42:1-10
Song: "What a Friend We Have in Jesus"

Modern pop-culture slang is filled with portmanteaus—combinations of two or more words into one new word. One such term that has gained popularity with teens and young adults in recent years is "frenemy." It's an enemy disguised as a friend.

Job's friends strike me as being "frenemies." When they heard about Job's suffering, Eliphaz, Bildad, and Zophar did what most friends would: they left their homes and went to comfort him. Yet their words dripped with condemnation.

Although Job was the most righteous man to be found on earth at that time, his friends assumed his misery must have resulted from his sin. While their advice sounds logical on the surface, it flies in the face of the true nature of God's sovereignty and power.

God called Job to pray for these false friends despite their misleading advice. Earthly friends will disappoint us and even contradict God's Word. Yet only when we forgive them can we truly embrace the riches God wants to impart to us—the richness of His mercy, love, and grace (see Matthew 6:15). What "frenemies" can we pray for today?

Dear Heavenly Father, please forgive my sins, and help me to forgive those who have sinned against me. May they come to know Jesus Christ as Savior and Lord. I pray in His precious, holy name. Amen.

Changing Fear

Oh, that their hearts would be inclined to fear me and keep all my commands always, so that it might go well with them and their children forever! (Deuteronomy 5:29).

Scripture: Deuteronomy 5:23-29
Song: "Savior, Teach Me Day by Day"

As I've matured, my concept of fear has changed. Fear of punishment teaches children right from wrong. My father often used negative fear to make me want to follow the rules, to choose to honor my responsibilities, to do what was right. I vividly recall often pausing at the back door before entering our kitchen. I had to assess if there might be any reason to fear my father's anger that day.

This hesitation continued until I went away for college. Sadly, during those years I feared God my Father too and was so afraid of His potential punishments. Such fear influenced me to make both good and bad choices.

Today's lesson speaks to me of the type of *positive* fear that inspires reverence and worship towards God the Father. Knowing of His great love for me, I understand now why I strive to obey His commandments and follow His rules. It is out of respect and trust, not my old negative fear. Happiness and joy bloom as we trust God on the journey of faith. Have you grown past your negative fear?

Father, I accept Your loving-kindness. You did not give me a Spirit of fear, but a Spirit of power, of love, and of a sound mind (see 2 Timothy 1:7). In Your holy name, amen.

October 27–31. **Joyceanna Rautio** resides in Naples, Florida, and is a business consultant committed to living by Christ's values. She enjoys studying Scripture, international travel, and outdoor adventures.

Sing to the Lord

May they sing of the ways of the LORD, for the glory of the LORD is great (Psalm 138:5).

Scripture: Psalm 138
Song: "Sing Praise to God Who Reigns Above"

As an eager teenager, I rushed to join our church's choir. My motivation? Panic! My minister had given a lesson in Sunday school saying that God would take away the gifts He had given us if we did not use them. At least that's what I *thought* he said.

Having sung duets with my older sister in Christmas pageants, I really believed I could sing. (Actually, my singing was more like making a joyful noise unto the Lord—yet with extra enthusiasm.) A choir member eventually explained that I was neither a soprano nor an alto, so I could not lose a "gift" I had never been given!

Singing in a church choir is a way to offer sincere praise and worship. But singing amidst the congregation can also be a joyful way to bring glory to the Lord.

As I sought other ways to serve, I began to see that my voice could honor God in many other ways: reading Scripture aloud for the congregation, for instance. And I could share joy by visiting the elderly at home, speaking words of comfort.

Have you ever overestimated the gifts the Lord has given you and been disappointed? Or have you perhaps hesitated to seek ways to use your gifts to serve God? Keep seeking. The Lord will always put a willing person to work in His kingdom.

O God, I know You love me and welcome all my off-key songs of praise and worship. Singing or speaking, may my voice always praise Your ways. In Christ's name, amen.

Here I Am, Lord

When the LORD saw that he had gone over to look, God called to him from within the bush, "Moses! Moses!" And Moses said, "Here I am" (Exodus 3:4).

Scripture: Exodus 3:1-6
Song: "Hear Me, O Father"

Were you ever content with your daily life, but God wasn't? Did you ever expect Jesus to ask you to push a "reset button"— to change the direction you so carefully planned to go? It happened to me when I attended a Christ-centered renewal weekend three years ago.

Talk about a life-changing experience! For the first time in my life, I fully experienced the unconditional love of Jesus, and then I understood Pentecost. I always knew the spark of the Holy Spirit was within me, and at times it burned like a campfire or fireplace. Now an intense newness of the Spirit is a raging bonfire within me, and I love knowing that I'm a vessel of the third person of the Trinity, listening for His guidance.

Identifying with Moses, I find that I am eager to say: "Here I am, Lord." And now I want people to know I am a Christian. I placed a fish symbol on my new car. I regularly attend worship services. I became a communion minister and joyfully volunteer to serve at the table. Only God knows where my journey with Christ will go. But it all follows from "Here I am."

Heavenly Father, I am humbled that You sent Your only Son to die for me. I offer my everlasting thanksgiving that Jesus gave His first gift, the Holy Spirit, to the world. As I listen for Your still, small voice, may I hear how You wish me to serve. In the name of the Father and of the Son and of the Holy Spirit, I pray. Amen.

Outdoor Splendor and Majesty

The earth is the LORD's, and everything in it, the world, and all who live in it; for he founded it on the seas and established it on the waters (Psalm 24:1, 2).

Scripture: Psalm 24
Song: "My God, I Thank Thee"

I loved riding a bicycle throughout Yosemite National Park. What a wonderful way to experience God's majesty and splendor in this special place on earth! It was also a perfect way to celebrate the end of my oldest sister's 30-year teaching career in California.

Outdoor activities had always appealed to both of us, so we could hardly wait to settle into our cabin at Yosemite before exploring the grandeur. Taking an early-morning ride, we arrived at the base of Yosemite Falls just after daybreak. How exhilarating to be surrounded by such beauty in God's creation! Only a few visitors were out so early to soak up the magnificence of the cascading waterfalls.

We gave thanks for the peaceful morning quiet of the park, sharing it with the abundant wildlife. In our hectic lives jammed with daily tasks, how often do we stop to recognize the awesomeness of this planet we inhabit? God expects us to luxuriate in His creation as well as to protect it for others to enjoy. Opening our eyes to such a duty will help insure the splendor remains available for generations to come.

Lord God, let me strive to cherish the beauty and riches of the world You've created. Give me the wisdom and will to conserve its resources. Please teach me to be a worthy steward of this fragile earth we call home. In Jesus' name, amen.

The Power of Prayer

In the morning, LORD, you hear my voice; in the morning I lay my requests before you and wait expectantly (Psalm 5:3).

Scripture: Psalm 5
Song: "Savior, Who Didst Healing Give"

I was on a month-long trek, visiting local churches and cathedrals throughout France with my journalist client and friend. Headquartered in Cambodia, Michelle focused on getting interviews for the 50th anniversary of Cambodia's independence from France. My focus? Praying daily for my friend Elizabeth, who was suffering with cancer. Yes, my mission was to light candles and offer up healing prayer in as many churches as we could fit into our journey.

Two memorable prayer opportunities caused me to reflect quietly on today's healing ministry of Jesus. One occurred in the Basilica of Saint Nazaire and Saint Celse, located within the walls of the restored medieval town of Carcassonne in southern France. The other occurred after struggling to climb the endless Great Inner Staircase to the Abbey at the top of Mont Saint Michel on the coast of Normandy. While praying for Elizabeth's recovery, I experienced the peace that passes all understanding. These were moments of spiritual growth that remain fresh in my heart even now.

Scripture encourages us to pray for the healing of the body, mind, and spirit of others. But do I fully trust that God listens to my healing prayer requests? Lord, help me!

Lord, I praise You and give You thanks for Your ever-present healing grace. Please use me as an instrument of Your peace and healing today. Through Christ, amen.

DEVOTIONS®

November

May your unfailing love be with us, LORD, even as
we put our hope in you.

— *Psalm 33:22*

Gary Wilde, Editor   **Margaret Williams,** Project Editor   Photo iStockphoto | Thinkstock®

DEVOTIONS® is published quarterly by Standard Publishing, Cincinnati, Ohio, www.standardpub.com.
© 2013 by Standard Publishing. All rights reserved. Topics based on the Home Daily Bible Readings,
International Sunday School Lessons. © 2011 by the Committee on the Uniform Series. Printed in
the U.S.A. All Scripture quotations, unless otherwise indicated, are taken from the *HOLY BIBLE,
NEW INTERNATIONAL VERSION®. NIV®.* Copyright © 1973, 1978, 1984, 2011 by Biblica. Used by
permission of Zondervan. All rights reserved. *The New King James Version* (NKJV). Copyright ©
1982 by Thomas Nelson, Inc. *The Holy Bible, New Century Version®* (NCV) © 1986, 1988, 1999,
2005 by Thomas Nelson, Inc., Nashville, Tennessee.   Volume 57 No. 4

God Is Watching

The LORD is on his heavenly throne. He observes everyone on earth; his eyes examine them (Psalm 11:4).

Scripture: Psalm 11
Song: "My Trust Is in the Lord"

I'm no longer shy about saying grace in a restaurant while holding hands with my friends. Wait staff who observe us praying will often comment, as will a manager or two. Most often servers say things like, "If more people prayed before meals, the world would be a much better place." Several take time to tell stories about why they seldom attend church anymore. Some have commented, however, that they feel God is watching them.

For me, such meal times have become unexpected opportunities to invite people to church. One encounter this February occurred because I missed a highway exit and ended up at a tiny diner. "Ginger" was my lively server. She was a young, divorced mother struggling to raise three little boys. "I've started taking the boys to different churches, looking for a Sunday school program they all like." She was already saving money to buy each son a promised children's Bible.

Ginger explained that she was "turning her life around" and wanted her sons in church every Sunday. I encouraged her to keep searching and trust God to bless her along the way. And I've been praying regularly for her and her family ever since.

Father, I pray that You guide all the Gingers in this world as they seek closer relationships with You. Please help them know how much You love them. In Jesus' name, amen.

November 1, 2. **Joyceanna Rautio** resides in Naples, Florida, and is a business consultant committed to living by Christ's values. She enjoys studying Scripture, international travel, and outdoor adventures.

A Temple to God

The glory of the LORD entered the temple through the gate facing east. Then the Spirit lifted me up and brought me into the inner court, and the glory of the LORD filled the temple (Ezekiel 43:4, 5).

Scripture: Ezekiel 43:1-12
Song: "God Is in His Temple"

A house of the Lord might be a chapel, a church, a basilica, a cathedral, or a meeting house. What images flashed in your mind as you read this list of structures? Perhaps you saw steeples, towers, numerous steps, flying buttresses, stained-glass windows, lofty ceilings, rows of pews? Did you automatically sense the glory of the Lord filling any of these places of worship and prayer?

One other structure filled with the Spirit might come to mind: a believer's physical body. The New Testament tells us that our bodies are temples of the Holy Spirit (see 1 Corinthians 6:19). But I ask myself: How often am I truly aware of the awesome responsibilities that go with this reality? Do I try to make healthy food choices to keep my temple fueled for serving? Do I take a regular brisk walk to get the exercise my temple needs?

We can glorify the Lord by honoring and caring for the bodies He gave us. And how wonderful to know that the Lord is within us as we enter His houses of worship, filled with His glory and grace!

O God, thank You for Your loving presence in my life. As I travel on my journey of faith and service, help me honor You today by respecting my earthly body as a temple of Your Spirit. In the name of Jesus, amen.

Quilted Together in Unity

The children of Reuben and the children of Gad called the altar, Witness, "For it is a witness between us that the LORD is God" (Joshua 22:34, *New King James Version*).

Scripture: Joshua 22:21-34
Song: "Blest Be the Tie That Binds"

I remember when I was young, sitting underneath the quilting loom and listening to my grandmother and my aunts talk as they quilted. The quilts were made from pieces of old clothing. Each piece was discussed: what garment it had come from, who had worn it, how old it was. Every quilt was being made for a specific purpose and a specific person. Wedding quilts were the most popular with baby quilts also being honored.

Quilts were originally designed to take something old and worn out and remake it into something new and useful. Most of the time quilts had a specific pattern. But there was something called a "crazy quilt" in which the scraps were joined together in a helter-skelter fashion.

As I grow older, I can see how God's church is like a quilt. He joins us into a beautiful design that only He can see. All we may see are the various odd-shaped pieces, but we blend together into a wonderful, beautiful, useful whole. As we come together to worship, we can bless each other. For each of us fits exactly where we are supposed to be.

Lord, thank You for making me a part of Your church. Thank You for fitting me into Your grand design and using my gifts for Your glory. In Jesus' name, amen.

November 3–9. **Conover Swofford** resides in Columbus, Georgia. She has been a freelance writer for more than 25 years.

God, Our Peace

Gideon built an altar there to the LORD, and called it The-LORD-Is-Peace (Judges 6:24, *New King James Version*).

Scripture: Judges 6:24-32
Song: "Wonderful Peace"

I couldn't find my cat, and I'd looked all over the house for her. Although I knew I hadn't left the front door open, I feared she might have gotten outside somehow. She is an indoor cat—being outside could be dangerous for her. So I hunted and prayed and grew frantic.

After several hours, I found her curled up and sound asleep in my bottom bureau drawer. How she had gotten in there, I had no idea, but there she was. She wasn't worried and had no idea that I was. She slept as if she didn't have any cares at all.

When I picked her up, she awoke and studied me for a minute, then went right back to sleep. As I held her in my lap, I thought about what a good object lesson she was. She lived her life without stress or anxiety. She expected to have food when she was hungry, water when she was thirsty . . . and to be completely taken care of.

All of those things God has promised us. If we leave everything to Him, He will give us His peace that passes all of our understanding. We can curl up and sleep, knowing that we are completely in His care.

Almighty and everlasting God, please help me to give all my worries and cares over to You and to trust You to take care of me. Today, I seek to remember that Your name is peace and that You delight in conveying that peace to my innermost being. In the holy name of Jesus, prince of peace, I pray. Amen.

Giving That Costs

But I will surely buy it from you for a price; nor will I offer burnt offerings to the Lord my God with that which costs me nothing (2 Samuel 24:24, *New King James Version*).

Scripture: 2 Samuel 24:17-25
Song: "We Give Thee but Thine Own"

As we were riding home from church one Sunday, my 8-year-old daughter excitedly told us that her Sunday school class was going to collect a special offering to give to one of the missionaries that our church supports. "Do you need some money for that?" I asked her.

Earnestly, she said to me, "Mama, I want to give *my* money, not yours." I was impressed. When we got home, I sat down with her, and we came up with a list of some things she could do to earn money. Positive that the rest of our family would like to help out, I had her call her grandmother and two of her aunts who lived close by.

Everyone had something that she could do. And everyone was impressed with her attitude. For the next two weeks, my daughter did all kinds of little jobs. She proudly put all of the money she earned into a special piggy bank and took it to church on Sunday. Along with the other members of her class, she happily put all of her money into the offering plate.

I was proud of all of them. And I continue to learn good things from our children.

Lord, please give me a cheerful attitude as I give back to You my tithes and offerings. I hope, daily, to give You my all. Thank You for all Your many blessings. In Jesus' name I pray. Amen.

God Our Refuge

You are my strong refuge. Let my mouth be filled with Your praise and with Your glory all the day (Psalm 71:7, 8, *New King James Version*).

Scripture: Psalm 71:1-8
Song: "How Sweet and Awesome Is This Place"

My friend and I were hiking in the Appalachian Mountains in north Georgia. We had overestimated our strength and sat down exhausted in the middle of nowhere. A storm was forming, and we watched it approach. Could we find shelter?

The only place available was a nearby outcropping of rock. We squeezed ourselves under it just as howling winds and rain tore through the trees above us. Although the space was small, it kept us dry.

We sat there and watched the lightning striking around us. Rains poured down furiously for about 15 minutes, and then . . . calm. When we crawled out of the space, my friend pointed upward. A rainbow curved in brilliant hues just above the mountaintop. Glory!

The air smelled fresh and clean, and our rest had refreshed us. I picked up a small, sharp stone and etched these words into the rock that had sheltered us: God Our Refuge. Then we started back down the mountain talking about the many things in this world that remind us of God's awesomeness and constant care. That was one unforgettable hike.

O Lord God in Heaven, You are awesome. Thank You for Your mighty power at work in the world and in my life. Open the eyes of my heart to be more aware of Your presence today. In the precious name of Christ my Lord I pray. Amen.

Best for the Beloved

I wait for the LORD, my soul waits, And in His word I do hope (Psalm 130:5, *New King James Version*).

Scripture: Psalm 130, 131
Song: "Sweet Hour of Prayer"

Ten-year-old Caitlin wanted a puppy. She wanted a puppy very badly. She pleaded and she wheedled and she pouted and she promised. All sorts of good behaviors would follow, if *only* she could have a puppy!

In vain did her parents explain to her that she was allergic to dogs. They took her to the pet store to show her that being around dogs made her eyes puff up and her nose run. Caitlin didn't care. The trip to the pet store was a mistake because it just made the little girl more determined than ever.

Finally, as kindly as they could, Caitlin's parents told her, No. Caitlin cried and cried but her parents couldn't change their answer. Having a puppy just wasn't good for their precious daughter, and it was their job to seek the best for her.

I believe that most any time we say, "God didn't answer my prayer," we mean that He didn't give us what we asked for. However, God promises to hear and answer, whether it's Yes, No, or Wait. Even we adults ask God for things that will hurt us. So He kindly tells us, No. Later, we may even see the divine wisdom in such denials. For true parental love requires doing what's best for the beloved child.

Lord, thank You for having my best interests in Your heart, even when You say No. I trust You to walk with me through this day with Your love. Please keep shaping my desires toward the things of Your kingdom. Through my Lord Christ I pray. Amen.

God's Acceptance

At the end of these days . . . the priests are to present your burnt offerings and fellowship offerings on the altar. Then I will accept you, declares the Sovereign LORD (Ezekiel 43:27).

Scripture: Ezekiel 43:22-27
Song: "There Is Power in the Blood"

My 15-year-old daughter walked hesitantly toward me, and I could sense something wrong. I smiled and said, "Tell me."

She started to cry, murmuring, "Don't hate me."

Appalled she would think that, I immediately put my arms around her. "No matter what it is, I won't hate you," I told her. "I could never hate you."

She pulled away from me, looked at me and said, "I'm pregnant." Vastly relieved that it wasn't something worse, I said, "So I get to be a grandmother!"

"Aren't you mad?" my daughter asked.

I hugged her again. "Honey, I'm not thrilled over the circumstances. But I am thrilled that we will have a baby in our family."

Perhaps we think that we have done something so awful that God doesn't love us any more. But that can't happen. True, the consequences of our self-destructive ways can bring much pain. But no matter what we've done, God looks at us through the sacrifice that Jesus made, and He accepts us, calling us to ever-increasing dependence upon Him. Nothing can separate us from the love of God, certainly not our sins.

Lord, I have done some very wrong things in my life. I have hurt other people and grieved Your Spirit. Help me to make amends where I can—and from now on to live more lovingly and kindly. In Jesus' name I pray. Amen.

One Sweet Substitute

"**Son of man, this is what the Sovereign** LORD **says: These will be the regulations for sacrificing burnt offerings and splashing blood against the altar when it is built**" (Ezekiel 43:18).

Scripture: Ezekiel 43:13-21
Song: "Teach Me Thy Way, O Lord"

I simply love cheesecake, and one particular recipe is my favorite. Over the years, many people have asked me for that precious gastronomical formula.

One of my friends, Polly, came to me and told me she'd made the cheesecake—but it didn't taste like mine. I was surprised and puzzled.

Then Polly told me that because she wanted to make it "more healthy," instead of cream cheese she'd used ricotta. Instead of sugar, she used artificial sweetener. Instead of sour cream, she used plain yogurt. *This was my recipe?* "Nothing wrong with substituting, Polly," I said. "But the result won't be my cheesecake!"

Sometimes we can get away with substitutions, and sometimes they make for a better end product. But as the great prophet Ezekiel surely knew, when we receive God's recipe for holiness, we're better off following it closely.

The Lord has promised to direct our paths if we let Him. If we lean to our own understanding, we might get diet cheesecake, but who would want *that*?

Father, direct me in the way I should go this day, and help me to follow Your pattern for my life. I thank You from the depths of my heart for my sweet substitute, Jesus, who lived the perfect life for me and took my place on the cross. In His name, amen.

The Only Well with Water

"My people have committed two sins: They have forsaken me, the spring of living water, and have dug their own cisterns, broken cisterns that cannot hold water" (Jeremiah 2:13).

Scripture: Jeremiah 2:5-13
Song: "Springs of Living Water"

Our youngest daughter, Harmony, has a plush pink blanket that she drags around the house. We affectionately call it Fuzzy. When she's playing with toys, Fuzzy lays within reach. When she watches a video on TV, there is Fuzzy beside her. Fuzzy takes a nap with her, rides in the car seat with her, and sits on the floor next to her seat at the table.

But when Harmony falls down and scrapes her knee, she doesn't reach for Fuzzy. She reaches up to Mama. While she can hug her precious Fuzzy, it cannot hug her back. In moments of need, only Mama will do.

Loving something is good, but *being loved* is better. Jeremiah lamented that Israel didn't seem to know the difference. They had shiny objects to captivate their attention. They had the idols of foreign gods to love. Yet, when they needed a satisfying Savior, a personal God to love them back, idols just couldn't cut it.

How eagerly we try to fulfill our longings with something other than God. But He alone can quench our soul's thirst.

Lord, forgive me for drinking the dust from empty wells. Redirect my cravings toward Your Word and yourself. I don't want to settle for anything less. In Jesus' name, amen.

November 10–16. **Matthew Boardwell** is an avid nonfiction reader and enthusiastic musician. He is husband to Pam, father of nine, and minister at his church in Erie, Colorado.

Long Dry Spells

On that day living water will flow out from Jerusalem . . . in summer and in winter (Zechariah 14:8).

Scripture: Zechariah 14:1-8
Song: "It's Beginning to Rain"

In 1570 rain fell near the Pacific coast of Chile. There wouldn't be another significant rainfall in that place for 400 years. Imagine four centuries without any noticeable moisture at all! Even though that record dry spell ended in 1971, the Atacama Desert is still the driest place on earth.

The prophet Zechariah foretold a terrible season of national and personal disasters for Jerusalem. Things would go from bad to worse through war, defeat, cataclysm, and abuse. At last, the day of the Lord will arrive when He will provide an escape and make things right. After that long dry spell, a healing stream of water will flow from the heart of the city.

How dreadful it will be while they wait for the drought to end! How long will it be before they taste His mercy again? Only God knows, but He can be trusted. He has a plan, He is in control, and His people will ultimately be restored.

Life comes with dry seasons when the mercies of God seem distant memories. Hardship and loss can strain our faith while we wait for deliverance. However, we can rely on God's faithfulness. He is bigger than our troubles, and He has a plan to bring us through them to healing.

Sovereign God, my situation is not a surprise to You. You know my hurts and see my difficulties. In the middle of this, I know that You still care. Deliver me, I pray. In the meanwhile, help me trust You with all my heart. Through Christ, amen.

Springs from Within

"Let anyone who is thirsty come to me and drink. Whoever believes in me, as Scripture has said, rivers of living water will flow from within them" (John 7:37, 38).

Scripture: John 7:37-44
Song: "Come, Thou Fount of Every Blessing"

Where I grew up in west Michigan, fresh water was never far away. A shovel and 15 minutes of effort could easily bring you to water. Many properties even had their own springs, so the landscape there is lush.

I've since spent over 20 years in semi-arid Colorado, where rain is a treat and water costs property owners dearly. Each summer when I turn on my sprinkler system, I long for the abundance of fresh water again.

When Jesus stood up at the feast, He was interrupting a joyous annual ceremony. On the seventh day of the festival, water was drawn seven times from the famous pool of Siloam and poured out at the altar while the crowds shouted and sang the praises of God. At the height of that clamor, Jesus announced that He was the fulfillment of all they celebrated. If they would believe in Him, He could give them the spiritual water they longed for—and place a fresh spring inside them.

Jesus still calls over the clamor. He invites us to believe and promises the Holy Spirit's permanent presence when we do. Every believer's heart will have its own life-giving spring.

Jesus, the living water, You promised that if I believe in You, I will have You living within me, filling me up and overflowing from my life. I do believe. I want Your water. I need Your Spirit. Fill me to overflowing for Your glory. In Your name, amen.

Eternal Refreshment

"For the Lamb at the center of the throne will be their shepherd; 'he will lead them to springs of living water. And God will wipe away every tear from their eyes'" (Revelation 7:17).

Scripture: Revelation 7:13-17
Song: "Shall We Gather at the River?"

Our young family made the 8-hour trip from Santa Fe, New Mexico, to the Grand Canyon in one day—in summer. We were new to the Southwest, so the amazing Painted Desert landscape was novel to us for the first hundred miles. But after a few hours, the sunbaked scenery tended to dull our senses.

I marveled that Navajos and explorers had traveled this dusty, barren land for centuries without cruise control or air conditioning! Lake Powell was such a refreshing sight after all that reddish-grey sand. The blue water and green irrigated grass seemed to glow with vibrant color.

God offers that kind of refreshment to those who endure hardship for His sake. At the end of their road they'll be safely home—no scorching sun, drought, or thirst. They will live in His shade and drink from His springs of life-giving water.

The vibrant refreshment of Heaven is hard to envision from earth, and we can only fall back on beautiful but finite analogies. But what unimaginable joys must await those who keep traveling toward God! The Lord is as eager to share them as we are to enjoy them.

Living God, I can hardly wait to arrive at home with You. Thank You for the pleasures of life that offer glimpses of glory. Still I know they will pale when Heaven is fully in view. Sustain me until I reach the end of my journey. In Jesus' name, amen.

Never Want Another!

"Everyone who drinks this water will be thirsty again, but whoever drinks the water I give them will never thirst. Indeed, the water I give them will become in them a spring of water welling up to eternal life" (John 4:13, 14).

Scripture: John 4:7-15
Song: "Only Jesus"

Together our family built a new white picket fence around our yard. With all the cutting, assembling, priming, and painting, the project took a few weeks out in the Colorado sunshine. Throughout the project our favorite sight was Mama on the back porch with a gallon jug of ice water.

We all enjoyed it. We craved it. But she was the one who went to fetch it, again and again. It would have been great if one draft of water could have quenched our thirst for the whole project. That would have saved my wife a lot of time and trouble.

The woman Jesus met at the well thought the same thing when He offered her His new water. "You mean I'd never have to make the daily trek to this well again? You mean I wouldn't have to face the scowls of my judgmental neighbors anymore? That's my kind of water! How do I get some?"

Of course, Jesus wasn't talking about physical water for bodily thirst. In this case, water served as a metaphor for eternal life in an empty soul. One drink of that new life and you'll never need another. (In fact, you'll never *want* another.)

Father, when my soul was empty, I sought to fill it and satisfy my spiritual thirst. The disappointment only revealed how much I needed You. Now, by Your grace, I have the eternal life of Christ and my soul is satisfied. Thank You, through Christ. Amen.

The Water of God's Word

That person is like a tree planted by streams of water, which yields its fruit in season and whose leaf does not wither—whatever they do prospers (Psalm 1:3).

Scripture: Psalm 1
Song: "Psalm 1"

To settlers on their westward trail, a long row of cottonwoods was a welcome sight. While yellow prairie grass survives on the occasional shower, giant trees like these need a steady source of moisture. The trees meant there was a river. In their shade, there would be enough water for both livestock and travelers.

On the banks of a river almost anything can flourish. And the person who continually drinks from the cool water of God's written Word flourishes like those cottonwoods. The psalmist sings about how that person avoids wretched influences, bears fruit, withstands heat, and prospers in everything.

With a steady stream of truth, correction, and encouragement, any believer can grow healthy and strong. The church where I learned to follow Jesus had flaws like any church. But its great strength was a deep love of Scripture. They taught me to delight in the law of the Lord. Thus I grew familiar with the Bible's heroes. I learned its life-giving principles that still sustain me. Best of all, I received the good news of God's love and forgiveness in Christ. So, may I help others drink deeply from God's Word as well.

O God, thank You for Your written Word. Thank You for those who brought it to me. I want to keep loving the Bible, and I want others to delight in it too. Show me how I can help them find nourishment and strength from Scripture. Through Christ, amen.

A Swelling River of Life

Their leaves will not wither, nor will their fruit fail. Every month they will bear fruit, because the water from the sanctuary flows to them (Ezekiel 47:12).

Scripture: Ezekiel 47:1-12
Song: "River of Living Water"

Tiny Nicollet Creek in northern Minnesota isn't all that impressive, just a spring burbling out of the marshy ground and dribbling into Lake Itasca. But its waters continue flowing over 2,500 miles later where the mighty Mississippi River measures more than a mile wide and empties into the Gulf of Mexico.

This fourth-longest river in the world begins with a trickle. A similar scene unfolds when Ezekiel sees the New Jerusalem. Flowing from the restored temple was just a trickle of water. As it flowed, the stream increased in depth and breadth, producing life in the desert.

God's kingdom is often depicted as something tiny growing to enormous proportions. Its imperceptible progress is nonetheless relentless and inevitable, like a mustard seed becoming a tree, a bit of yeast permeating the whole loaf, or a tiny child who is born to save and rule the world.

Sometimes the work is too small and its progress too slight for us to notice. At those moments our part in the kingdom appears insignificant. But time is all this swelling river needs to become the mighty force that nourishes and heals the nations.

My God and King, Your kingdom grows in power every single day. I am privileged to be part of it. Give me a glimpse of its greatness, even when my portion of it seems so small. Flow through me to extend Your kingdom in my world. In Jesus' name, amen.

Just Read the Sonogram

"See, the former things have taken place, and new things I declare; before they spring into being I announce them to you" (Isaiah 42:9).

Scripture: Isaiah 42:5-9
Song: "Living by Faith"

The excitement at their wedding two years ago was nothing compared to this. Now they were ecstatic and exuberant—not nervous, stiff, or subdued. News of their first baby released unbounded joy. "Look at this sonogram picture! You can see every detail, even that he is sucking his thumb!"

Our Lord keeps anticipation alive by announcing new adventures before we experience them. His Word is the spiritual sonogram that forecasts what we need for life and godliness.

The prophets heralded Jesus' advent. He came. And he claimed victory over life and death. Jesus said, "In this world you will have trouble. But take heart! I have overcome the world" (John 16:33).

Before He ascended to Heaven, Jesus promised the Comforter as a gift. He came. So we have the power of the Spirit to help us face every challenge. After this life there are eternal mansions for us, Jesus promised. "Before they spring into being," we know these things are real. We anticipate, just like first-time parents can plan for the new baby. History confirms, but promises excite. Read the spiritual sonogram!

Lord, You will surprise me today with Your presence. Work in me and through me. I have great anticipation of my future with You, beginning now! In Jesus' name, amen.

November 17–23. **Bob Mize** is a minister, chaplain, and freelance writer living in Lubbock, Texas. He and his wife, Charlotte, have three grown children and five grandchildren.

But What Kind of King?

"My kingdom is not of this world. If it were, my servants would fight to prevent my arrest by the Jewish leaders. But now my kingdom is from another place" (John 18:36).

Scripture: Isaiah 42:10-16
Song: "Crown Him with Many Crowns"

"You are a king, then?"
"Yes."
"What kind of king, though?" Not "kingly" in those days, and not today. Not dying a heroic death on the front line of war, but dying the shameful death of a common criminal, accomplishing victory in my heart. Not born of royalty, but to an obscure couple, growing up in a hick town: "Nazareth! Can anything good come from there?" (John 1:46).

Not a gold crown, but a crown of thorns, pressed into His scalp by mockers. No thick robe draped with gold chains, but one seamless garment for which His executioners gambled. No influential cabinet and entourage, but a small group of rough men from various walks of life. Not riding a white horse leading the charge of a massive army, but riding the colt of a donkey, welcomed by a crowd that would later demand His death.

No physical sword, but the sword of the Spirit. No kingdom plotted on a map, but a spiritual, universal kingdom, made up of every heart enthroning Him. Not a physical throne in some future earthly kingdom, but the throne of my life.

O God, may I honor King Jesus in all that I say, do, and think today. I bow before Him, offer my time and energy, spend time in His presence. Blessed, praised, worshipped, hallowed, and adored be Jesus Christ on His throne of glory in Heaven! Amen.

Broken to Be Better

The sacrifice God wants is a broken spirit. God, you will not reject a heart that is broken and sorry for sin (Psalm 51:17, *New Century Version*).

Scripture: Psalm 51:1-13
Song: "Spirit of the Living God"

Dan began his home-building career with the goal of becoming wealthy. The American Dream: hard work, long days, reinvested profits. The stuff success is made of, right?

It didn't work. Three bankruptcies and a divorce later, he was broken. He'd grown up in a Christian home, but it "didn't take." Pondering his plight brought him to a powerful repentance.

But he had a new beginning with his grown son, who had a special creativity in building affordable start-up homes. The big difference, though, was a spiritual one. Dan and his son made a promise to the Lord to give 10 percent of the company profit to kingdom work. Above personal giving, the company itself would tithe.

At year 20 the company had completed 4,000 homes. Of greater importance to Dan was the fact that in one calendar year the company gave away over $9 million dollars to spiritual ministries worldwide. Dan was broken to be better. And this promise is true: "The Lord is close to the brokenhearted and saves those who are crushed in spirit" (Psalm 34:18).

Broken? Our Lord is the rebuilder.

Heavenly Father, in the name of Jesus and for His kingdom, turn my brokenness into boldness. Empower me with Your Spirit to share what is truly important. Thank You, in the name of Your Son my Savior. Amen.

Wait Quietly

It is good to wait quietly for the salvation of the LORD (Lamentations 3:26).

Scripture: Lamentations 3:19-26
Song: "Be Still My Soul"

The youth's "wilderness trek" included a new challenge this year: eight daylight hours alone in the wilderness. Water and food allowed, but no electronics. Emphasis: quietness . . . being still before the Lord . . . doing nothing but *waiting on the Lord*.

After three hours, the teens began trickling back into base camp, admitting their defeat. Each said something like, "I just can't take the silence for that long . . . the quiet freaked me out."

Stay in silence! It may be harder for our youth, who are so conditioned to electronically produced stimuli. But it is tough for most of us to be still and quiet. Waiting seems like torture rather than a spiritual blessing.

Noise pollution is real, especially in urban areas. And often our tendency is to create sounds rather than seek quiet. We keep the TV constantly on, ear buds always in, car radios blaring. Even our worship assemblies rarely include times of silence.

I've noticed though that blessings come my way when I seek quiet, remove distractions, and intentionally become still before the Lord. Could you try it for awhile today? Ask the Lord's help in creating a time and place just for you and Him. Then wait quietly upon the Lord.

Dear God, in Your presence I wait and quiet my soul before Your mighty power. Help me rest and wait in Your presence, so that when I go back "into the world," You can minister to others through me. In Jesus' name I pray. Amen.

You Look Like Your Dad!

Praise be to the God and Father of our Lord Jesus Christ! In his great mercy he has given us new birth into a living hope through the resurrection of Jesus Christ from the dead(1 Peter 1:3).

Scripture: 1 Peter 1:1-7
Song: "Father of Mercies"

Sid went to the grocery store to buy steaks for grilling. As he rounded an aisle, he glanced up and was shocked to see a man at a distance who looked amazingly like his father. He wanted a longer look, but didn't want to stare.

He looked down at his basket, but then stole another glance. *Surprise!* He was looking into a huge mirror behind the meat displays. Now he knew why people said, "You look like your dad."

We have been "chosen . . . [by] the Father" (v. 2)" to look like Him. It happens gradually as we "are being transformed into his image with ever-increasing glory, which comes from the Lord, who is the Spirit" (2 Corinthians 3:18). God provides the "new birth into a living hope through the resurrection of Jesus Christ . . . into an inheritance that can never perish, spoil, or fade" (vv. 3, 4). In Christ we are "shielded by God's power" (v. 5), even though we "have had to suffer grief in all kinds of trials" (v. 6). We can rejoice greatly in a gift from God, a gift that is worth more than gold. God became a man so we can know what God looks like—so we can, some day, look just like Him.

Lord Jesus, help me look like You in word and deed today. May I think, speak, and act in Your name, having Your mind and following in Your steps. In the name of the Father and of the Son and of the Holy Spirit, I pray. Amen.

Communities for Christ

All the believers were together and had everything in common (Acts 2:44).

Scripture: Acts 2:37-47
Song: "Bind Us Together, Lord"

My cousin took us to visit a Hutterite Community in northern Montana. These 120 people live in a close-knit, exclusive colony. They have the same origins as Mennonites and Amish, but are modern and open to visitors and photographers. These gentle people are self-sufficient, building their own houses, growing their own food, making all their own clothing, furniture, and modern equipment for their kitchens and farm operations.

Along with four other colonies in the state, they farm hundreds of thousands of acres of wheat, plus provide most of the eggs and 99% of all the milk sold in Montana. Their goal is to preserve their Austrian/German religion, from their roots dating back to the 1500s.

Many such social experiments have dotted the history of every country. But what is "community" in the biblical sense? Have Christians missed something? Being the Lord's people is more than preserving a certain language, style of dress, or foods. We are to share material goods, meet together, eat together, and worship, doing it all with glad and sincere hearts. Most importantly, we are to love as Jesus loved.

God, Creator and Sustainer, help me be a vital and vibrant part of Your community, encouraging others in their citizenship in Christ. May I remember today that everything I have is really on loan from You. May I be a good steward of the goods—and people—whom You have placed in my care. Through Christ I pray. Amen.

You Are an Heir!

I pray that the eyes of your heart may be enlightened in order that you may know the hope to which he has called you, the riches of his glorious inheritance in his holy people (Ephesians 1:18).

Scripture: Ezekiel 47:13-23
Song: "Count Your Many Blessings"

I like inheritance stories, especially those with a surprising twist. In 1992, Cara Wood, 17, was working in a diner east of Cleveland. She was outgoing, a good employee, and a favorite of customer Bill Cruxton. Bill was an elderly widower with no children. He became friends with Cara, whom he always requested as his waitress. Cara became so important to Cruxton that he rewrote his will, making her the beneficiary of his estate. When Cruxton died of heart failure at age 82, the young waitress inherited half a million dollars!

Often I think of my spiritual inheritance, a greater one than any amount of money or land. Actually, a list of lands and boundaries sounds boring to me—like genealogies—until I realize my name is included in them! I am part of the inheritance of Israel. I am in the lineage of the Christ.

Are you giving thanks to the Father for the riches of His inheritance? It's waiting in Heaven for you, but determine to enjoy it now, every day—especially, the indwelling presence of your Lord Jesus Christ.

Mighty Father, thank You for adopting me by the blood of Jesus Christ. I am profoundly grateful for every spiritual blessing that is mine in Him. Give me a joyful heart in my fellowship with Him today! In His name, amen.

Plugging in to the Past

My soul is downcast within me; therefore I will remember you from the land of the Jordan (Psalm 42:6).

Scripture: Psalm 42:5-11
Song: "I Sing the Mighty Power of God"

My 90-year-old mother suffers from short-term memory loss. She can't remember last week or yesterday, or even things that happened 10 minutes ago. Sometimes she has a sense of loss—a glimmer of her present mental failings—and it makes her sad.

Whenever possible I take our conversations back to long ago, happier times. We talk about things that make us laugh, like the time my naughty brother, while forced to stand in the corner, continued his wayward ways by tearing off a large section of the wallpaper. This story is old and familiar territory, and we both laugh at the same time.

It feels good to remember together. When King David's soul was down in the dumps, he too had a remedy. He remembered God and His exploits. His mind went to the promised land and to Mt. Hermon on its northern border, that pinnacle where many believe Jesus was transfigured. David brought to mind the great deeds done by God the Father for His children. He "plugged in" to the old stories of God's faithfulness. Then, even in hard times, David was able to connect with good memories, declaring his faith in God's unfailing love.

Lord, when I am overwhelmed by the circumstances of my days, I will remember You. I will praise You for Your faithfulness to me . . . always. In Jesus' name, amen.

November 24–30. **Jan Pierce** lives in Vancouver, Washington. She and her husband travel annually to India where they support churches, orphanages, and schools.

God, the Artist

By the word of the LORD the heavens were made, their starry host by the breath of his mouth. He gathers the waters of the sea into jars; he puts the deep into storehouses (Psalm 33:6, 7).

Scripture: Psalm 33:1-9
Song: "For the Beauty of the Earth"

Here in my beautiful Pacific Northwest it's rhododendron time. It's also iris, peony, rose, and azalea time. Our yards absolutely burst with color this time of the year, and somehow we faithful ones forget the previous months of dreary rain.

God created the heavens above, and He created the seas. He spoke the trees and the flowers and all our world into existence. Sometimes I take a close look at the structure and make-up of just one garden bloom—the delicate petals with silky texture, the darker depths of the cup shapes, the elegance of the stamens poking their heads out and above it. I marvel at the intricacy of just one blossom.

Even in death flowers carry on a process that is beautiful in its order. The blossoms wilt and drop to the ground, and the seed pod remains to begin the life cycle once again next season.

How amazing is our God. What an artist! Verse 8 says, "Let all the earth fear the LORD; let all the people of the world revere him." Study just one tiny piece of God's creation and marvel at His creative majesty. Father of all creation, I stand in awe.

O God, the king of glory, I thank You for the beautiful world You've given me to enjoy. Your awesome beauty and power speak to me every time I open my eyes to truly see. May I honor You with my life this day! In Jesus' name, amen.

Trusting Prayer

The eyes of the LORD are on those who fear him, on those whose hope is in his unfailing love (Psalm 33:18).

Scripture: Psalm 33:10-22
Song: "In Thee, O Lord, I Put My Trust"

George Müller trusted God. We see from his journal entries that his faith in God's provision was rock solid. He believed God wanted him to build an orphanage. He already had scores of children living in four homes, but neighbors complained of noise and overcrowding. So George prayed and journaled . . .

December 23, 1845: This is now the 50th day since I have come to the conclusion to build. Not even one penny has come in since December 10th.

December 24, 1845: No further donations have come in, but my hope in God is unshaken.

January 3, 1846: One of the orphans gave sixpence for the building fund . . . I went out to look for a piece of ground.

January 31, 1846: It is now 89 days since I have been daily waiting upon God about the building.

December 9, 1846: It is now 400 days . . .

July 7, 1847: Work on the building was begun today.

Rather than speak of disappointments, no visible results, or rising expenses, Müller chose to hold fast to the belief that God would provide, and He did. Can we, too, hope in God's love that way? Lord, let it be so!

Father, forgive me when I become impatient in prayer. Give me ears to hear Your will and the strength to pray faithfully for Your provision. As You reveal Your will, let me trust You to fulfill it! In Jesus' name, amen.

Reach Higher

Train yourself to be godly. For physical training is of some value, but godliness has value for all things, holding promise for both the present life and the life to come (1 Timothy 4:7, 8).

Scripture: 1 Timothy 4:4-11
Song: "No Cross for Me?"

According to popular culture these days, we've got plenty of reasons to feel guilty about our lifestyles. We're supposed to care about the health of our food supply, rallying against genetically engineered produce. We're encouraged to eat eight to 10 servings of colorful fruits and vegetables daily and exercise faithfully to stay fit and trim. We should drink eight full glasses of water daily and take vitamin supplements. We should eat more lean protein and less sugar.

Don't misunderstand. I actually agree with the above causes. But Paul told Timothy there was something much more important than physical fitness, which only benefits our lives here on earth. He said it was far more important to train ourselves in godliness. After all, living a life pleasing to God has benefits both now and all through eternity.

We train in godliness through prayer, study, and meditation on the Word and in serving one another in love. When we set our hearts on such godly training, we're reaching right past the confines of life here on earth. We're reaching higher to grasp onto eternal values.

God, I want my priorities in life to be all about You. May I honor You by a life dedicated to walking with You—and a heart set on eternal values. In Jesus' name, amen.

The Weight

Restore us again, God our Savior, and put away your displeasure toward us (Psalm 85:4).

Scripture: Psalm 85:1-7
Song: "God of Grace and God of Glory"

We're all familiar with the heavy heart that accompanies a break in relationship with family or friends. It's as though a cloud hangs overhead, as though we're carrying a heavy load. Whether we're interacting with disobedient children, counseling a wayward teen, or navigating the waters of misunderstanding, our hearts feel the burden.

There's a good reason for these heavy hearts—God wants His children to live in harmony. The heaviness is a direct result of being out of step with God's best for us. When there's disobedience, defiance, or selfishness in relationships, our souls long for resolution of the problem and restoration of loving bonds.

In Psalm 85, the psalmist cries out for a restoration of his relationship of love with his Savior. It's as if a child were begging his or her parent, "Please don't be mad at me."

Thankfully, our Father in Heaven desires the very same, a relationship of love and forgiveness. He will respond to our heart cries. He'll remove the weight of sin from us and turn our mourning to joy. We'll be revived and given new life so that we can once again praise Him.

Merciful Father, thank You for always offering me the gift of forgiveness. Help me to remember that this is hardly a cheap grace: It came at the cost of Your Son's precious blood. Thank You so much! Now may I be willing to keep my relationships with others free of the weight of sinful behaviors. In Jesus' name, amen.

Too Good to Be True?

This man will not be your heir, but a son who is your own flesh and blood will be your heir (Genesis 15:4).

Scripture: Genesis 15:1-6
Song: "Amazing Grace"

The woman sobbed as her family members gathered around her in prayer. She'd abandoned two sons, given birth to six children by five different men, and been married and divorced eight times. She had just prayed for forgiveness and cried tears of joy. "It's too good to be true. How could God love me?" Nevertheless, she basked in God's love, soaked it up and gloried in it until her death from cancer just two years later.

The woman was my mother-in-law, the mother my husband grew up without, and the one he met again at age 19. It was his privilege to share God's plan of salvation with his mother and stand with her as she came to the understanding that, sinful though her life had been, God loved her enough to die for her. She was totally forgiven, advancing to the waters of baptism.

Abraham thought he had to settle for second-best. He'd received a promise of children too numerous to count, but here he was an old man with no son. So he would give up on God's full blessing and name a servant as his heir.

God had a better plan. Abraham would have the full blessing—a son of his own. Too good to be true? Not with the amazing, promise-keeping God we serve.

Father in Heaven, You are good and gracious, all the time. Though I don't deserve Your love, I thank You that You offer it to me each day. I receive it with all my heart. In Jesus' name I pray. Amen.

I've Got Your Back!

For the LORD will go before you, the God of Israel will be your rear guard (Isaiah 52:12).

Scripture: Isaiah 52:1, 2, 7-12
Song: "Father, Lead Me Day by Day"

Part of the human condition is this: though we're surrounded by people, we can feel very alone. Family and friends may seem emotionally distant. Our busy schedules may prevent times of fellowship, sharing, and a place to "be real." Often the deepest cry of our hearts is to be heard and understood.

Here is the good news—God is available. He's ready to listen. God loves His people, both corporately and individually. The community of believers offers us some of the love and support we need, but our deepest cries of the heart will always and only be met by God himself. He longs to interact with us through prayer, meditation, and the prompting of His Holy Spirit.

In the end times God will reveal himself in all His splendor and might. In that day all the earth will see His power, and every knee will bow to His Son.

And to think that this very day those of us who serve Him have the assurance He will both go before us and be "our rear guard," our protection! We don't have to be lonely or afraid. We have the Father of creation to love and protect us. He has our backs each and every day of our lives.

Father God, I run to You in times of trouble, for You have promised always to be present, never to leave me. Thank You for being my protector and my shield against the enemy of my soul. Today I give myself into Your care once again. Make me strong to do Your will in all things! In Jesus' name I pray. Amen.

My Prayer Notes

_____

_____

_____

_____

_____

_____

_____

_____

_____

_____

_____

_____

_____

_____

_____

_____

_____

_____

_____

_____

_____

_____

DEVOTIONS®

December

[God] has spoken to us by his Son, ... The Son is the radiance of God's glory and the exact representation of his being, sustaining all things by his powerful word.

— *Hebrews 1:2, 3*

Gary Wilde, Editor   **Margaret Williams,** Project Editor   Bible Art © Standard Publishing

DEVOTIONS® is published quarterly by Standard Publishing, Cincinnati, Ohio, www.standardpub.com. © 2013 by Standard Publishing. All rights reserved. Topics based on the Home Daily Bible Readings, International Sunday School Lessons. © 2012 by the Committee on the Uniform Series. Printed in the U.S.A. All Scripture quotations, unless otherwise indicated, are taken from the *HOLY BIBLE, NEW INTERNATIONAL VERSION®. NIV®.* Copyright © 1973, 1978, 1984, 2011 by Biblica, Inc.®. Used by permission of Zondervan. All rights reserved. The *New King James Version* (NKJV). Copyright © 1982 by Thomas Nelson, Inc. *King James Version* (KJV), public domain. Scripture quotations marked (*NLT*) are taken from the Holy Bible, *New Living Translation.* Copyright © 1996, 2004, 2007. Used by permission of Tyndale House Publishers, Inc., Wheaton, Illinois 60189. All rights reserved.

Volume 58 No. 1

God's Amazing Grace

The LORD our God is merciful and forgiving, even though we have rebelled against him (Daniel 9:9, *New Living Translation*).

Scripture: Daniel 9:3-10
Song: "Grace Greater than Our Sin"

Daniel sought the Lord God in prayer and petition, in fasting, and in sackcloth and ashes. His prayer to the Lord was a brutally honest confession; it wasn't pretty.

The people had turned away from God and His laws. Living in rebellion and wickedness, they had refused to listen to the prophets. Even so, divine mercy and forgiveness would not come to an end.

I can relate! At times I've feared to tell the Lord what I had done wrong. He already knew, of course, but I was still afraid to reveal myself to Him. However, when I finally came to the place of humble confession, He gave me His forgiveness and peace.

Wherever you are today, regardless of what you've done, please don't be afraid to talk to God and tell Him just how it is, in all honesty.

Confessing our sins can be difficult, and even scary, at times. But the great news is that God can always handle anything we tell Him; He is surprised by nothing. And, thankfully, He responds not with anger and wrath, but with mercy and healing.

Lord, release me from fear, that I may come to You, openly and humbly, my whole life before You. Then empower me to make restitution as needed. In Jesus' name, amen.

December 1–7. **Tyler Myers** lives in Ohio. He works in printing and enjoys being with his family and his lovable Golden Lab. He also enjoys Christian music and jumping on the trampoline.

One Requirement for Forgiveness

O my God, lean down and listen to me. Open your eyes and see our despair. . . . We make this plea, not because we deserve help, but because of your mercy (Daniel 9:18, *New Living Translation*).

Scripture: Daniel 9:11-19
Song: "I Will Sing of the Mercies of the Lord"

Daniel continued to pour his heart out to God for his people, and things were bad—really bad. Not only had the people experienced the bitter consequence of shame for their sin, but the solemn curses and judgments written in the Law of Moses had been poured out upon them as well.

Nevertheless, hope was not lost. In verse 18, Daniel pleaded with God, not on the basis that the people deserved His help and forgiveness, but purely on the basis of His mercy. Think about that for a moment: Daniel's petition wasn't a prayer that begged God to find some small bit of worthiness in the people.

No. While Daniel had a healthy, reverential fear of God, he knew God's mercy and grace were greater than anything the people had done wrong. And he knew a plea to God for help could be made—in the midst of sinfulness—on the basis of His undying mercy.

Isn't that exactly the kind of heavenly Father our Lord Jesus showed us? As He put it: "I came not to call the righteous, but sinners to repentance" (Luke 5:32, *KJV*). There is only one qualification for God's saving help: you have to be a sinner.

Heavenly Father, thank You for Your mercy, forgiveness, and grace that's greater than anything I do (or have done) wrong. Through Christ's name, amen.

A Great Day Coming!

Let us be glad and rejoice, and let us give honor to him. For the time has come for the wedding feast of the Lamb, and his bride has prepared herself (Revelation 19:7, *New Living Translation*).

Scripture: Revelation 19:1-8
Song: "I Wish We'd All Been Ready"

With all of the challenges, demands, and difficulties in life, it can be easy to lose sight of what's really important. Granted, lots of things in life are purely trivial and of no consequence: if you forget napkins for a picnic, don't despair (if you're a guy) — you can wipe your mouth off on your shirt sleeve just as well.

Other things, though, shouldn't be taken lightly. An athlete needs to spend time training properly, eating healthy, and getting plenty of rest if he's to be in top form for victory. Students need to read and study well, so they'll be prepared on test day.

But of all the important matters in life, here's the most crucial: knowing Jesus Christ the Lord and being prepared for the wedding feast of the Lamb. We don't know exactly when it will happen, but Jesus promised us that He would come a second time into the world. And among the things He will do at that time is this: "Mark my words — I will not drink wine again until the day I drink it new with you in my Father's Kingdom" (Matthew 26:29, *NLT*).

What a great day that will be! A day to get ready for, during each day of our lives.

Father, help me to stay focused on what really matters. Having my heart right with You is more important than anything else. In the name of Christ, I pray. Amen.

What World Are You Living For?

Blessed are those who wash their robes. They will be permitted to enter through the gates of the city and eat the fruit from the tree of life (Revelation 22:14, *New Living Translation*).

Scripture: Revelation 22:8-14
Song: "This World Is Not My Home"

We live in a world of amusements, bright lights, glamour, and thrills. There is so much to tempt us, so much that promises fulfillment. Sometimes I've given into that kind of temptation, entertaining myself with TV and music that were hardly uplifting.

The ways of this world can be so alluring . . . but what world am I living for? When I come to my senses, I realize that I can live for this very temporary world, or I can live for Christ. His eternal kingdom offers so much more to me, including a peace that passes all understanding.

Nevertheless, living for Christ and His kingdom will cost me! In our Bible passage, the people who enter the city gates to eat from the tree of life haven't lived for selfish pleasure. Rather, they've had to wash their robes (in the cleansing blood of the Lamb), relinquish their sins, and immerse their lives in His way of life.

While the good things we do can never earn our salvation in Christ, righteousness—out of pure gratitude—is the heart's desire of the Christian. And good works will be the fruit of a heart and soul that's been redeemed by the love of Christ. A world filled with that kind of fruit sounds ever so tempting.

Dear Heavenly Father, because of Your grace and power, I don't have to give into temptation, no matter how enticing. I thank You, through Christ my Lord. Amen.

In the Dark About "Why"?

John tried to talk hHim out of it. "I am the one who needs to be baptized by you," he said, "so why are you coming to me?" (Matthew 3:14, *New Living Translation*).

Scripture: Matthew 3:13-17
Song: "Jesus, Savior, Pilot Me"

This passage convicts and challenges me. Jesus Christ the Lord—God the Father's only begotten, perfect Son—went to the Jordan River to be baptized by John. Think about what an amazing privilege that would be: baptizing Jesus Christ. Did John selfishly jump at the opportunity to baptize Jesus, so he could have bragging rights? No, in fact, the opposite happened: this amazing preacher tried to talk Jesus out of it.

From John's point of view, it just wasn't right, didn't make sense to him. But thankfully, John obeyed His Lord.

I wonder how many times I've missed out on a great opportunity to serve, simply because I didn't understand the "why"? The Lord calls . . . and I reason my way out of obedience. Have you been there too?

Though it can be comforting and reassuring to know *why*, the Lord is never obligated to reveal His reasons. Our part is to love God, trust Him, and obey Him—even when we don't fully understand. I love the way a wise, experienced missionary once put it: "Never doubt in the darkness what God has shown you in the light."

Heavenly Father, thank You for the times when I understand why You want me to do something. And thank You for always being trustworthy, even when I don't understand why. You are the wisest parent of all. I love You. In Jesus' name, amen.

A Fine Example

God had mercy on me so that Christ Jesus could use me as a prime example of his great patience with even the worst sinners. Then others will realize that they, too, can believe in him and receive eternal life (1 Timothy 1:16, *New Living Translation*).

Scripture: 1 Timothy 1:12-17
Song: "Saved, Saved!"

The biblical Paul wasn't always the radical, on-fire, sold-out-to-Jesus Christian he's often remembered for being. In fact, to say that he was the opposite sounds a bit understated.

Before his conversion, he was known as Saul, a man consumed with hatred for the Christian faith. Constantly persecuting and seeking to destroy Christians, Saul truly believed he was doing God's will. Thus, he had no remorse for his actions . . . until Christ confronted him on the road to Damascus. (For the whole story, read Acts 9.)

Saul's conversion to Christ is inspiring in itself. But it also serves as a wonderful example of our Lord's great patience with sinners. Anyone who hears Paul's story can realize that they too can find forgiveness and new life—no matter how rotten the "old life."

No matter who you are or what you have done, please don't fall for the lie that you have been "too bad" to come to Christ. Like the raging Saul, you are just the one He is waiting to meet.

Dear Heavenly Father, thank You for being so gracious and patient with me. Even in spite of all my sins, You give me encouragement from Paul's life, and the promise of Your Word, that I am forgiven through the same cross. In Jesus' name, amen.

Cleansing Already Provided

The Son radiates God's own glory and expresses the very character of God, and he sustains everything by the mighty power of his command (Hebrews 1:3a, *New Living Translation*).

Scripture: Hebrews 1:1-9
Song: "I Need You to Love Me"

The Christian sister trio, BarlowGirl, has a hit song, "I Need You to Love Me." It's a moving song about God's amazing mercy toward us when we fall short. And it conveys the powerful theme that one should not pretend that they somehow deserve what they already have.

That song agrees with the wonderful message found in the second part of Hebrews 1:3, "When he had cleansed us from our sins, he sat down in the place of honor at the right hand of the majestic God in heaven." Notice the tense: "When he had cleansed us from our sins . . ." is clearly in the past. Jesus Christ the Lord isn't still attempting to pay our sin debt. He successfully completed the mission His Father had given Him to do; our debt has been paid in full.

Are you striving to attain God's acceptance, love, and forgiveness, based on your performance? Our Lord wants us to know that, because of the atonement He made for us, we never need strive for his cleansing power of His forgiveness. His love is eternal, and the cleansing has already been provided.

Merciful Lord of my life, thank You for the powerful, reassuring truths in Your Word. Thank You for loving me and for paying my sin debt in full. Help me to honor You with my life, and be thankful, always—thankful that I can receive the cleansing forgiveness You provide. In the name of Jesus I pray. Amen.

The Delight of Priority

The LORD your God is testing you to find out whether you love him with all your heart and with all your soul (Deuteronomy 13:3).

Scripture: Deuteronomy 13:1-8
Song: "More Love, More Power"

I was 13 and my 17-year-old brother was transferring anhydrous ammonia (a chemical fertilizer that is toxic in its gaseous form) from the large bulk tank to a small applicator tank on the back of the tractor. When he disconnected the transfer hose, he forgot to shut off the valve on the applicator, and the gas began spewing out. Through the noxious cloud I could see him as he tried desperately to shut off the valve. When he began to collapse, I was terrified—but did what I had to do. I ran into the cloud and dragged him out to safety.

There is almost nothing we won't do for those we love. But even if those we cherish try to lead us off the path of devotion to our Lord, there should be no hesitation; we must choose Him instead. In grand hyperbole, Jesus echoed the words in our Scripture today, recorded by Moses, when He declared that unless we "hate" (see Luke 14:26) our own family, we cannot be His disciples.

It's a tremendous claim to stake upon our hearts, this demand for a love that encompasses and transcends our devotion to all others. But it's a demand that He has earned the right to deliver.

Lord, Your love and sacrifice deserves and demands all that I am and all that I have. Guard my heart, O Lord, that none may compete with You. Through Christ, amen.

December 8-14. **Doc Arnett** is a bi-vocational minister in northeast Kansas. He and his wife, Randa, both work at Highland Community College.

The Delight of Devotion

May your hearts be fully committed to the LORD our God, to live by his decrees and obey his commands, as at this time (1 Kings 8:61).

Scripture: 1 Kings 8:54-62
Song: "More Love to Thee, O Christ"

Over the past 40 years or so, I've officiated at a few weddings. The ones I've enjoyed the most involved couples that I knew well. The ones I've enjoyed the least were for strangers, people whose only inclination for church arose when they wanted a place for a wedding. But for all of them, I've wondered whether or not the love and devotion they held and pledged on that day would last through the years.

We've all known those moments of intense feeling, the excitement and enthusiasm that grips us, as we launch ourselves into some new project, new hobby, new job, or even new relationship. It is not unusual that the devotion wanes; other interests or unexpected demands come along to drain away our time and commitment. In short, we change. People take up new hobbies, new causes, even new spouses.

It doesn't matter much whether I maintain my youthful interest in model cars, bass fishing, or rock music. But my devotion to my spouse is different; it matters quite a bit! And what matters even more is whether or not our devotion to Christ continually increases over the years. It matters to Him, the one who can then keep us devoted to every other rightful commitment.

Lord, remind me of the joy of Your salvation this day. May every moment of my life reveal that my devotion to You is constantly increasing. In Christ's name, amen.

The Delight of Reverence

Let us be thankful, and so worship God acceptably with reverence and awe, for our "God is a consuming fire" (Hebrews 12:28, 29).

Scripture: Hebrews 12:22-29
Song: "Our God Is an Awesome God"

"Hey, God, it's Alex. You know, right here in Highland . . ." I have no reason to doubt that the young man leading our prayer at the beginning of a college Bible study was at least as devoted as I am to Jesus Christ. I have no right to judge him or anyone else as to their relationship with the Lord. But I do believe that the flippant way he began his prayer did not convey the reverence and awe that our God fully deserves—the Almighty King of the universe.

We live in a day that seems to have lost the sense of due reverence for anyone or anything. Teenagers address the elderly by their given names with no title of respect. Workers treat their supervisors as less than their peers. Citizens speak of the elected rulers of their nation with disdain. And even self-professed Christians use the name "God" merely as an exclamation.

Reverence and awe are not only modeled, taught, and commanded in Scripture, they are inescapable expressions for those whose hearts are humble before Him. If we understand our own nature and anything at all of His, we will come before Him with fear and trembling.

Lord God, Your power, Your love, Your holiness, Your mercy, Your compassion, and Your magnificence exceed my ability to comprehend. Yet I will worship You in love, in fear, in reverence, and in gratitude. In the name of Jesus, amen.

The Delight of Worship

Let the hearts of those who seek the LORD rejoice (1 Chronicles 16:10).

Scripture: 1 Chronicles 16:7-15
Song: "Forever"

My wife, Randa, and I have sung together for nearly 25 years. She is a better singer and musician than I am; she has a better ear for pitch and is much better at singing harmony. But neither of us was gifted with an amazing voice, and I think we sound better together than either of us does alone. I like that.

I am always a little leery of applause when we sing at church, though. In fact, I like it best when we finish a song and hear a reverent silence, perhaps including a whispered "Amen" or a "Thank You, Jesus."

There are gifted singers and there are people gifted for worship. There are those with wonderful voices and those with a wonderful love for praising God. And, rarely perhaps, there are gifted singers who are anointed for worshipping God.

Those anointed for worship and for leading worship, know that the focus of true, spiritual worship must be upon the Lord alone. Those who love Christ absolutely rejoice in praising Him. There is a lifting liberation in losing ourselves in His adoration. It is the purest joy that I have known upon this earth. And, thankfully, it is a joy that will not cease through the ages but will fill us all, throughout eternity.

Lord God, thank You for allowing me the privilege of worshipping You. Let my heart fully rejoice in its adoration of You, my Savior. In Christ's name, amen.

The Delight of Praise

Let my teaching fall like rain and my words descend like dew, like showers on new grass, like abundant rain on tender plants. I will proclaim the name of the LORD. Oh, praise the greatness of our God! (Deuteronomy 32:2, 3).

Scripture: Deuteronomy 32:1-7
Song: "Holy, Holy, Holy"

Across much of Kansas, especially in the central and western parts, an extended drought continues through late winter. Hay and feed prices have nearly doubled in the past two years. Last summer, corn sprouted, grew quickly in the spring rain, then withered in the splintering heat of summer. Pastures browned into useless stems and blades.

We have been spared its extremes in the northeastern corner of the state, but the drought has taken its toll here as well. Last fall, when I was planting a new shrub, I dug down a foot deep and never found any moisture in the ground. We continue well below average precipitation. But today, as I write this on the second Saturday of March, it is raining.

Those who live upon the land understand the blessing of rain and how vital it is for the crops, for the pastures, for the water table. They understand, more than most, the delight of God's good mercy sent upon "the righteous and the unrighteous" (see Matthew 5:45).

Lifting our hearts in sincere praise to God, we know the blessing that comes with exalting His name. It revives the spirit, refreshes the heart, and rekindles the fire of devotion.

God and Father of all, let those who would be lifted up, lift up the name of the Lord! You alone are worthy of all my praise. In the name of Your Son, I pray. Amen.

The Delight of Sacrifice

Through Jesus, therefore, let us continually offer to God a sacrifice of praise—the fruit of lips that openly profess his name (Hebrews 13:15).

Scripture: Hebrews 13:6-15
Song: "We Bring the Sacrifice of Praise"

As a minister and preacher, I've sometimes thought about what it would be like to be a priest in the days of ancient Israel. I think it would be more like working in a slaughterhouse than doing the work of a modern minister. Needless to say, I'd rather be me today than a Levite 3,000 years ago!

Through Moses, God taught us that His worship involves sacrifice. The blood of the offered lambs prophesied and pre-figured the offering of the Lamb of God. In another place, Paul speaks of offering our bodies as living sacrifices.

It is a delight to many of us to lift up the name of Christ and to worship Him, to "openly profess his name," especially in the safety of a church sanctuary.

But I think that a greater sacrifice is lifted, and perhaps a greater blessing is received, when we make our profession in other settings. Sharing our faith with the server in our favorite restaurant or with the person who fixes our car or as we visit to pray for a sick neighbor or a relative in the hospital. These venues give us additional opportunities to offer up the sacrifices in which God delights.

O Lord, my Father, may I never shy away from professing Your name in the world. Give me the wisdom that comes from above, and lead me to prepared hearts ready to hear of Your goodness. In the precious name of Jesus, I pray. Amen.

The Delight of Submission

O come, let us worship and bow down: let us kneel before the LORD our maker. For he is our God; and we are the people of his pasture, and the sheep of his hand (Psalm 95:6, 7, *King James Version*).

Scripture: Psalm 95:1-7
Song: "Come, Let Us Worship and Bow Down"

When I was in my mid-30s, my mom finally got something off her chest one day. "You have always been a rebellious child," she wrote. I had no idea she'd viewed me that way throughout my years of growing up. Now, a quarter-century later, I can look back at that letter with a bit of a grin on my face. At the time, not so much.

A price comes with noticing things are not as they should be. At times my life would have been easier if I had been considerably less discerning about injustice and unfairness, particularly in regard to my own situation.

I learned, eventually, that yielding to God brings a far greater peace, a far deeper satisfaction, than trying to force things to my liking. I learned, also, that those who are not in submission to others are not in submission to God. We cannot walk in pride against our employer, our supervisor, our minister, our neighbor, or our spouse . . . and walk humbly with our God.

The sheep who eagerly turn into the pen, who readily run to their shepherd, and who delight in the stroke of his hand are the sheep who reap the reward of satisfaction and security.

O Good Shepherd, thank You for making me a lamb of Your own redeeming, for tending to me, and keeping me in the security of Your pasture. In Your name, amen.

"Catch Me, Daddy!"

Cry out, "Save us, God our Savior; gather us and deliver us from the nations, that we may give thanks to your holy name, and glory in your praise" (1 Chronicles 16:35).

Scripture: 1 Chronicles 16:35-41
Song: "I Am Trusting Thee"

My preschooler climbed to the top of the playground slide and found herself staring down a very steep slope. Unsure if she could manage it herself, she wisely yelled for Daddy. Then, as soon as she cried out, down she went.

Why such faith? She saw him nearby and knew he'd stop her from hitting the ground. She'd experienced his care daily and had no reason to doubt him as she stood at the top of a scary precipice. His love toward her was constant and trustworthy.

David sang a song of praise and trust as the ark was carried to the high place. Then he set up patterns for daily praise and sacrifice. Why? Because "his love endures forever" (v. 41).

What a difference it makes to rely only on God's love. We can bring every irritation to Him and know He'll walk through it with us. His love endures for the day, for the week, for the season, forever. Let's ask Him to catch us as we enjoy sliding into His strong embrace. He is sure to be there all the time.

Dear God and Father, I thank You for a love that lasts through all stages and circumstances of my life. Forgive me for going forward purely on my own at times. I want to rely on Your enduring love and constant presence with me today. I pray this prayer in the name of Jesus, my merciful Savior and Lord. Amen.

December 15–21. **Sara Schaffer,** of Broomfield, Colorado, loves to delve into the Word and share it with others through writing, speaking, and singing.

Celebrity Sighting

The trumpeters and musicians joined in unison to give praise and thanks to the LORD . . . Then the temple of the LORD was filled with the cloud (2 Chronicles 5:13).

Scripture: 2 Chronicles 5:2-14
Song: "We Have Seen His Glory"

At a campaign rally years ago, I arrived three hours early to get a spot close to the stage. Soon hundreds of others came and pushed their way forward. The noisy crowd's cheers increased as the buses rolled in and the candidates took the stage.

Enfolded by the masses, I clapped and yelled loudly as the men of the hour eloquently gave us smiles and promises. And soon I was pushing through the crowd to shake hands with these political celebrities. I drove home elated and satisfied.

When the ark of God arrived at the temple, the Israelites saturated the streets with worship. Then, to everyone's amazement, God himself arrived on the scene. His presence filled the temple and overwhelmed the people with His glory.

Ever been taken aback by God's glory? Like the Israelites, we may sense His presence in times of worship and celebration. However, sometimes circumstances seem to block our closeness to Him. Nevertheless, remember this: though I had to push past others to meet well-known politicians, it is God himself who comes into our lives and reaches for us. In those moments, let us deeply enjoy our tender, personal celebrity sighting.

Dear Lord, You are holy, holy, holy. I worship You and long for Your touch. Please reach through my circumstances and bless me with Your presence. I look forward to the day when I will worship and know You face to face. In Christ's name, amen.

Traveling Truth

The heavens declare the glory of God; the skies proclaim the work of his hands (Psalm 19:1).

Scripture: Psalm 19
Song: "Indescribable"

One day young mother Brett brought her two little children, Belle and Peter, outside into a starry night to tell them something special: God exists, and He sees and hears us. Though she couldn't see God, Belle felt sure He was protecting her. Her mama also taught her to pray, to be truthful, and to work hard.

Belle and her family were slaves in upper New York in the latter eighteenth century. Belle endured abuse, separation from family, and constant discrimination, even after receiving her freedom. At age 46 she set out to be a traveling missionary and changed her name to Sojourner Truth.

Facing extreme pain and heartaches, Sojourner found comfort in the stars of the night sky. She knew of God as the skies proclaimed His works, and she continued to speak the truth to many until her death in 1883.

According to the psalmist, the reality of God surrounds us. Are we joining in the chorus? Do our hearts thrill at the rising sun? And how will we respond to God's greatness and beautiful creation this Christmas season? Perhaps it starts with something as simple as looking up at a night sky . . . and telling someone you love that God exists.

O God, creator of Heaven and earth, thank You for the evidence of Your glory in the stars. Give me eyes to see and praise You as I go through my day. In Jesus' name I pray. Amen.

Glorious Experiences

Awake, harp and lyre! I will awaken the dawn (Psalm 108:2).

Scripture: Psalm 108:1-6
Song: "I Love to Walk with Jesus"

One summer morning I headed downstairs, grabbed my coffee, and sat at the dining room table. Through a foggy mind, I prayed and began my Bible study. In my study guide, the final assignment for that day encouraged me to watch a sunrise and experience God's glory. Still yawning after my second shot of caffeine, I decided to skip the suggested exercise.

The next morning I went through the same routine, but the unfinished exercise nagged at my conscience. Looking toward the deck, I noticed a lawn chair draped with a blanket right in front of the sliding glass doors. I knew God was taking away any excuses. Smiling at this not-so-subtle hint, I slid the door open and faced the chair east.

As I sat there, the changing sky entranced me. God's amazing celestial artwork mesmerized me like the flames of a campfire often do. Yes, this beautiful dawn sky brought tears to my eyes, and praise filled my heart. I could almost see David strumming his harp and adoring his Lord God in those sweet few moments of a new day.

What small assignment are you putting off? I pray God grants us hearts that long to obey and praise Him. What glorious experiences surely await us as we follow His leading.

O God, I praise You right now. Fill me to overflowing—so I can't keep quiet about Your love and glory. You are an amazing God. Be exalted over all the earth . . . and in my life today. Through Christ I pray. Amen.

The Hope of Glory

We boast in the hope of the glory of God (Romans 5:2).

Scripture: Romans 5:1-5
Song: "Precious Lord, Take My Hand"

My grandmother lay on the bed, mostly quiet and still, as she had been for several days. Illness had diminished her strength, and the only sounds she made were faint murmurings.

I gently asked, "Grandma, will you give Josh a hug for me in Heaven?" Josh, my first husband, had died in an accident at age 27. Just before getting very sick, Grandma had been able to attend our wedding. Without opening her eyes she said, "Yes."

"Will you give Grandpa a hug for me, too?"

"Yes, yes. Many hugs," came her soft response.

I consistently witnessed Grandma's life boasting in the hope of God's glory. She knew she was headed to Heaven and confidently gloried in her sufferings. She practically glowed as she lay on that bed, revealing the continual flow of God's love pouring into her heart.

Perhaps you face a time of suffering. Will you persevere? Maybe you *have* been persevering. In that case, what qualities of character have been developing in you as a result?

Or like my grandmother, you may have developed such grace and faith that you rest peacefully in the hope that doesn't disappoint. Wherever we are in our spiritual journeys, may we press on until the glory of God is ours to enjoy completely.

Dear Lord, often my hopes disappoint me. May I develop the faith to live fully on the eternal, glorious hope that only You can offer. Even in my suffering, may I glorify You so others can see Your love flowing through me. In Jesus' name I pray. Amen.

Invisible Significance

There was no guest room available for them (Luke 2:7).

Scripture: Luke 2:1-7
Song: "To God Be the Glory"

At a beautiful old church in a small Minnesota town, Ted was the janitor for 18 years. His job included cleaning, making repairs, doing lawn care, and removing snow—all of which he did exceptionally well.

However, Ted also went beyond his janitorial duties. When someone came into the church to talk, Ted listened and advised. If a pallbearer was needed at a funeral service, Ted stepped in. During his tenure, Ted even walked several brides down the aisle!

Ted served in an important behind-the-scenes ministry. He wasn't the preacher or the superintendent of the Sunday school or the church board president. He was a servant seeking God's glory.

Jesus came *into* the world but was not *of* the world. The King of kings entered into a tiny, unremarkable stall apart from the swarming crowds in Bethlehem. Then, for most of His life, He focused on being a good son and a good carpenter, thoroughly unknown to the world at large.

Are you in an invisible, unremarkable, insignificant place? If so, just like Jesus and my grandpa Ted, you can find opportunities to glorify Him there with the gifts He has given you.

Father, thank You for sending Your Son to enter the world apart from fanfare and fame. In light of His example, forgive me for seeking so much approval when I already have Yours. May I glorify You throughout this day. In Jesus' name, amen.

Glimpses of Glory

Suddenly a great company of the heavenly host appeared with the angel, praising God (Luke 2:13).

Scripture: Luke 2:8-20
Song: "Go, Tell It on the Mountain"

In February of 2013, a meteor burst through the atmosphere with a blaze of light. Headlines about the phenomenon lit up the Internet and newspapers. Firsthand observers driving in Russia recorded their sightings with dashboard cams.

The global media broadcast the remarkable amateur videos. They showed a meteor's bright, sudden appearance and brilliant tail coursing downward. Then the heavenly rock exploded into thousands of fragments that hit the earth.

How much more indescribable the brightness of angels in the heavens! And yet God gave this glimpse of glory to ordinary shepherds, who ran to Bethlehem and then saw the king in His stable.

Jesus' arrival literally "hit" the earth—like a miracle meteor—and all people throughout time have felt, to some degree, His impact (see John 1:9). His willing descent to humanity is remarkable and brilliant, waiting for a soul-deep response.

God has given us glimpses of His glory, and He entrusts each of us with the potential impact of the incarnation on individual human lives. Can we, this Christmas, recapture our amazement at Christ's birth? Can we "go, tell it on the mountain"?

Dear Father, what a Christmas gift is Your incarnate Son, Jesus! Give me the courage and passion to tell others of the real impact of this holiday. However they respond, may You be glorified in my way of life and in my words. Through Christ, amen.

Interested in Faith, But . . .

Without faith it is impossible to please God, because anyone who comes to him must believe that he exists and that he rewards those who earnestly seek him (Hebrews 11:6).

Scripture: Hebrews 11:1-6
Song: "Faith Is the Victory"

My friend never knew her mom and dad. She grew up "in the system," and family love is foreign to her. She says "I don't do Christmas," but she's entranced by the decorated trees, lights, and yuletide music. Yet she doesn't want to be around families at Christmas because she's "uncomfortable." I think that's code for being miserable about what she missed in her childhood.

I pray for her soul and converse with her about God and His love for her. Finally, she said, "I try to talk to Him, but I don't know how. I just feel worse after that." She can't use the word *pray*, but that's what she's trying to do, and I receive encouragement from that.

She is interested in faith . . . but has none. Her life experiences seem to have robbed her of any confidence that the future holds better days. How I want her to know the hope and assurance I've been so graciously given. Slowly, as we both wait on the Lord, may He touch her heart and lead her to faith.

Almighty and most merciful God, give me the humble spirit of a child—and of the childlike people I know. Help me to live so that others will want to know You as I do. Keep me ever mindful: all I am and have comes from Your gracious hand. In the name of the Father and of the Son and of the Holy Spirit, I pray. Amen.

December 22–28. **Lanita Bradley Boyd** is a teacher, writer, speaker, wife, mother, grandmother, and friend who lives in Fort Thomas, Kentucky. She especially enjoys mentoring younger women.

Faith Through the Storm

I have prayed for you, Simon, that your faith may not fail. And when you have turned back, strengthen your brothers (Luke 22:32).

Scripture: Luke 8:19-25
Song: "Peace, Be Still"

Helen leaned against me and sobbed. "My father had so much faith!" she wailed. "He would be so disappointed in me. I just can't pray. I've tried, and I just can't bring out anything to say to God. I guess I'm mad at Him for taking Dad so suddenly. But what can I do about it?" Her pleading eyes met mine.

"I remember feeling somewhat that way when my dad died," I started cautiously. "Would it help if you knew I was praying for you? Lots of folks are praying for your peace and comfort, but I mean praying what you would pray if you could."

She smiled through her tears. She was almost joyful as she answered, "Oh, yes! Please do." So together we prayed, and for weeks I prayed the thoughts and ideas Helen wanted to bring before the Father but felt she could not.

Finally one day she came to me, smiling. "I'm finally able to pray again," she said.

At times we've got to lean on the faith of others—as the disciples depended on Jesus' faith to get them through the storm. We also lean on Jesus to carry us through. And mostly His help comes by way of the friends He sends to us.

Almighty Heavenly Father, I come before You on behalf of my friend who cannot pray for herself. Please heal her, dear God, and help her to return to You in full submission, knowing that Your ways are higher than ours. In Your Son's name, amen.

Help!

"I do believe; help me overcome my unbelief!" (Mark 9:24).

Scripture: Mark 9:15-24
Song: "I Know Whom I Have Believed"

One activity at our church's women's retreat was to share our favorite Bible passage and tell how it had influenced our lives. That can be a challenge when so many Scriptures are beloved.

For example, I had long before settled on Psalm 37:4 as my life's theme: "Delight yourself in the Lord, and he will give you the desires of your heart." Through this verse I understand that drawing close to Him changes the desires of my heart—and I love that idea.

We were eager to hear what our friend Ruth had chosen because she was a spiritual leader and mentor to all of us. She was the Christian woman we all wanted to emulate. So it was a shock when she said her most cherished verse was, "I do believe; help me overcome my unbelief." Ruth? She knew unbelief?

On that retreat I learned that everyone has their crises of faith, their moments of doubt or seasons of unbelief—even the strongest Christian disciples. Sometimes our faith falters, our confidence in Christ weakens, and our trust seems distant and misplaced. At those times, we can join the boy's father, my friend Ruth, and countless other believers in saying, "I choose to keep believing, but . . . *help!*"

Almighty and wise God, ruler of the universe, I appreciate Your power and Your majesty as well as Your grace and mercy toward me. Thank You for wise mentors who reveal Your strength by letting me see their own weaknesses. In the name of Jesus, who lives and reigns with You and the Holy Spirit, amen.

Light in the Darkness

The true light that gives light to everyone was coming into the world (John 1:9).

Scripture: John 1:1-9
Song: "Here I Am to Worship"

As people around the world today honor the birth of Jesus, John gives us a broader picture of the event. Yes, Jesus was a baby, born to Mary, honored first by shepherds and later by the Magi. But He was more. He is the Word, Son of God, who came to live as humans live, to know the joys and sorrows of ordinary persons here on earth. Amazing—that God the holy trinity made himself available to us on earth.

At Christmas Eve services, someone lights a single candle in the darkened church. The next candle is lit from it, and so on, until the room blazes with light. So it is with our lives as Christians. We may feel insignificant in Jesus' plan to spread the gospel throughout the world. But our light, in combination with the lights of others, can set the world ablaze.

Thankfully, Jesus, in some significant way, through conscience and the natural law, has already enlightened the hearts of every human to the truths of *general* revelation: "For since the creation of the world God's invisible qualities—his eternal power and divine nature—have been clearly seen . . . so that people are without excuse" (Romans 1:20). Therefore, we serve Jesus by shining forth the *specific* revelation of His incarnate personhood, adding to what all peoples already know of the Creator's glory.

Father, may the revelation of Your glory in creation move all persons to seek out Your true nature—and discover the great event of the incarnation! Through Christ, amen.

Growing in Faith

See what great love the Father has lavished on us, that we should be called children of God! . . . The reason the world does not know us is that it did not know him (1 John 3:1).

Scripture: Matthew 17:14-20
Song: "Love Lifted Me"

My parents didn't know the term "positive reinforcement," but that's what they demonstrated as I was growing up. If I had a test scheduled, they'd say, "I know you can do well." When I faced a challenging piano recital, they'd say, "You'll have a great performance." Unfortunately, their faith in me was sometimes misplaced! Whereas I usually studied hard for a test, I did not practice my piano lessons so dutifully. Yet they simply continued to love me.

Our faith in God is never misplaced, but often it isn't strong. In Matthew 17, even the disciples—those who were with Jesus every day—did not have enough faith. So how can we increase our faith?

Prayer is the answer. As Richard Trent says, "Prayer is not getting man's will done in heaven, but getting God's will done on earth. It is not overcoming God's reluctance but laying hold of God's willingness."

Sitting in silence or telling Him our problems, listening for His guidance or seeking it from His Word—time with God increases our faith. No matter how often we fail, what counts is that we are making an effort with a heart open to Him.

Father, I thank You for the love You show to me. I thank You for Your Word that helps me to grow closer to You. Strengthen my faith today! In Jesus' name, amen.

How Strong Is My Faith?

When Jesus heard this, he was amazed at him, and turning to the crowd following him, he said, "I tell you, I have not found such great faith even in Israel" (Luke 7:9).

Scripture: Matthew 15:21-31
Song: "My Task"

Marie was born with Ring 14 Syndrome, a rare genetic disorder characterized by slow physical and mental development, seizures, immune deficiencies, and short life expectancy. She is now 7 years old, primarily due to her parents' diligence in providing for her health care. They have educated themselves, traveled when necessary, worked with Marie as instructed, and raised money for treatment research.

At the same time, this child's life is covered with the prayers of numerous faith-filled believers. Their faith clings to the power of the great physician.

In today's story, a mother challenged Jesus to the point that He healed her demon-possessed daughter. Her faith made a marvelous difference for her child.

Today our faith can make a difference for children we know personally, but also for ill, starving, and abused children throughout the world. We may never know the results of our prayers, of course. But we can believe that our Lord is responding to them. From the homeless in our own cities to those on the other side of the world, our praying in faith can make a difference.

Father, I ask Your blessings on suffering children throughout the world. Please give them the food, shelter, and love that they need. In the name of Jesus, amen.

What a Comeback!

Immediately Jesus reached out his hand and caught him. "You of little faith," he said, "why did you doubt?" (Matthew 14:31).

Scripture: Matthew 14:22-36
Song: "Turn Your Eyes upon Jesus"

Hank was a bank officer and church treasurer, and no one had reason to doubt his trustworthiness. One day, however, bank auditors noticed some discrepancies in an account, and he was called to answer for the shortfall. Soon it came out that Hank had "borrowed" money to fund his gambling habit. "I was going to pay it back soon," he said.

And, of course, he paid it back immediately; he had no choice. No charges were filed, but he lost his position at the bank. And another qualified person became church treasurer.

The discovery of Hank's fallibility gave him an opportunity to start anew. He went to Gamblers Anonymous meetings, reordered his priorities, and changed his habits. Again he is a productive member of his congregation, loved and respected for his renewal and his faithfulness. Though he took his eyes off Jesus for a time—as did the great apostle Peter one stormy night— His Lord and master caught him amidst a free fall into potential devastation.

We all fall, some more noticeably than others. Peter made a habit of taking his eyes off Jesus, but how he came back on the Day of Pentecost!

Father, thanks for Your Son and His willingness to die for me—and to catch me when I fall. Help me keep my eyes on Him, this day and always. Through Christ, amen.

A Holy Place . . . Right Here

When you pray, go away by yourself, shut the door behind you, and pray to your Father in private. Then your Father, who sees everything, will reward you (Matthew 6:6, *New Living Translation*).

Scripture: Matthew 6:1-8
Song: "In the Garden"

I know a holy place in Michigan. It overlooks the Tahquamenon River, and I found it when a group of us spent a week at our church camp many years ago. I returned several more times.

In the afternoons, during our free time, I would grab my Bible and notebook and head down the path into the forest. The voices from the beach faded away as I came to the fire pit in a clearing. As I sat on a log, I watched the river move past me, and I heard the water lapping on the banks.

There, I met God. I heard His voice in the pages of His Word, I confessed my failures, I journaled . . . and my relationship with Him deepened. I left the fire pit feeling refreshed and with a new sense of purpose.

But I knew I needed my own holy place—a place where I met God alone—and that I couldn't just save it for the times in Michigan. In fact, I'm coming to see, more and more, that the "holy place" is wherever I am when my heart opens to my heavenly Father's presence in prayer.

Lord, help me remember that wherever I spend time with You is a holy place. I need that time if I'm to grow and become more like You. Through Christ, amen.

December 29–31. **Deborah Christensen,** of Addison, Illinois, is a writer and editor for Lighthouse Christian Products. She loves to cook and spend time with family and friends.

All That You Need

God is able to bless you abundantly, so that in all things at all times, having all that you need, you will abound in every good work (2 Corinthians 9:8).

Scripture: 2 Corinthians 9:7-15
Song: "Jesus Is All I Need"

What does it mean to us to "have all we need"? Since we didn't have any money for lightbulbs, I recall doing laundry on a ringer washer by candlelight. At the time, it did not make sense to me that I should have to do this, as God's dedicated servant. It didn't make sense, until I read the verse above.

You see, we wanted to abound in every good work. We wanted to do exactly what God wanted us to do. We gave our time, our tithe, our talents to the Lord. Then we asked him to bless our efforts.

My husband's parents were coming for Thanksgiving, but we had no extra money for an extra special meal. (We'd "enjoyed" a can of mushroom soup for our breakfast that morning.) Then we prayed, asking God to help us.

The day before our family arrived, there was a knock on the door. People from a large church brought boxes and bags full of potatoes and pumpkin and cranberry sauce and . . . oh, so much more. Their explanation: "We are providing this in appreciation for all you do for others."

A Thanksgiving dinner was all I had prayed for. Food for our dinner—and food for days after was what we received.

Thank You, **Lord,** for providing for our needs at that time, and many other times, and in all the days ahead. In Jesus' name, amen.

Excel in Giving

Since you excel in everything—in faith, in speech, in knowledge, in complete earnestness and in the love we have kindled in you—see that you also excel in this grace of giving (2 Corinthians 8:7).

Scripture: 2 Corinthians 8:1-14
Song: "All Because of God's Amazing Grace"

People from Macedonia faced fierce drought. Very poor, but very happy to do what God wanted. Encouraged to give an offering, even more than they could afford, they gave. There was no holding back.

"Excel in this grace of giving." It means going over and above what is expected. That is what the people from Macedonia did. Paul encouraged the Corinthians to do that. God wants us to do that too.

God wants us to excel in this grace of giving.

Grace is unmerited favor, a good thing we receive through no good deed that we do. This says to me that I need to give to those who don't deserve it.

Give to those who don't deserve it! Give to those who have made bad choices! Give to those who have taken advantage of me! Yes, that is grace. It's unconditional.

But if we excel in everything, won't we burn ourselves out in service to the Lord? I love how Oswald Chambers speaks of this: "It is impossible to get exhausted in work for God. We get exhausted because we try to do God's work in our own way."

Lord, I don't know why You have asked me to do this. I don't know how I can. Please help me. In Jesus' name, amen.

Grace That Transforms

As far as the east is from the west, so far has he removed our transgressions from us (Psalm 103:12).

Scripture: Psalm 103:1-13
Song: "Give Me, O Lord, a Heart of Grace"

John Newton composed one of the most beloved Christian songs ever written. It came from the depths of his heart and told how God had reached into his life years after he'd followed in his father's footsteps and went to sea. Eventually, Newton captained a slave ship. But while he guided his ship through a violent storm, he cried out, "Lord, have mercy upon us."

Newton believed that God used that storm to reach him and that His grace began its work in his life. He marked May 10, 1748, as the day he gave his life to Christ, eventually giving up the slave trade to become an Anglican priest. While serving as a minister, he wrote hymns with poet William Cowper for his church. Among them was "Amazing Grace."

Part of his epitaph reads this way: "Once an infidel and libertine, a servant of slaves in Africa, was, by the rich mercy of our Lord and Saviour Jesus Christ, preserved, restored, pardoned, and appointed to preach the Gospel which he had long laboured to destroy."

This beloved song is a testament to God's redeeming grace. Newton clearly saw the reality of his sin and the power of God to forgive him. He was lost and God found him.

Lord, I thank You for Your grace. Even though I don't deserve it, You remove my sins from me as far as the east is from the west. You forgive me and wash me clean. You do for me what I can't do myself. You make me right with You. Through Christ, amen.

The Instruction Sheets

"Keep my commands and follow them. I am the LORD"
(Leviticus 22:31).

Scripture: Leviticus 22:26-33
Song: "Thy Word Is a Lamp"

I got up quickly when the doorbell rang. I knew who it was. The large delivery man with the big box on his shoulder made his way up to my office. When he finished delivering all the boxes, I opened them one at a time. They contained the various pieces of my new office furniture.

Each box came with an instruction sheet. Sometimes the instructions didn't make sense, so I tried to do it in a different way—a way that made sense to me. That never worked. I wasted time and had to undo all my work and do it the way the instruction sheet directed me. My office finally took shape, though, and I felt some real satisfaction as each piece of furniture worked the way it was supposed to.

Then it occurred to me: *What if I followed God's commands as closely as I followed those instructions?* Sometimes His commands don't make sense. I don't always understand them, and I prefer to do things my way.

But something amazing happens when I live God's way. He begins to change me, softening my will to the things that touch His heart. Then I experience a closeness to Him that fulfills the original purpose of any command from Heaven: the complete freedom of divine fellowship.

Lord, Your commands are for my good! Help me remember that they aren't burdensome but point down the pathway to knowing You better. In Jesus' name, amen.